Enforcing Regulation

Law in Social Context Series

Editors:
Keith Hawkins, Oxford University, Centre for
Socio-Legal Studies
John M. Thomas, State University of New York at
Buffalo, School of Management

Board of Advisors:
Richard L. Abel, Professor of Law, University of
California, Los Angeles
Marc Galanter, Professor of Law, University of
Wisconsin
Herbert Jacob, Professor of Political Science,
Northwestern University
Richard O. Lempert, Professor of Law, University
of Michigan
Albert J. Reiss, Jr., William Graham Sumner
Professor of Sociology, Yale University
Klaus A. Ziegert, Professor of Law, University of
Sidney

Studies of law, legal institutions, and legal processes have
become prominent in virtually every area of social sciences.
This series is established to encourage and to publish
research which will increase understanding of the role of law
in society. The series encourages the preparation of
manuscripts that are accessible to scholars in many fields
and from many countries.

Enforcing Regulation

edited by

Keith Hawkins
John M. Thomas

Kluwer–Nijhoff Publishing
A member of the Kluwer Academic Publishers Group
Boston   The Hague   Dordrecht   Lancaster

Distributors for North America:
Kluwer Boston, Inc.
190 Old Derby Street
Hingham, Massachusetts 02043, U.S.A.

Distributors Outside North America:
Kluwer Academic Publishers Group
Distribution Centre
P.O. Box 322
3300AH Dordrecht, The Netherlands

Library of Congress Cataloging in Publication Data

Main entry under title:

Enforcing regulation.

(Law in social context series)
Contents: The regulatory process. The enforcement process in
regulatory bureaucracies / Keith Hawkins and John M. Thomas.
Selecting strategies of social control over organizational life / Albert
J. Reiss, Jr.
1. Administrative procedure—United States. 2. Administrative
law—United States. 3. Administrative procedure.
4. Administrative law. I. Hawkins, Keith. II. Thomas, John, M.
(John Michael), 1938–   III. Series.
KF5407.E53 1983   342.73'066   83-4378
ISBN 0-89838-148-7   347.30266

Printed in the United States of America.

Contents

Preface

"To the present day", wrote James O. Freedman in *Crisis and Legitimacy,* "Americans have failed to develop or agree upon a coherent philosophy of governmental activism in economic matters." The general premise of this collection of original essays is that the study of regulatory enforcement can provide a valuable framework for understanding the ways in which governments intervene in everyday social and economic life. Moreover, as various topical approaches to regulatory reform are debated, it is important that proposals for change be informed by an understanding of the way regulatory bureaucracies carry out the essential tasks of enforcement. New approaches should reflect knowledge of patterns of enforcement common to many problems of regulation, as well as practices unique to particular regulatory tasks. To this end, the authors of the chapters in this book address a number of important issues in the enforcement process: the feasibility of adopting formal procedures to control the discretion of enforcement officials; the process by which enforcement officials judge violators and attempt to secure compliance with the law; the impact of resource constraints on enforcement practice; the relationship between enforcement officials and the regulated; the impact of legal sanctions and the threat of prosecution on strategies for negotiating compliance; the influence of professional ideologies and values on enforcement outcomes; and analysis of the difficulties encountered in initiating comprehensive, proactive strategies of enforcement.

The idea for this book grew out of a panel on the use of discretion in regulation which we organized at the 1980 annual meeting of the Law and Society Association in Madison, Wisconsin. *Enforcing Regulation* is the first of two volumes on the subject of regulation in the Law in Social Context series. The second will focus on the problem of policy formation in the regulatory process. We would like to acknowledge the generous assistance and encouragement of Philip D. Jones of

Kluwer-Nijhoff, Boston, in the completion of this book and, most important, in the development of the Law in Social Context series. We would also like to acknowledge gratefully the invaluable assistance of Wende Birkbeck, William J. Weiksnar and Mindy Zoghlin of the Center for Policy Studies, State University of New York at Buffalo in the preparation of the manuscript.

I THE REGULATORY PROCESS: ISSUES AND CONCEPTS

1 THE ENFORCEMENT PROCESS IN REGULATORY BUREAUCRACIES

Keith Hawkins
John M. Thomas

Introduction

The explosive growth over the past two decades in government programs designed to regulate the workplace, consumer rights, the environment, and many other areas, has been well documented [Bardach, 1979; Bardach and Kagan, 1982; Lilley and Miller, 1977; Weidenbaum, 1978]. More recently, the intensity of this movement has been accompanied by strong appeals for moderation and change based on judgments of the economic impact of regulatory policies [see Schultz, 1977]. Prompting this debate has been an increased awareness that social, or protective, regulation encompasses fundamental problems involving the role of corporations in society and tradeoffs between efficiency and equity. The impact of regulation on these basic values has led one historian of the field to note: "Regulation . . . is a complex and sometimes intractable topic, but nonetheless, an irresistible one" [McCraw, 1982: vii].

Fortunately, these concerns have also brought about an interest in understanding the nature of the regulatory process itself: the day-to-day decision-making behavior of regulatory agencies, particularly those informal bureaucratic practices that affect performance and have unintended consequences. This work has become broadly multidisciplinary, including the fields of sociology, law, political science,

3

organization theory, and the economics of decision making. In part, this interest is reflected in a changing conception of American administrative law, part of whose task is to govern the regulatory process. The received wisdom of traditional administrative law has been that regulatory agencies are capable of implementing clearly definable, objective goals requiring technical expertise [see Freedman, 1978]. Today, however, it is recognized that the expert model has become irrelevant, if, indeed, it ever existed in practice. Administrative law is now more properly viewed from a political and organizational perspective — a balancing of competing demands and interests through the actions of a government bureaucracy [see Stewart, 1975; Rabin, 1977]. The purpose of this chapter is to present an overview of the principal concepts and issues in regulatory enforcement from this perspective.

The Nature of Protective Government Regulation

The debate over the design and enforcement of protective regulatory laws is complicated by the nature of the problems that these regulations address. Unlike many areas of traditional economic regulation, the problems governed by the legal framework of protective regulation are, for the most part, not specific to any one industry. The number of potential targets of regulation confronting the agency bureaucracy is vast, resulting in resource constraints on finding violations as well as patterns of partial enforcement [see Diver, 1980]. The field of protective regulation represents what Fuller has termed a class of "polycentric" legal problems [Fuller, 1960]. The administrative process is confronted with numerous economic and political tradeoffs and the need to think ex ante about the allocation of scarce resources. This is particularly clear in the environmental protection area, but these characteristics are also present in such diverse areas as consumer protection, worker health and safety, and housing code enforcement [see Boyer, 1972: 117; Ross and Thomas, 1981]. In the political arena, protective regulatory issues have been defined as evils to be eliminated by the lawmaking process rather than conflicting objectives to be accommodated. As Wilson has pointed out, these are a class of regulatory problems that impose "diffused benefits" and "concentrated costs": the public at large is the perceived beneficiary, while corporations and industry confront increased burdens through legislation [see Wilson, 1974: 143]. The political definition of these problems has resulted in a legalistic enforcement ethos. Bardach and Kagan have summarized this characteristic as follows: "In the most significant regulatory areas, the law has been deliberately structured to prevent capture, to program inspectors to apply regulations strictly, to pressure enforcement officials to apply formal penalties to violators and to adopt a more legalistic and deterrence-oriented stance vis-a-vis regulated enterprises"

[Bardach and Kagan, 1982: 57]. This creates conflict, however, because a principal goal of protective regulatory enforcement is the elimination of a highly undesirable condition or practice. These offenses lend themselves to what is termed a "compliance orientation" in law enforcement where it is felt that negotiation between the regulator and the regulated is important to correct a problem.

A significant trend in the protective regulatory movement has been the search for more effective ways to control the behavior of the large corporate enterprise [see Stone, 1980]. One aspect of this effort has been an increased willingness on the part of the federal government to promote the use of criminal sanctions as a means of deterring corporate regulatory offenses [see McAdams and Miljus, 1977]. Traditionally, criminal penalties were viewed as ancillary to other sanctions, and applied as a last resort when other legal controls proved unworkable [see Harvard Law Review, 1979]. An example of the more recent prominence given to criminal penalties is the case of *U.S. vs. Park,* 421 U.S. 658 (1975). In this case Acme Markets, Inc. *and* its chief executive officer, J. R. Park, were found guilty of violating the 1938 law against storing food, shipped in interstate commerce, in a rodent contaminated, unsanitary building. In interpreting the Food and Drug Administration (FDA) legislation, the Supreme Court upheld the conviction and argued that a corporate officer with the authority and responsibility to prevent or correct a violation of the FDA act, and who does not do so, may be held criminally liable for the violation. Recent legislation in environmental regulation also supports this trend. The 1972 amendments to the Federal Water Pollution Control Act provide for the criminal prosecution of corporate officers for abuse of the environment by their organizations. First offenders face imprisonment up to one year and fines of $2,500 to $25,000 per day; additional offenses can be punishable by up to $50,000 per day and a prison term of up to two years. In practice, however, many regulatory agencies have been loathe to use available criminal penalties. While the teeth in such remedies have been sharpened by the courts and Congress, their implementation by agencies has been more problematic. Edelhertz has summarized this phenomenon in the case of IRS and SEC regulation as follows: "Except in rare instances agency enforcement officials are prone to avoid considering cases for criminal prosecution. Agents or auditors alert to criminal issues lose their goal in a climate of discouragement and delay, or in the course of administrative and civil settlement negotiation" [*Subcommittee,* 1978: 8]. Moreover, the compliance orientation in regulation tends to create uncertainty and ambivalence about the role of criminal sanctions. The use of these sanctions by officials is frequently influenced by their perceptions of the underlying goals of the law being enforced.

The field of administrative law has become complicated by the fact that many protective regulatory statutes incorporate a goal that embodies what has been

termed the "utilitarian ethos" in the American legal tradition, specifically economic efficiency [Kagan, 1978: 10]. The Consumer Product Safety Act, for
example, states that the promulgation of standards shall include consideration of
the public's need for the product involved, the probable impact of a regulation on
the cost and availability of the products, and efforts to achieve objectives which
minimize adverse effects on competition and commerce (*Consumer Product
Safety Act of 1972*, 15 U.S.C. § 2058 (c)(1)(1976)). Similarly, the Toxic Substances Control Act of 1977 specifically requires the administrator of the act to
consider the economic impacts of proposed action and not to "impede unduly or
create unnecessary economic barriers to technological innovation" while fulfil-
ling the "primary purpose" of the statute (*Toxic Substance Control Act of 1977*, 15
U.S.C.A. § 2601(b)(1978 Supp.)). Again, the Occupational Safety and Health
Administration (OSHA) legislation of 1970 states that the "feasibility" of
standards should be considered relevant to the attainment of the highest degree of
health and safety protection for the employee, and feasibility has been interpreted
to allow the secretary of labor to take account of economic dislocation in enforcing
OSHA regulations (*Occupational Safety and Health Act of 1970*, 29 U.S.C. §655
(b)(1976)). The end result of legislation that attempts to accommodate both goals
is a high degree of policy-making and enforcement discretion available to the
regulatory agency. Indeed, regulatory control is fundamentally influenced by the
way agency officials interpret the conflict between the protective issue, which led
to the law, and pressures for economic efficiency which arise in particular cases.

Regulatory agencies are created to take sides on the issue of control. Their
statutory mandates and legal powers are explicitly committed to the guiding
principle of regulation: it is proper for government to restrain social and economic
activity through law in certain circumstances. Yet the behavior of agencies and
officials reveals a considerable ambivalence about the use of law in regulating
conduct [Kadish, 1963; Hawkins, 1980]. The recognition that economic activity is
the source of material prosperity is coupled with moral unease about associating
such conduct with the stigmatizing effects of legal sanctions. This dilemma
between tolerance and restraint represents contrasting ideological positions about
the propriety of regulation.

Thus regulatory agencies, in effect, find themselves assailed on two sides by
interested publics or constituencies with different positions on the question of the
extent to which legal rules justify intervention in economic life. One such public
might be regarded as "activist" because of its vigorous commitment to a policing
mission. This group urges substantial restraint on what it views as serious harms
caused by unregulated activity, even though this may impose heavy costs upon
productive enterprise. Activists have few qualms about employing law to mitigate
the consequences of unfettered economic activity. The formal procedures of the
law are in the forefront of what is regarded as "enforcement" and these tend to be

viewed as an index of such policing activity. So far as the activist public is concerned, agencies run the risk of criticism of ineffectiveness or co-optation by business interests if they appear to be insufficiently aggressive. The "business" public, on the other hand, takes a very different position. It is, in the extreme, critical of the very principle of regulation, which it sees as an unjustifiable inroad by government into free enterprise. This results, it is claimed, in productive industry suffering under the burdens of constraints imposed by overbearing bureaucracies.

These contrasting views are the stuff of political debate and activity, as recent conspicuous attention given by government to the alleged burdens of regulation suggests. Regulatory agencies meanwhile remain caught between these two opposing constellations of interests. Their behavior in implementing statutory mandates reflects the dilemma between what Kagan [1978] has called "stringency" and "accommodation" and expresses the ways in which they adapt to these conflicting values. The dilemma is played out in the creation and refinement of regulatory policy and is made all the more poignant by expectations aroused through the provision of complex legal sanctions among the tools of regulatory control. This is not to suggest that agencies adopt a relatively static position between the activist and business publics, but rather that they may be observed to shift towards or away from greater stringency in response to their definitions of a significant audience. The essay by Shover et al. (see below, chapter 6) shows that such shifts over time are paralleled by regional variations in regulatory enforcement. This study suggests that it is possible to discern such variations in agency enforcement policy (in this case, federal surface mining regulation) as a response to more localized differences in the agency's perceived environment.

The tension between the conflicting values of stringency and accommodation has been observed recently by a number of writers as reflected in two contrasting systems, styles, or strategies of regulatory enforcement [e.g., Hawkins, forthcoming; Kelman, see below, chapter 5; Mileski, 1971; Reiss, see below, chapter 2; Reiss and Biderman, 1980]. This work has focused on contrasting conceptions of enforcement in which punishment (stringency) or compliance (accommodation) are central values. The contrast is analytically helpful in thinking about enforcement strategies that are, on the one hand, directed towards meting out punishment for harm done and, on the other, those that are concerned with securing conformity to a rule or standard.

The Problem of Enforcement in Regulation

The problem of enforcement is an acute one in regulation for reasons that are intrinsic to the nature and task of regulatory control. The problem, essentially, is one of an all-pervasive uncertainty. In the first place, the concept of regulation implies a toleration of conduct that causes, or possesses the potential for harm, not the eradication of existing harmful acts. This tolerance requires administrative choice as to the kind and level of harmful activity deemed to fall within the regulatory agency's mandate, as well as discretion as to its enforcement at the field level.

The notion of tolerance is closely linked with a second source of uncertainty, namely a major dilemma surrounding the objectives of enforcement. "Launched on a wave of concern about a specific social problem," Kagan writes [1978: 9], "regulatory agencies typically are charged with a single publicly emphasized *police mission*" (his emphasis). The common conception of policing is that harms or evils falling within the ambit of the law should ideally be repressed or eradicated. In keeping with the conception of a policing mission, the regulatory law establishing and defining the legal mandate and creating the enforcement bureaucracy also provides in theory for the ultimate use of legal sanctions for noncompliance. Where the sanction is criminal, the law, in effect, aligns the conduct subject to regulation with more familiar rulebreaking addressed by the traditional criminal code. In other words, a sanction associated with *repressive* law enforcement is made available to further the interests of *regulatory* law enforcement. As discussed earlier, however, missionary zeal is diluted by other objectives in realization of the fact that unrestrained policing in pursuit of an ideal of full enforcement has major implications for economic efficiency. The choice about the degree of commitment a regulatory agency should display to a policing style of enforcement, therefore, "actually involves fundamental problems of equity: what is the just allocation of the costs of ameliorative measures?" [Kagan, 1978: 11] This choice is made doubly difficult, for, apart from the value question, there are problems in making the necessary predictive decisions.

A final part of the uncertainty surrounding regulatory control stems from the issue of moral ambivalence. Regulatory control may lack the moral mandate necessary for the legitimacy of an agency's enforcement work. Law enforcement, in general, tends to be associated with conduct widely regarded as *mala in se*, yet the acts, events, and states of affairs subject to regulatory control do not often lend themselves to easy moral categorization. Instead, they are typically regarded as *mala prohibita*, matters where a breach is not often viewed as morally reprehensible (see below, chapter 3). This is so because in many types of conduct covered by the regulatory laws there are technical and economic constraints upon the regulated that have major implications for the issue of choice in rulebreaking (see below, chapter 3). Many areas of regulatory control have only recently been defined as requiring intervention through law, and, as a result, there is an uneasiness about exerting control by means of direct legal orders. What may, in short, be "illegal" is often not regarded as "criminal" [Conklin, 1977].

The political and moral ambivalence surrounding regulatory activity presents significant problems at the policy-making level as well as at the field or street level of enforcement. In both cases enforcement authority is not secured on a perceived political and moral consensus about the harms subject to control nor about the appropriate degree of intervention [Hawkins, forthcoming]. An initial zeal for a policing mission may generate certain expectations about appropriate strategies of control. But enforcement activity in practice must contend with seemingly endless "good" grounds for non-compliance or partial compliance put forward by those who find themselves unwilling or unable because of financial circumstance, technology or time to conform with the law.

The need for regulatory agencies to maintain legitimacy in a political environment can disrupt the ongoing relationship with the regulated that enforcement officials, such as inspectors, feel is necessary to carry out enforcement tasks. An example is found in Schuck's analysis of meat packing regulations [Schuck, 1972]. As is the case with many instances of regulatory control, the enforcement of packing regulations has combined the tendency of an agency (the Department of Agriculture (USDA)) to overregulate with an industry's propensity to find ways to get around legalistic applications of the law. Schuck observed, however, that if regulations were strictly enforced, no meat processor could remain open; hence, inspectors inevitably had enormous discretion to decide which rules to enforce and how. The USDA traditionally allowed inspectors to apply regulations in a flexible manner, recognizing that reasonableness can be important in achieving a measure of compliance. Each inspector was assigned to, and worked in, one plant. In all plants an informal system of taking gratuities — a system known as "cumshaw" — was accepted and commonplace. Through this system inspectors developed widely shared norms about the acceptance of such gifts. Accepting an occasional bundle of meat, "cumshaw," was felt by inspectors to be insignificant as a bribe, but very important in maintaining the ongoing cooperative relationship needed for effective enforcement. As Schuck graphically notes: "much in the meat inspector's daily life — the pressures of his work routine, temptations by the packer, the job socialization process, the traditions of the industry, the conventional morality of his fellow inspectors, the general bribery statute, and the imperative of 'getting the job done' . . . tells him that he may accept gratuities from the packer with a clear conscience" [Schuck, 1972: 83].

Unfortunately for the inspectors, however, the USDA adopted a rigidly legalistic position against them when the gratuity system became public and politicized. In response to political pressure, the agency publically redefined the behavior of inspectors as corruption.

The political concerns of regulatory agencies to demonstrate efficiency through aggregate results can result in pressure on enforcement officials to "close" cases. In these circumstances, inspectors, investigators, and prosecutors respond to the need to manage case flow — the control system — rather than to the specific requirements of individual cases [Ross and Thomas, 1981]. Cases with the greatest probability of being closed out quickly take precedence; and since evaluations of the performance of street-level officials are based on measurable, aggregate indicators of productivity, they have no incentive to adopt a flexible accommodative style of regulatory enforcement. This can create serious problems for an enforcement strategy that requires the investigation and analysis of the underlying causes of regulatory violations. Inspectors subject to such productivity measures will tend to overlook less obvious violations and potentially intractable problems, merely reporting those that are clearly identifiable or amenable to rapid processing through the system.

Enforcement Policy and the Regulatory Bureaucracy

The regulatory agency has primary responsibility for the development of substantive policy together with the implementation of that policy. Policy formation can be viewed as the "law-in-action," a process whereby the agency interprets and translates legislative goals into rules, standards, and plans of action; the problem of implementation encompasses the enforcement of these agency directives and includes the operating routines used by field-level personnel and applied to targets of regulation, decisions about the application of regulations, and means for obtaining compliance with rules. Policy formation necessarily implies decision-making about enforcement. Policy includes assumptions about effective strategies for achieving compliance with rules and regulatory goals. In addition, enforcement is typically governed by policy decisions about the case management process; for example, the allocation of resources between proactively identifying cases versus responding to complaints [see chapter 7 below], and establishing priorities among the potential targets of regulation [see Rosenthal and Levine, 1980].

The nature of regulatory legislation, its clarity and goal specificity will influence enforcement policy. Legislation that specifies a clear intent to protect the environment, for example, may be interpreted more stringently than a statute that attempts in more ambiguous terms to define the public interest by balancing the objectives of environmental protection *and* economic progress. [Sabatier, 1977: 425] In a study of the implementation of the 1971 federal regulation freezing wages, prices, and rents, Kagan found that agency officials frequently used the nature of the law to justify a particular norm of enforcement. He noted that "the freeze order stated an explicit and stringent rule rather than a series of conflicting considerations and goals" [Kagan, 1978: 73]. This specific mandate resulted in an interpretation of the agency task as the "implementation of predetermined policy,'' rather than accommodation and negotiation tailored to the circumstances of individual cases. Such interpretations can become a source of ''procedural rationality'' — a means of coping with the complexity of the decision-making task [Simon, 1978: 9].

The policy formation process is also influenced by perceptions of the procedural requirements in legislation. In recent years, regulatory cases have included a requirement of formal proceedings designed to insure due process safeguards [see DeLong, 1979; Stewart, 1975]. Although these requirements are followed, agency professional staff often consider them a waste of time, inefficient, and irrelevant. As a consequence, what Joskow and Noll refer to as the ''informal regulatory process'' — the day-to-day interaction and bargaining between the agency and the regulated — becomes a critical factor in policy formation [Joskow and Noll, 1982: 52–53].

An important policy issue in regulatory enforcement is the allocation of resources among competing demands. There are few studies that have focused on this dimension of enforcement policy — the way priorities are established and resources allocated among competing commitments [see Galanter, 1972], though recently this aspect of the policy-making process in OSHA has been subjected to careful analysis [see Kelman, 1981; Zeckhauser and Nichols, 1978]. Historically, the Federal Trade Commission (FTC) has been a focus of both academic study and investigative probes. There have, for instance, been indictments of the agency for its failure to devote resources to the more important responsibilities of its statutory mandate [see Posner, 1969; Edelman, 1964], and an early Nader group investigation concluded that the agency was ineffective because it failed to go after major firms that routinely broke the law, choosing instead to pursue small violators in order to give an appearance of active regulation [Turner, 1970]

In general, agencies impose priorities, often implicitly, because they do not have the resources to perform every function delegated by legislation. Formal and informal policy that allocates enforcement resources is a means of controlling the behavior of field-level officials who have the power to commit the agency to the investigation and prosecution of specific violations. An important relationship exists between policy norms governing resource allocation and the exercise of discretion in individual cases. In a recent study of the Internal Revenue Service (IRS) that analyzed the relationship between resource allocation and enforcement [Long, 1979], it was hypothesized that ''important areas of discretion are exercised not by individual law enforcement officers, but by the law enforcement agency more generally in setting broader policies.'' This research examined the relationship of resource allocation to (1) choice of sanction — civil versus criminal, and (2) decisions about the auditing of returns. It was found that few criminal sanctions were used and that this was positively correlated with the amount of resources allocated to criminal investigation. In addition, the relatively large allocation of resources devoted to civil investigation (audits) was related to the organizational policy of maximizing total enforcement coverage. The time and cost of criminal investigations are substantially higher than civil, thus "transferring more resources into the criminal area may produce an increase in criminal conviction, but only at the price of greatly reduced enforcement coverage" [Long, 1979: 11]. In this case, allocation priorities were determined by efficiency criteria that arguably bore little relationship to the goal of deterrence. The IRS study also examined the use of a formal management policy known as the "Audit Plan," which incorporates the number of audits within each income class to be carried out the next fiscal year, and allocates this responsibility among geographical regions and districts. As in the case of choice between sanctions, this pattern of resource allocation occurred primarily in response to least-cost criteria. Because higher income returns are more complex and time-consuming, it was found that resources were allocated disproportionately to the examination of lower income returns [Long, 1979: 15].

Another important issue in the relationship between policy making and enforcement practice concerns the way the law is mobilized — how cases enter the regulatory process. In the case of housing code enforcement, for example, there is a strong tradition of responding to individual complaints [see Ross and Thomas, 1981]. Similarly, a major criticism of OSHA regulation has been its policy of responding to all employee-initiated complaints. A shortcoming of the complaint-oriented policy is that it is not necessarily congruent with strategies targeted at specific classes of victims or identifying the underlying issues in regulatory problems (see below, chapter 7). An inherent limitation of such a reactive approach is that, by definition, it must operate on a case-by-case basis where, according to Black:

> Cases enter the system one by one, and they are processed one by one. This creates an intelligence gap about the relations among and between cases. It is difficult to link patterns of illegal behavior to single or similar violators and thus to deal with the sources rather than merely the symptoms of these patterns [Black, 1973: 134–135].

Conversely, the possibility of negotiating compliance or imposing legal sanctions on the basis of information about recurrent patterns of illegality can be enhanced by proactive enforcement policy.

Regulatory policy making frequently results in "overinclusiveness" — rules that are too general, stringent, and costly, if fully enforced (see below, chapter 8) This occurs because the agency bureaucracy resists the costs of information and analysis necessary to design rules that reflect unique economic conditions. Adjustment to this problem then takes place in the course of enforcement where the agency relies upon the discretion of officials in individual cases. At the enforcement stage officials can adjust the dictates of rules to information about particular regulatory problems and specific organizations. As Kagan (see below, chapter 3) points out, in contrast with the police, regulatory agents generally have the time to analyze a situation. Moreover, they interact, for the most part, with organizations that respond rationally to the enforcement process. This is not to say that all enforcement officials either adopt, or are capable of implementing, such a strategy. A great deal of enforcement decision making either simply exacerbates the problem of unreasonableness that follows from overinclusive rules [Bardach and Kagan, 1982], or is too routinized and oriented to closing cases and silencing complaints (see below, chapter 7). A high degree of professionalism is necessary to adapt overinclusive rules to the requirements of individual regulatory problems. Professionalism requires an ability to resolve the stringency-accommodative dilemma by using both strategies depending upon the nature of the regulatory problem, the actions of the regulated, and the "career" of an individual case.

The distinction between compliance and deterrence systems of social control is fundamental to the problem of implementing regulatory policy. As Reiss (see below, chapter 2) states, a compliance system is primarily concerned with preventing violations and remedying underlying problems; a deterrence system, with detecing offenses and punishing violators. Much enforcement activity in regulation can be seen in terms of a compliance system where the objective is to ameliorate a social problem such as unhealthy or unsafe working conditions, pollution, or impure food and drugs. Effecting a remedy, so far as the regulated are concerned, often means taking some positive action involving expenditure of money and time. Thus a treatment plant has to be bought, installed, and made to work efficiently if the problem is one of air or water pollution control. Hazardous machinery must be fenced to make workplaces safer; houses in disrepair must be renovated to meet minimum standards of housing. Enforcement agents who employ a compliance strategy adopt tactics that rely heavily on privately practiced, low-visibility bargaining and bluffing [Hawkins, 1983]. The formal processes of the law tend frequently to be used with extreme reluctance because association with the law taints, and is damaging to the ultimate ends of enforcement. The formal law is more useful in a compliance system as a threat, where the discrepancy between law enforcement that is theoretically possible and that which is actually practiced is exploited by field-level agents. This threat is typically employed as part of an array of enforcement tactics that are all characterized by a continuing personal contact between regulator and regulated in which amicable social relationships are valued not only as a means of easing the job, but also as a means of assisting in the discovery of future problems and the detection of violators [Hawkins, forthcoming].

In a deterrence system, on the other hand, the enforcement style tends to be accusatory and adversarial, leading to routine reliance on formal legal processes. The preoccupation is not with putting a problem right but with punishing wrongdoing. This kind of enforcement behavior is backward-looking in the sense that it is directed towards the harm done, the detection of the lawbreaker and the imposition of a just sanction; however, it is also forward-looking in the sense that it is directed towards the prevention of further rulebreaking by the offender and (presumably) those who might be similarly tempted. To the extent that enforcement relies more heavily on formal legal processes, it depends less on private negotiations and is more concerned with proving that a violation took place [Reiss and Biderman, 1980; Reiss, see below, chapter 2]. Indeed rulebreaking in this instance usually possesses a discrete, categorical quality far removed from the problems of, say, occupational ill-health or dirty water. Adjudication in public by a third party is the means of settling the issue — not informal, private negotiation.

Compliance and deterrence systems are enforcement responses to contrasting kinds of rulebreaking. The deterrence system tends to be associated with *incidents* or *acts* of wrongdoing that by their very nature, are relatively unpredictable, thus allowing no personalized relationships to be established between enforcement agent and rulebreaker. A compliance strategy, in contrast, emerges in the context of some degree of personal relationship between the enforcement agent and his clientele. Although it is known that the police adopt a compliance strategy when they are involved in continuing relationships with certain kinds of rulebreakers (drunks, vagrants, prostitutes, for example), this approach is much more evident in the enforcement of regulation. There are three reasons in particular for this. First, much rulebreaking behavior in regulation does not consist of clear-cut acts but is episodic, repetitive, or continuous. Many of the activities or states of affairs that regulatory agencies seek to control is of this kind: dangerous machinery in factories, dilapidated housing, or chimneys belching smoke. Second, it is relatively easy for personal relationships to grow up where enforcement agents deal with only a limited sector of the public (as defined by the kind of economic activity subject to regulation) and where they will make contact on a relatively regular basis in the course of monitoring compliance. Third, victims are often not dramatically evident to the enforcement agent. Rather they may be diffuse, remote, and exist in the aggregate, leading in areas such as occupational health or water and air pollution to difficulty in thinking of "victims" as such since the conditions caused by regulatory problems are often only manifest several years later. Harm may, of course, be immediate and obvious (workers do, after all, lose limbs in factory accidents), but in many cases regulatory control is concerned with harm that is vague, uncertain, and distant as in the case of toxic substances and certain problems of worker health. This often makes it extremely difficult to establish a causal link between the rulebreaking and any subsequent possible "victimization." This encourages enforcement agents again to embark on a prospective enforcement strategy that seeks to correct a problem, rather than directly punish those responsible.

These contrasts point to two very different conceptions of law enforcement. In a deterrence system, law is enforced, in theory, when an offender is detected, prosecuted, convicted, and punishment is set in the ceremony of the trial. In a compliance system, however, law is enforced by attainment of the purpose of regulation: in practical terms, when an enforcement agent is satisfied that compliance with standards representing the broad aspirations of the statute has been secured.

The Regulatory Process

Enforcement policy is developed and implemented through interactions between, on the one hand, agency officials and professionals and, on the other, between the agency bureaucracy and interest groups, legislators and the regulated. From this perspective, there are two concepts that are useful for understanding the nature of the regulatory process: *bargaining* between the agency and its environment, and the *social construction* of regulatory tasks.

Bargaining

The concept of bargaining is central to both the formal and informal processes of regulation. Not only do enforcement officials in a compliance system tend to rely upon tactics of informal negotiation, the law itself frequently provides for bargaining in formal proceedings, particularly over type of remedy [Bardach and Kagan, 1982: 141]. Bargaining has become institutionalized in certain agencies, such as the Securities and Exchange Commission (SEC), through the use of "consent decrees" — a formal agreement not to violate a regulation again, negotiated by the agency and authorized by a court [see Clinard, 1979: 144; Thomas, 1982: 128; and Bardach and Kagan, 1982: 142]. From an organization theory perspective, bargaining is fundamental to the regulatory process because of goals shared by the agency and the regulated enterprise. Both organizations are concerned with conserving resources and minimizing interference with established routines. To attain these goals, negotiation defines a process where compliance is a mutually beneficial outcome for each bureaucracy: "compliance emerges as a product of the power-mediating efforts of both parties, as compliance demands fewer resources from both agencies and business firms than do adversarial activities to impose and thwart punitive sanctions" [Vaughn, 1982: 384].

Maintaining the legitimacy of bargaining in regulatory control is essential to an effective resolution of the stringency-accommodation dilemma discussed previously in this chapter. Excessive legalism in the enforcement of rules can preclude effective bargaining; at the extreme, legal means displace regulatory ends. On the other hand, the need for accommodation can lead to a view that bargaining takes place outside the "public interest" [Kagan, 1978: 13]. Bargaining also suffers a loss of legitimacy if it occurs by default as a response to resource constraints, unclear policy objectives, agency conflict, or inadequate incentives. Furthermore, bargaining becomes an obstacle to regulatory goals if it is excessively routinized, and employed in such a way that more fundamental questions about regulatory problems are not addressed (see below, chapter 7). Silbey's study of a state consumer protection agency analyzed the consequences of a bargaining process that, in effect, becomes an end in itself, rather than a means of remedying the underlying causes of a problem: "The law enforcement agency may succeed in obtaining by some standards a satisfactory result but is individualized to an extreme; it does not provide the opportunity or conditions able to remedy the situation that gave rise to the need for law enforcement in the first place" [Silbey, 1980: 15–16].

The nature of the bargaining process can influence the adoption of compliance or deterrence strategies of regulatory enforcement by agencies. According to Reiss (see below, chapter 2), a compliance system is associated with trust between the regulator and regulated where trust is necessary to carry out the principal functions of monitoring and the prevention of regulatory offenses. To the extent that bargaining is employed in a way that promotes trust, it contributes to the implementation of regulatory objectives. It can help reduce, as Bardach notes, "the delays, misunderstandings, and the confusion attending the implementation process" [Bardach, 1979: 416]. When the process fails to build trust, however, there is likely to be greater resort to a deterrence system — the use of penalties based upon assumptions of blameworthiness.

Bargaining in the regulatory process can create problems of control and accountability. Here the influence of discretion in day-to-day enforcement actions is highly significant. In the pollution control area, for example, it has been hypothesized that:

> the accretion of many small exceptions in the policy process amounts often to a significant deviation from the policy norm from which the regulatory agency began. The more this is so, the more it must be clear that large amounts of regulatory action have little or nothing to do with the achievement of any over-all systemic result, and much more to do with achieving a tolerable day-to-day working arrangement. That is what a bargaining arrangement is largely about [Holden, 1966: 29].

Political pressures on agencies to apply rules more stringently lead to managerial efforts to control the discretion available to enforcement officials [Bardach and Kagan, 1982: 54]. A perverse consequence of excessively legalistic demands, however, is the denial that discretion is not only inevitable, but necessary for effective bargaining. There is no doubt that enforcement agents must balance potentially conflicting objectives in the exercise of discretion. As Danaceau states, "it is both desirable and possible for inspectors to respond to the concerns and anxieties of business and industry without jeopardizing either the goals of the programs they represent or their own positions as enforcement officers" [Danaceau, 1982: 143]. This task demands a capacity for flexibility, which, in turn requires discretion. Such a positive view of discretion, however, is not to deny that serious abuses can occur [Davis, 1969]. An extreme form of abuse occurs when discretion leads to the creation of nonexistent authority in encounters with the regulated. Thus a study of housing code enforcement examined a case where one inspector spontaneously invented a law that he felt was needed to obtain compliance [Ross and Thomas, 1981].

Social Construction

A second concept that aids in understanding the regulatory process concerns the way tasks and problems are defined. In organization theory, this perspective, referred to as the "social constructionist view," focuses primarily on the interpretation of reality by individual members of bureaucracies [see Pffefer, 1982: chapter 6]. Understanding interpretative work is important because there are few objective indicators of successful performance and because political mandates are vague and conflicting. Definitions of the "public interest" to be served are derived from perceptions about the regulated, interest groups, and other government institutions. Noll has termed these various sources — such as the courts, executive agencies, the press, affected parties, and the regulated — "theatres of external judgement" [Noll, 1976: 45]. The social construction perspective helps explain why some policies or rules will be enforced by lower-level officials and others neglected. The enforcement of rules is strongly mediated by inspector interpretations of their relationships with the regulated. [See Hawkins, 1983; Mileski, 1971; Nivola, 1978; Lipsky, 1976, 1980] These judgements are, in turn, related to beliefs about the cause of violations and evaluations of the harm caused by offenses and assessments of the moral status of the violators [see Hawkins, forthcoming]. Consequently, assumptions about the motives of regulated organizations are an important factor in the creation of meaning in the regulatory environment. Kagan and Scholz, (see below, chapter 4), for example, have identified the way these judgments are used to develop "implicit theories of noncompliance" that govern the enforcement strategies of regulatory officials.

The process of social construction can lead to institutionalized, shared values that, in effect, become ideologies with considerable influence on agency policy. It has been recently noted that the role of ideology "is a topic much neglected in the study of implementation'' and that ''much of what occurs depends upon the orientation of the enforcement agency toward the underlying goal of the law, and analogous orientations among regulated organizations'' [Clune and Lindquist, 1981: 1064]. An important source of regulatory ideology can be the values of high level professions in the agency. A study of OSHA, for example, analyzed the impact of the values of key officials trained in safety engineering or industrial hygiene, who strongly believed that the costs of regulation should be incidental to continued risk reduction in the workplace [Kelman, 1981: 250]. This set of beliefs exerted a strong influence both on definitions of offenses and on the exercise of discretion by inspectors. OSHA inspectors tended to internalize this value system in the enforcement of violations. Yet as the author goes on to argue: ''there is a cost to infusing this sense of mission. Many American inspectors, armed with their goal of finding violations, appear to be steamrollers'' [Kelman, 1981: 187]. In the extreme, following the Reiss framework, such an ideology is congruent with a deterrence system based upon detecting and penalizing the violator, in contrast to the negotiation of compliance.

The deterrence system of social control may serve as a master framework for some regulatory officials and some social scientists (particularly economists) by which the regulatory world is interpreted. It provides a definition of the regulated enterprise as a rational actor fully capable of being deterred through the imposition of adequate penalties and an increase in the probability of detection. This, however, is not necessarily always an accurate interpretation. Moreover, one consequence of adopting such a ''limited view of the enforcement compliance environment'' at the field or street level may be that opportunities for voluntary compliance by the firm are lost, resulting in an ineffective regulatory process [Beckenstein and Gabel, 1980: 20].

Conclusion

Enforcement practice is heavily influenced by the role that organizations play in regulation. While lay conceptions of lawbreaking and law enforcement are probably founded on ideas of the lawbreaker as an individual actor and enforcement by a public police, in regulation much of the potential for violation rests with corporations and other organizations, or at least with individuals who are part of organizations. Given the complexity of many regulated bureaucracies, differing levels of organizational and legal responsibility, and differing opportunities, incentives, and motives for engaging in regulatory misconduct, this has major implications for the enforcement strategy adopted by regulatory officials. Some of these issues are touched on in this volume by Kagan and Scholz, but the regulated organization as the object of law enforcement is a topic ripe for research [see Stone, 1980; Vaughn, 1982].

Also high on any agenda for research on the regulatory process should be the study of enforcement practice as a part of agency behavior. Just as it is essential to know how policy is formed in the regulatory bureaucracy, it is also important to know how that policy is transmitted downwards through the organization and implemented at the street level. The size of most regulatory bureaucracies, the complexity of the problems in the arena to be regulated, and the inevitable existence of a rather autonomous and dispersed inspectorate, all make the issue of how to control discretion at the field level crucial. At the same time, however, we need to know more about the ways in which implementation is shaped by virtue of an enforcement agent's membership in an organization. At the organizational level, for example, an agency committed to a strategy of compliance might well end up enforcing regulations so as to produce evidence of activity rather than evidence of effectiveness, simply because the former is much easier to display than the latter. (That such evidence is required is another kind of testimony to the essential political vulnerability of regulatory agencies.) However, a similar irony might be evident on an individual level where enforcement agents may well seek to display their activity (rather than their effectiveness) to their superiors, because regulatory organizations may in fact find it easier to monitor activity rather than effectiveness.

It is important to recognize that perceptions and evaluations of enforcement problems affect policy decisions. McKean has observed that regulatory policy analysts rarely consider ''the implications that enforcement costs have for deciding whether or not to regulate and what form of regulation to adopt. Such analysts usually assume perfect compliance, rarely experiencing any judgments about the degree of effectiveness that might be expected'' [McKean, 1980: 270]. More significantly, perhaps, policy makers fail to understand field-level actions that fundamentally influence enforcement costs. Such actions include inspection, bargaining, and monitoring — that is, the behavior of agents who are supposed to apply standard operating procedures designed to control the exercise of discretion. In general, these points illustrate the role of enforcement practice as a constraint on rational policy making in regulation. As Diver has noted, agencies have tended to neglect the ''inherent nature of the enforcement function,'' and in so doing have contributed significantly to regulatory failure [Diver, 1980: 298].

An understanding of the enforcement process can have significant implications for the design of legislation. Regulatory lawmaking typically includes both an effort to specify substantive goals *and* a means for achieving these goals. The latter implies a set of requirements imposed on the agency to insure its cooperation with the law. This can come in the form of statutory provisions mandating formal review mechanisms, reporting requirements, and decision-making procedures [see Rosenbaum, 1982: 15]. Consequently, knowledge of the way the agency bureaucracy develops and implements enforcement policy can be of considerable value at the lawmaking stage of regulation. The problem of policy formation in regulation is the subject of a second volume in this series.

References

Bardach, Eugene (1979). Reason, Responsibility and the New Social Regulation, in Burnham and Weinberg (eds.); *American Politics and Public Policy*. Cambridge, Mass.: The MIT Press.

Bardach, Eugene and Robert Kagan (1982). *Going by the Book: The Problem of Regulatory Unreasonableness*. Philadelphia: Temple University Press.

Beckenstein, Alan R. and H. Landis Gabel (1980). Organizational Compliance Processes and the Efficiency of Antitrust Enforcement. Presented at the 1980 meeting of the Law and Society Association, Madison, Wis., June 5–8.

Black, Donald J. (1973). The Mobilization of Law, 2 *Journal of Legal Studies* 125.

Boyer, Barry B. (1972). Alternatives to Administrative Trialtype Hearings for Resolving Complex Scientific, Economic, and Social Issues, 71 *Michigan Law Review* 111.

Clinard, Marshall B. (1979). *Illegal Corporate Behavior* Washington, D.C: LEAA, U.S. Department of Justice.

Clune, William III and R. E. Lindquist [1981]. What "Implementation" Isn't: Toward a General Framework for Implementation Research, *Wisconsin Law Review*, (Volume 1981, No. 5) 1044.

Conklin, John E. (1977). *Illegal, But not Criminal: Business Crime in America*. Englewood Cliffs, N.J.: Prentice-Hall.

Danaceau, Paul (1982). Developing Successful Enforcement Programs, in Bardach and Kagan (eds.) *Social Regulation: Strategies for Reform*. San Francisco: Institute for Contemporary Studies.

Davis, Kenneth Culp (1969). *Discretionary Justice*. Baton Rouge: Louisiana State University Press.

DeLong, James V. (1979). Informal Rulemaking and the Integration of Law and Policy, 65 *Virginia Law Review* 257.

Diver, Colin S. (1980). A Theory of Regulatory Enforcement, 28 *Public Policy* 257.

Edelman, Murray (1964). *The Symbolic Uses of Politics*. Urbana, Ill.: University of Illinois Press.

Freedman, James O. (1978). *Crisis and Legitimacy*. London: Cambridge University Press.

Fuller, Lon L. (1960). Adjudication and the Rule of Law, 1960 *Proceedings of the American Society of International Law*.

Galanter, Marc (1972). The Deployment Process in the Implementation of Legal Policy. Proposal to National Science Foundation. Law School, State University of New York at Buffalo.

Harvard Law Review (1979). Developments in the Law — Corporate Crime: Regulating Corporate Behavior Through Criminal Sanction, 92 *Harvard Law Review* 1227.

Hawkins, Keith (1980). The Use of Discretion by Regulatory Officials: A Case Study on Environmental Pollution in the United Kingdom. Paper presented at the Conference on Perspectives on Regulation: Law, Discretion and Bureaucratic Behavior, sponsored by the Baldy Center for Law and Social Policy and the Oxford University Centre for Socio-legal Studies, State University of New York at Buffalo, May.

———. (1983). "Bargain and Bluff: Compliance Strategy and Deterrence in the Enforcement of Regulation", 5 *Law and Policy Quarterly* 35.

———. (forthcoming). *Environment and Enforcement: Regulation and the Social Definition of Pollution*. New York: Oxford University Press.

Holden, Matthew, Jr. (1966). Pollution Control as a Bargaining Process. Unpublished manuscript.

Joskow, Paul L. and Roger C. Noll (1982). Regulation in Theory and Practice: An Overview in Fromm (ed.), *Studies in Public Regulation*. Cambridge, Mass.: MIT Press.

Kadish, Sanford H. (1963). Some Observations on the Use of Criminal Sanctions in Enforcing Economic Regulations, 30 *University of Chicago Law Review* 423.

Kagan, Robert (1978). *Regulatory Justice*. New York: Russell Sage.

Kelman, Steven (1981). *Regulating America, Regulating Sweden*. Cambridge, Mass.: MIT Press.

Lilley, William III and James C. Miller III (1977). The New Social Regulation, 47 *The Public Interest* 649.

Lipsky, Michael (1980). *Street-level Bureaucracy*. New York: Russell Sage.

———. (1976). Toward a Theory of Street-level Bureaucracy, in Hawley and Lipsky (eds.) *Theoretical Perspectives on Urban Politics*. Englewood Cliffs, N.J.: Prentice-Hall.

Long, Susan B. (1979). The Internal Revenue Service: Examining the Exercise of Discretion in Tax Enforcement. Paper presented before the 1979 Annual Meeting of the Law and Society Association. San Francisco.

McAdams, Tony and Robert C. Miljus (1977). Growing Criminal Liability for Executives, *March–April Harvard Business Review* 36.

McCraw, Thomas K. (ed.) (1982). *Regulation in Perspective*. Cambridge, Mass.: Harvard University Press.

McKean, Roland N. (1980). Enforcement Costs in Environmental and Safety Regulation, 6 *Policy Analysis* 269.

Mileski, Maureen A. (1971). *Policing Slum Landlords: An Observation Study of Administrative Control*. Yale University PhD. Dissertation.

Nivola, Pietro S. (1978). Distributing a Municipal Service: A Case Study of Housing Inspection, 40 *Journal of Politics* 59.

Noll, Roger G. (1976). *Government Administrative Behavior and Private Sector Response: A Multidisciplinary Survey*. California Institute of Technology Social Science Working Paper No. 62, October.

Pedersen, William F. (1975). Formal Records and Informal Rulemaking, 85 *Yale Law Journal* 38.

Pfeffer, Jeffrey (1982). *Organizations and Organization Theory*. Boston: Pitman Publishing Inc.

Posner, R. (1969). The Federal Trade Commission, 37 *University of Chicago Law Review* 47.

Rabin, Robert (1977). Administrative Law in Transition: A Discipline in Search of an Organizing Principle, 72 *Northwestern University Law Review* 120.

Reiss, Albert J. and Albert D. Biderman (1980). *Data Sources on White-collar Law-breaking*. Washington, D.C.: Government Printing Office.

Rosenbaum, Nelson (1982). Statutory Structure and Policy Implementation: The Case of Wetlands Regulation, in Mazmanian and Sabatier (eds.), *Effective Policy Implementation*. Lexington, Mass.: Lexington Books.

Rosenthal, S. and E. Levine (1980). Case Management and Policy Implementation, 28 *Public Policy*. 381.

Ross, H. Laurence and John M. Thomas (1981). Blue-Collar Bureaucrats and the Law in Action: Housing Code Regulation in Three Cities. Paper presented at the 1981 meeting of the Association for Public Policy Analysis and Management, Washington, D.C., October 23, 1981.

Sabatier, Paul A. (1977) Regulatory Policy-making: Toward a Framework of Analysis, 17 *Natural Resources Journal* 415.

Schuck, Peter H. (1972). The Curious Case of the Indicted Meat Inspectors, *Harper's Magazine,* (September).

Schultze, Charles L. (1977). The Public Use of Private Interest, *Harper's Magazine.* (May).

Shapiro, Susan (1979). Thinking About White-collar Crime: Matters of Conceptualization and Research. Unpublished manuscript, Yale University.

Silbey, Susan (1980). Mediation: A Means of Cooperating with Business. Presented at the 1980 meeting of the Law and Society Association, Madison, Wisconsin, June 5–8.

Simon, H. A. (1978). Rationality as Process and as Product of Thought, *American Economic Association Proceedings* 68 (May) 1.

Stewart, Richard B. (1975). The Reformation of American Administrative Law, 88 *Harvard Law Review* 1669.

Stone, Christopher (1980). The Place of Enterprise Liability in the Control of Corporate Conduct, 90 *Yale Law Journal* 1.

Subcommittee on Crime-U.S. House of Representatives (1978). *White-collar Crime.* Washington, D.C.: U.S. Government Printing Office.

Thomas, John M. (1982). The Regulatory Role in the Containment of Corporate Illegality, in Edelhertz and Overcast (eds.), *A Research Agenda on White-collar Crime.* Lexington, Mass.: Lexington Books.

Turner, James S. (1970). *The Chemical Feast.* New York: Grossman.

Vaughn, Diane (1982). Toward Understanding Organizational Behavior, 80 *Michigan Law Review* 1 377.

Weidenbaum, Murray (1978). The Impacts of Government Regulation. Working paper No. 32, Center for the Study of American Business. St. Louis: Washington University.

Wilson, James Q. (1974). The Politics of Regulation in James McKie (ed.) *Social Responsibility and the Business Predicament.*

Zeckhauser, R. and A. Nichols (1978). *The Occupational Safety and Health Administration: An Overview Prepared for the Senate Committee on Government Operations.* U.S. Senate Committee on Government Operations, August. Washington, D.C.: U.S. Government Printing Office.

2 SELECTING STRATEGIES OF SOCIAL CONTROL OVER ORGANIZATIONAL LIFE

Albert J. Reiss, Jr.

Generic Social Control Strategies

We shall regard social control as organized behavior *intended* to control the behavior or activities of others [Janowitz, 1975; Zald, 1978]. Our main purpose is to make problematic the choice between two generic forms of social control, *compliance* and *deterrence*. To simplify the exposition, it is limited to the conditions under which law and legal agents of social control opt for one or the other of these generic forms. What is said seemingly applies, within specifiable limits, to all organizations.

Compliance and Deterrence Systems of Social Control.

Compliance and *deterrence* forms of law enforcement have different objectives. The principal objective of a compliance law enforcement system is to secure conformity with law by means insuring compliance or by taking action to prevent potential law violations without the necessity to detect, process, and penalize violators. The principal objective of deterrent law enforcement systems is to secure conformity with law by detecting violations of law, determining who is responsible

Support for this investigation was provided by the National Institute of Justice, U.S. Department of Justice, under Grant # 80-IJ-CX-0106.

for their violation, and penalizing violators to deter violations in the future, either by those who are punished or by those who might do so were violators not penalized.

There are a number of ways that we can compare and contrast these systems. For one, although both compliance and deterrence law enforcement systems are oriented towards *preventing* the occurrence of violations, compliance systems are *premonitory,* attending to conditions that induce conformity or to foreboding of harm. By contrast deterrent law enforcement systems are *postmonitory,* reacting to violations that have occurred. Agents are oriented towards apprehending violators and penalizing them to prevent future violations. Each system, then, aims to prevent violations but they differ in the means of prevention.

Although penalties may be used in either system, they are integral only to deterrence systems. Deterrence systems assume that penalties have causal effect, the principal of which is to prevent future violations. Compliance systems, correlatively, either reward or withhold imposing penalties to induce states of compliance. Penalties when invoked in compliance systems are seen principally as *threats* rather than as sanctions to be carried out. Sanctions typically are suspended and withdrawn on demonstration of a state of compliance. Where penalty systems primarily manipulate punishments, compliance systems principally manipulate rewards. The rewards used vary among control organizations but they include such diverse incentives as money grants and subsidies, privileges such as licensing, tax abatement, and assumed or limited liability.

Many, if not most, social control systems are organized as a mixture of compliance and deterrence models of law enforcement. Still when faced with a potential or actual violation, the two systems behave differently. When faced with a potential violation, the deterrence-based system will mobilize its detection system to await the actual violation so that it may catch and punish violators; the compliance-based system correlatively will attempt to prevent its occurrence. To prevent violations, compliance systems may use *threats* of punishments, but to actually carry out a punishment is a signal of its failure to prevent the non-compliance. System responses differ also when actual violations are detected. Since compliance systems are based in rewards, negative sanctions typically take the form of threats to withdraw, or the actual withdrawing of, rewards. Where the reward is a privilege such as licensing, the threat will be to revoke the license. The punishments are more directly linked to compliance and the prevention of non-compliance. In deterrence-based systems, actual punishments are more generic in nature and less likely to be linked to specific forms of conduct.

There appear to be differences also in the process by which actual punishment is determined. Hawkins [1984] observes that penalties in a compliance system are the outcome of a long negotiation process. A penalty is resorted to when and only when it signals the termination of negotiation — a sign of exasperation with the violator. This appears to be the case in certain forms of compliance systems. More generally, where the relationship between enforcer and potential violator must be a continuing one, the penalty is assessed as a form of leverage to secure compliance. The violator has a choice between bearing the costs of compliance or the costs of the penalty. The efficacy of compliance enforcement depends in part upon the trade-offs between the costs of compliance and of penalties. Whether or not penalties are actually invoked to secure leverage for compliance, or, rather, to punish for failure to negotiate a reasonable agreement in good faith, the levying of a penalty in compliance systems is a mark of its failure to secure compliance, whereas the levying of a penalty is a mark of success in deterrence-based systems. In deterrence systems, penalties serve notice that all violators will suffer a similar fate; in compliance-based systems, they serve notice that the law enforcement system has been unable to secure compliance.

Compliance and deterrence law enforcement systems differ also in their organization for the mobilization of law. Compliance systems are organized to induce conformity either by providing incentives towards that end or using means that prevent unwanted conditions. They are primarily proactive in their mobilization [Reiss and Bordua, 1967:29, 40–41]. Deterrence law enforcement systems are organized to detect and process violations once they have occurred. They vary in their mix of proactive and reactive mobilization forms, but on balance depend upon reactive mobilization.

Violations are attended to in both compliance and deterrence enforcement systems, but the two systems recognize and process them differently. Deterrence law enforcement is mobilized by the detection of and search for violations and their perpetrators, whereas compliance systems are mobilized by observing the conditional states of systems and their propensities for compliance and noncompliance. The core violation in a compliance system is often dubbed a "technical" violation, behavior that violates a condition or standard that is designed to *prevent* harm or unwanted conditions. In contrast, the core violation in a deterrence system is *immediately harmful* behavior. Compliance systems, indeed, create standards for monitoring compliance and noncompliance that define a host of technical violations. The Securities and Exchange Commission in the United States, for example, has a host of regulations relating to bookkeeping and reporting; failure of registered parties to follow them constitutes a technical violation [Shapiro, 1980:245–48].

Typically, compliance and deterrence systems differ as well in their presumptions of sociocultural causality. Deterrence systems rest on presumptions about the causal effect of sanctions, especially the power of sanctioning violators to deter future violation. The deterrent penalties of the criminal law and penalties within the civil law are based for the most part on reactive mobilizations. The preventive and incentive strategies of administrative law depend principally upon proactive strategies. Compliance systems presume knowledge of what causes violations and of how to prevent them if causal conditions are manipulated.

Looked at yet another way, deterrence law enforcement systems seek to penalize persons or organizations for the harms they have caused, whereas compliance systems seek to avoid harms and their consequences. Compliance systems, consequently, are as concerned with insuring that laws are obeyed as in obtaining conformity once they are broken. Compliance systems focus on the viola*tion*, not the viola*tor*. Their central concern is to control occurrences and their consequences by inducing potential violators to comply with the law.

Designing Social Control Systems of Law Enforcement

The choice between compliance and deterrence strategies of social control is governed by both general and specific conditions of organizations. Below we explore some of these conditions that govern choice.

There are conditions where a choice can be made to pursue either a deterrent or a compliance strategy and some where either strategy seems a reasonable choice. Many organizations pursue mixed strategies of social control, opting for mixes of compliance and deterrent strategies. The typical administrative regulatory agency in the United States, for example, combines both compliance and deterrence strategies in administrative and civil proceedings; it also can opt to mobilize the criminal justice system to pursue deterrent strategies. Where choices exist, the trade-offs between detecting and sanctioning violators to prevent future harms and the immediate prevention of harms and their relative effectiveness in doing so often govern the choice.

Compliance strategies *will* be preferred whenever the processes of detecting violations and sanctioning violators are so complex and protracted or so costly that they are regarded as inadequate remedies for *continuing harm*. They are favored, then, because they provide the quickest relief to continuing harm. Injunctive processes, for example, are essentially compliance-oriented. They grant temporary or perpetual relief from a possible harmful course of action that cannot adequately be redressed by another action at law.

Whether or not one seeks to redress as well as to prevent harm is an important condition affecting the choice of a strategy. The choice between restitutive or reparative sanctions and the state's denial of life, liberty, or property, for example, rests upon resolving questions of who is to be considered victimized and whose harm is to be redressed by whom. Compliance strategies will be opted for where the possibilities of redressing serious and consequential harms to collectivities are negligible, even when the likelihood of harm is rare. The reasons are simple and obvious enough. There is little gain from deterring future behavior when the behavior penalized has been so harmful that it threatens collective life. Given the harmful consequences of radiation or the potentially harmful effects of gene splicing, for example, the system will opt for compliance rather than the punishment of violators. The offending parties in harm by radiation can indeed be victims of their own violation. The Nuclear Regulatory Commission thus is compelled in the first instance to opt for compliance rather than deterrence to control harmful consequences from the generation of nuclear power.

A condition of modern societies is that they are based on trust relationships. Whenever trust systems break down or are undermined in exacting obedience to law, there commonly is recourse to a compliance model of enforcement and its attendant methods of detection by surveillance and direct intervention. There are many examples of this devolution, or reversion, as trust systems are fragile. Shearing and Stenning [1981] demonstrate that private policing has grown rapidly as a substitute for public policing not only because private organizations can control policing for their own ends, but more importantly because private police are oriented primarily towards controlling *opportunities* for breaches of the law. Public police by contrast are oriented towards discovering breaches of the law, problem populations, and apprehension [Shearing and Stenning, 1981: 214]. Similarly, when local citizens lose trust in public policing they often respond with attempts to develop direct forms of surveillance and control through citizen watch and vigilante groups [Marx and Archer, 1971]. Moreover, a response to the breakdown of trust in public life, such as that in the hijacking of airplanes, is a resort to surveillance and compliance strategies where only those who pass scanning, screening, and, if necessary, personal searches are permitted to board commercial aircraft. In the face of terrorist activities, though the events be rare, those areas and persons whose protection is considered most vital will be surrounded with compliance law enforcement. Organizations likewise increasingly protect themselves against external subversion from those who cannot be trusted with direct observation, identification, and control of access and egress. Photo identification has come to dominate all former trust systems whether they be the borrowing of books from a university library or the entrance of persons to the Oval Office. Organizations are more interested in having those who would potentially harm them or their employees pass compliance tests than in reacting to infractions once they have taken place.

Deterrence systems generally arise when the occurrence of events in time and place are unpredictable and when their causes are imperfectly understood so that particular preventive actions cannot be undertaken. Correlatively, the more predictable any violation or the greater the certainty that a particular intervention will prevent violations, the more likely the organization will resort to compliance strategies. Compliance systems, consequently, often are associated with testing and licensing systems, especially ones that require some demonstration that conformity exists prior to undertaking a particular activity that could cause harm. The license itself can be seen as a conditional reward or at least as conditionally related to rewards; so long as one conforms, one is licensed to be rewarded. Parenthetically, we note that questions about the efficacy of such strategies must be separated from matters of belief in efficacy. Control of medical practice or the generation of nuclear power, for example, opts for both licensing practice and sanctioning malpractice; but the critical sanction is the withdrawal of the license to practice. And, control of the manufacture of drugs includes testing evaluation, licensing, and monitoring.

Compliance systems emerge whenever long-run consequences are far more serious than short-run harms and whenever long-run harms can be avoided only by short-run interventions. It is difficult, for example, to undo an election and its results by attempting to locate and punish persons who have voted illegally or to void the effects of illegal campaign financing. The main alternative to accepting a manipulated outcome is a new election. Such outcomes generally are too costly and too difficult to reconstitute, so that the system opts to avoid the consequences by adopting compliance procedures. Compliance is sought by setting standards and procedures for campaign financing, registration of eligible voters and their certification at time of voting, the development of technological and organizational means to cast and record votes, and by maintaining voting records that can be audited after an election. Similarly when delayed effects are understood, for example, how coal dust in mines causes both black lung disease and deadly explosions, enforcement emphasis falls more upon conditions that produce clean air in mines than upon punishing mine owners when infractions are detected.

Deterrence systems are generally ineffective when penalties against individuals, or especially against organizations, can be passed on and borne by others without inflicting grievous harm to any of the parties. Thus the fining of the corporation can be borne by consumers so long as it does not fatally damage the competitive position of the corporation. The alternative of setting the costs so high that it damages the interests that other parties have in the organization is often unacceptable since such parties are deemed innocent and it is unjust for them to bear such costs. Moreover, interested parties protect their interests by bringing political pressures to bear to reduce the penalties. In either case, the deterrent effect is limited because of the consequences of the penalties for affected but innocent parties. At times the penalties, when invoked, will be designated for the benefit of innocent and affected parties. More commonly, however, the failure of penalties to have a deterrent effect leads to the substitution of a compliance strategy.

The tort doctrines of negligence and liability for harm, including the special case of strict liability, rest on deterrent strategies. The presumption is that one will exercise ordinary care to avoid the costs of being found liable. Prudence may require that one protect oneself against claims of liability, but there is an element of deterrence there also since one's cost of protection may increase on being held liable. Tort doctrines are designed to redress injury and to reduce the risk of injury. The collectivization of risk either to injured or injuring parties are ways to ameliorate or minimize the consequences of harm to either party. But organizational risk-taking, either for the organization inflicting the injury or for the organization assuming the risk on its behalf, as, for example, by insuring against the costs of harm, is most likely when such risks are calculable. That is not always the case. Moreover, when, as noted previously, such risks can be reduced by preventable actions, there will be pressures to opt for compliance strategies, particularly where there are third-party interests for reducing the risk of injury. The compliance strategies adopted to insure safe consumer products are a case in point. There an organized intelligence system of hospital emergency treatment for injuries resulting from consumer products is used to get organizations to develop safe products rather than as a basis for enhancing the claims of litigants. Consumer product safety enforcement also exemplifies how a surveillance system is an essential ingredient of compliance enforcement.

All organizations, from the smallest to the largest, from the family to the modern state, rest on institutions of secrecy and their private as well as public protection. To a substantial degree, secrets are integral to trust since a condition of trust is the capacity to keep secrets. All organizations are vulnerable to the disclosure of their secrets. The greater the harm that can result from the disclosure of a secret, the greater the investment an organization has in preventing its disclosure. The punishment of violators for disclosing secrets is of limited value since it takes place only after the secret is disclosed and the organization harmed.

Secrets are integral to trust since the capacity to keep secrets is a condition of trust. Paradoxically, then, secrets are vulnerable to the very conditions that make them possible. The society that exists by surveillance and direct control is essentially without secrets whereas the society built on trust will maintain secrecy and individuality [Durkheim, 1947]. The greater the divison of labor and the larger the scale of its organizations, the more trust must be substituted for direct surveillance. Yet the larger the organization, the more vulnerable it is to the breakdown of trust relationships and the disclosure of secrets. Where such secrets are vital to the organization, it cannot, as noted, rely upon deterrent strategies. The resolution to this seeming paradox is to combine control by compliance surveillance with trust.

Compliance systems emerge where regulators or controllers can define a distinct population of potential violators and track them to exercise direct surveillance and control over them. Compliance systems, therefore, are more likely to be opted for by organizations to control the behavior of organizations or of persons in organized activities within and without organizations rather than to control the behavior of discrete individuals. Correlatively, deterrent strategies are opted for when organizations attempt to control the behavior of discrete and dispersed individuals.

Whenever compliance is directed towards discrete individuals — as it is for some behavior — compliance will be treated as a voluntary rather than as a required activity.

To be effective, then, compliance will be directed towards known populations that can be surveyed by direct observation or by some other means of monitoring behavior and evaluating conduct. Total institutions are compliance-oriented; the public streets and private places are not. Mob and crowd behavior are subject primarily to surveillance and directed or commanded intervention. Infiltration, spying, and related forms of intelligence collection are essential to compliance strategies and may be used for proactive detection in deterrence based systems but they are not an essential element of a deterrence strategy. Similarly, tactics such as harassment are compliance-inducing rather than simple deterrent strategies. When deterrent systems of justice fail, the police often substitute direct control systems such as harassment. Note, though, that harassment works only when a population is reasonably concentrated in space through participation in some form of organized activity. Thus one can harass prostitutes congregated in residential units or in a particular territory, but one cannot similarly harass call girls into conforming with stated law enforcement objectives for controlling their activity.

Organizations likewise are more likely to seek compliance when the same victims are repeatedly victimized by the same violators or when there is a very large number of victims for a very small number of violators. In either case, the violators are more easily detected, viewed, and controlled. Moreover, short of incapacitation strategies, few penalties are likely to work under these conditions. Organizations are more likely to victimize in these conditions than are persons. Note, however, that repeated violations in very small organizations such as families are more likely to be subject to compliance than deterrence strategies. Initial efforts to control the behavior of intrafamilial violence, for example, aim towards preserving the integrity of the organization by seeking compliance rather than by imposing penalties. Observe also that under these conditions the family also will be controlled by compliance strategies because it meets other requirements for those strategies. Penalties, for example, victimize innocent members.

The selection of compliance strategies as the means of social control often depends upon the degree to which controllers can manipulate *collateral security*. Given the vulnerability of trust as a means of social control, promises can be buttressed with collateral security. Indeed, where one cannot rely upon direct surveillance and control, and yet where relationships must continue, trust is necessary and promise essential. Where one can practically and legitimately levy and enforce penalties, deterrence is an alternative strategy for broken agreements, but where one lacks the power of deterrence, compliance strategies based on collateral security are viable. Hostages were originally forms of collateral security. One *gave* a most valued person in hostage to assure the voluntary agreement would be kept. Today the hostage is *taken* to insure compliance with a coerced agreement. Collateral securities are often used by organizations to insure that agreements will be carried out, i.e., their conditions complied with. Collateral is intended to guarantee both the validity and convertibility of tender or to insure performance of an agreement. If direct security fails, one may fall back upon the collateral. The greater the mistrust that agreements will be kept, or the more vulnerable to damage the parties to an agreement if it is not kept, the more likely they are to insist upon collateral security and the more likely that collateral will take the form of transferring possession of the collateral until the agreement is carried out. We note in passing that the institution of bail replaced the communal guarantees of appearance by direct control of the accused or later, the simple promise to appear. The bail bondsman of today is synedochically related to the surety or guarantor for the promise of the accused and it, in turn, is the synedoche of the hundred in early England.

Changes Affecting Deterrence Strategies

In modern democratic societies, deterrence systems depend upon the capacity to detect, to prove wrongdoing, and to adjudicate matters to which penalties are attached. The structure of modern democratic societies makes it increasingly difficult to satisfy these conditions so that most violations cannot be detected and penalized, most especially those involving violations of trust. Deterrent effects, accordingly, are substantially reduced because perceptions of risk of detection and of being penalized are judged low. In contrast, compliance systems are less subject to restrictions of detection and proof, and compliance rather than deterrence objectives are sought. We shall consider briefly the major changes in modern societies that bring about these conditions and their relationship to selecting compliance or deterrence strategies of control.

Extension of Entitlements

Historically three major changes have altered substantially the nature of wrongdoing and its control. The first of these was emphasized by Durkheim in pointing to the consequences of the elaboration of the division of labor. The common conscience that controlled behavior was weakened in all respects except that it strengthened the individual's position vis-a-vis the collectivity [Durkheim, 1947:172]. In particular, modern democratic welfare societies are characterized by the extension of entitlements (what Charles Reich [1970] characterizes as the *new property*): rights and benefits for which all are eligible. They also have extended

substantially the *right to privacy* of the place and person, making it more difficult
to directly observe and survey wrongdoing and to gather evidence concerning
lawbreaking [Stinchcombe, 1963: 151]. Moreover, such extensions make it more
difficult to formally adjudicate matters and administer penalties because of the
rights of the accused [Reiss, 1974].

A major consequence of these changes is that they have made it increasingly
difficult to detect wrongdoing in deterrence-based systems. At the same time these
changes have had less effect on compliance-based systems, most especially those
relating to organizational behavior. The basic systems of surveillance by inspection and of investigation, including audit, are far less restricted in compliance than
in deterrence based systems. What we wish to emphasize here is that techniques of
detection and proof that are considerably restricted in deterrence-based systems are
far more likely to be legitimated in compliance-based systems, especially where
one seeks to control the behavior of organizations or of organized activity.

Two other important consequences of these continuing changes are worth noting
because of their effect on wrongdoing and deterrence strategies of law enforcement. One of these is that the growth of the new property has changed substantially
the way that members of underprivileged classes commit crimes; the nature of the
new property of rights and privileges is to make it possible to commit a whole
series of law violations formerly the domain of the higher classes. These include
especially crimes of fraud and misrepresentation with respect to the new property.
The second consequence is that all classes, but especially the underclasses, can
bargain over their outcomes in a justice system given the difficulty of proving
matters in a formal system of justice that recognizes this extension of individual
rights. Not surprisingly, it is large-scale organizations in countries such as the
United States that have benefited most because of the extension of almost all
individual rights to organizations. An historic failure to constitutionally differentiate organizations from individuals as a class has enhanced substantially the
power of organizations before the law and of individuals who operate as their
agents.

Growth of Trust Systems

The second major change has been the shift historically from direct observation
and intervention to trust as the fundamental basis of relationships and transactions.

One might trace the evolution of strategies of social control from strategies
of control by surveillance to control by trust. It is mistaken to regard trust as an
element in primary group control, since the hallmarks of the simpler systems of
primary group control are surveillance, the absence of privacy, and coercion. It
was a simple matter in simple societies, it seems, to detect and deal with delicts,
since even crimes of stealth were difficult to accomplish without being observed or

easily detected. Simple societies and small groups can be seen as compliance-oriented in that the central element in compliance systems is the capacity to observe, monitor, and directly intervene in behavior. Without assigning causal attribution, we can trace a gradual evolution from systems based on surveillance to systems based on trust. Very simply put, where one cannot directly observe, yet seeks to control, the principal substitutes are collateral security and trust. The basic contention is that modern societies and their organizations are increasingly built on complex trust relationships.

To say that modern societies are built principally on trust relationships, however, is not to suggest that they are built primarily around institutions of trust. Indeed, the development of trust systems has markedly changed the nature of wrongdoing. In modern societies prototypical lawbreaking is a violation of organizational trust. Trust relationships are vulnerable to fraud, misrepresentation, and failure to abide by agreement. The inherent fragility of trust relationships leads to a parallel emergence of institutions built around mistrust and distrust as well as those of trust. There are, for example, a series of institutions that are designed to minimize the risk of harm when fiduciary responsibility is violated. There are institutions of distrust such as of collateral security and the collectivization of risk to minimize losses from harms due to a violation of trust.

Trust may be regarded as the principal means of organizing and controlling individual as well as organizational behavior in modern societies. The individual who ventures into the street trusts that those around him intend no harm. Exchanges among organizations are essentially trust agreements. The contract — the fundamental basis of all relationships — rests on the trust that it will be carried out, not that one will have to invoke machinery of enforcement to secure its fulfillment. Indeed, it is all too apparent that the power of law as a means of social control lies in its capacity to secure compliance by agreement; to enforce the law by deterrence is to acknowledge the failure of law as a fundamental instrument of social control.

The cardinal violations of modern societies, then, are violations of trust, with organizations as well as individuals being the victims as well as the violators. Apart from the protections afforded by the institutions of mistrust, whenever trust is violated the principal means evolved for coping with trust violations is that of a penalty for violating trust. While such penalties may take the form of simple restitution, they often require satisfying a collective interest as well. That collective interest takes the form of assigning penalties to deter future violations.

Growth of Organizations and the Complexity of Organizational Life

The third major change, the emergence of large-scale organizations, though related to a growing complexity of the division of labor, is both a cause and consequence of the shift from deterrence to compliance strategies. To a growing extent, lawbreaking occurs on the part of organizations, especially large-scale organizations. In capitalist societies such lawbreaking extends to the not-for-profit as well as government and profit-making organizations.

Organizations create more difficult problems of detection and proof given their greater capacity to avoid detection [Shapiro, 1980], to subvert the processes of investigation and proof [Katz, 1979], and to bargain over the outcomes of deterrence-based adjudication. Correlatively, organizational processes have remained more open to the very same methods of detection and proof where the goal is compliance. Indeed, so far as organizations are concerned, they may be required to engage in self-incrimination when compliance is at stake.

Inasmuch as most violations involving organizations are violations of trust and inasmuch as deterrence-based law enforcement systems are relatively restricted in their capacities to detect, prove, and sanction violations of trust, modern societies increasingly turn to compliance-based systems of control over violations of trust. One might readily question why modern societies do not legitimate within deterrence-based systems what is legitimated in compliance-based systems. There is no simple answer to that question, but the answer lies in part in opting for the prevention of harms because of their consequences to both injured and injuring parties. But it may lie also in the peculiar way in which the central institutions, including those of trust, are preserved in such societies. Where the state intends no injury as a consequence of its control and at the same time affords protection to the integrity of organizations, it is easier to legitimate forms of intervention that would otherwise be precluded in the interests of the injuring as well as the injured parties.

Conclusion

We have posed some propositions concerning the conditions under which modern democratic states attempt to control behavior, especially organizational deviance through compliance-based rather than deterrence-based systems. It is apparent that law enforcement agencies often are built around both. Still, if the basic thesis propounded is sound, then one should expect that two kinds of shifts will continue to take place in attempts to control individual and organizational lawbreaking and to prevent harms to individuals and organizations. One of these is that more and more systems of social control will be built around compliance rather than deterrent strategies. Both individuals and organizations will have to respond to compliance strategies. The prototypical enforcement strategy for both individuals and organizations will become more like that of the Internal Revenue Service than like that of a local police agency. The other is that deterrent law enforcement may be expected to shift more towards proactive rather than reactive forms of mobilization, especially towards the techniques of proactive law enforcement that are instrumental to compliance strategies of social control.

References

Durkheim, Emile (1947). *The Division of Labor in Society* (2nd edition, 1902). Translated by George Simpson. Glencoe: The Free Press.

Hawkins, Keith (1984). *Environment and Enforcement: Regulation and the Social Definition of Pollution*. Oxford: Oxford University Press.

Janowitz, Morris (1975). Sociological Theory and Social Control, 81 *American Journal of Sociology* 82.

Katz, Jack (1979). Legality and Equality: Plea-Bargaining in the Prosecution of White-Collar and Common Crimes, 13 *Law and Society Review* 431.

Marx, Gary and D. Archer (1971). Citizen Involvement in the Law Enforcement Process: The Case of Community Police Patrols, 13 *American Behavioral Scientist* 52.

Reich, Charles (1964). The New Property, 72 *Yale Law Journal*. 733.

Reiss, Jr., Albert J. (1974). Citizen Access to Criminal Justice, 1 *British Journal of Law and Society* 50.

Reiss, Jr., Albert J. (1983). The Policing of Organizational Life in Maurice Punch (ed.), *Control of Police Organizations*. Cambridge: MIT Press.

Reiss, Jr., Albert J. and David J. Bordua (1967). Environment and Organization: A Perspective on the Police, in David Bordua (ed.), *The Police: Six Sociological Essays*. New York: John Wiley.

Shapiro, Susan (1980). *Detecting Illegalities: A Perspective on the Control of Securities Violations*. Ann Arbor, Michigan: University Microfilms.

Shearing, Clifford D. and Philip C. Stenning (1981). Modern Private Security: Its Growth and Implications, in Michael Tonry and Norval Morris (eds.), *Crime and Justice: An Annual Review*. Chicago: University of Chicago Press.

Stinchcombe, Arthur (1963). Institutions of Privacy in the Determination of Police Administrative Practice, 69 *American Journal of Sociology* 150.

Zald, Mayer N. (1978). On the Social Control of Industries, 57 *Social Forces* 79.

3 ON REGULATORY INSPECTORATES AND POLICE

Robert A. Kagan

Governmental law enforcement, along with other activities of the modern state, seems to grow more and more specialized. Large urban police departments have special juvenile squads, vice squads, and bomb defusing squads, along with separate political intelligence units, traffic control sections and narcotics investigators. The Internal Revenue Service (IRS) has special enforcement agents for gambling casinos, petroleum companies, and banks. Still, most police officers and revenue agents start out with common training. The special units work within a unified bureaucratic structure and culture. A more extreme manifestation of the trend toward specialization is the establishment of a separate enforcement agency for each of the many regulatory programs enacted by an increasingly interventionist state.

These specialized regulatory enforcement staffs usually are not called "police." We call them "inspectors," or more innocuously, "safety consultants," "equal opportunity specialists," "auditors," "compliance agents," and "nursing home surveyors," but they are in fact special police forces for industry. They are legally empowered to intrude upon private property, examine books and records, take samples and measurements, and interrogate executives and workers in order to uncover evidence of noncompliance with the law. They issue citations that can lead to fines, expensive remedial orders, and, in some cases, criminal penalties. There are many types of inspectorates in the United States today, divided into broad categories based on the kind of protection they seek to provide, such as protection of health and safety, pollution control, prevention of fraud, and antidiscrimination.

Some regulatory inspectorates trace their origin to the nineteenth century. The Federal Bureau of Navigation, established in 1829, sent inspectors to check steamship boilers (to prevent explosions) and to examine sailing vessels for seaworthiness. In the late nineteenth century, the Interstate Commerce Commission required inspection of locomotives, brakes, switching, and signal equipment. By the turn of the century, many states had small inspectorates for factories, coal mines, dairies, and agricultural pests. Large cities provided for inspections to enforce ventilation, fire safety, and overcrowding rules in building codes.

Most present day inspectorates, however, were established or expanded to substantial size only in the 1960s and 1970s, as federal and state legislatures responded to the pressure of civil rights, consumer and environmental groups for "tougher" laws and more effective implementation. Compared to traditional police departments, therefore, most regulatory inspectorates are young institutions. As of yet, they share no overriding ethos of regulatory enforcement. Most people, including regulatory officials, do not think of worker safety inspectors, air pollution testers, and nursing home surveyors as members of a common occupation, sharing common problems and concerns.

In this respect, the contrast between regulatory inspectorates and police forces is striking. "Professionalization" of the police has long been a major concern. Much effort has been devoted to improving police training, enforcement and communication techniques, judicial and administrative due process controls, and imbuing police officers with a philosophy of law enforcement appropriate to a democratic society. Scores of researchers have studied police law enforcement practices in detail.

Few researchers, however, have studied and compared the practices of diverse, organizationally discrete, regulatory inspectorates. There are no "Academies of Regulatory Enforcement" comparable to modern police academies, no schools of regulatory justice comparable to schools of criminal justice. No novels or television series portray the moral crises of workplace safety or air pollution inspectors. We have few accepted notions, and hardly even a meaningful debate, about the norms of responsibility, fairness, and accountability that should govern inspectors' conduct, or what "professionalization" of inspectors might entail. One step in that direction, perhaps, is to develop a sense of what is distinctive about regulatory law enforcement by contrasting it with the more familiar characteristics of law enforcement by police.

This chapter will first point out certain basic commonalities between regulatory inspectorates and police departments. Succeeding sections will discuss differences

— in social function, in the nature of the offenders the police and inspectors typically deal with, and in the nature of the legal offenses they encounter. These differences, it will be shown, distinguish the enforcement tasks and problems experienced by regulatory inspectors from those experienced by police officers. A concluding section will note the implications of the preceding discussion for the "professionalization" of regulatory inspectors.

Throughout, observations about inspectors will be based primarily on unstructured interviews with enforcement officials (plus representatives of regulated firms) in state and federal agencies concerned with air pollution, occupational safety and health, quality of care in nursing homes, truck safety, municipal housing maintenance, the manufacture of pure food and drugs, processing of milk products, and blood banks.[1] The emphasis will be on regulatory enforcement and policing in the United States.

Commonalities

Police and inspectors both are law enforcement officials. Police officers, of course, perform many tasks other than law enforcement; indeed, to some observers, police would more accurately be described as "peacekeepers" or "order maintainers." [see Rumbaut and Bittner, 1979] Still, much police work stems from or involves the officer's authority and obligation to respond to violations of specific legal rules and to initiate legal action against serious violators. So, too, with regulatory inspectorates.

Police and inspectors both work "in the field," out of sight of their supervisors. They make decisions about the meaning of the law in face-to-face contact with complainants and suspects, directly exposed to offenders' expressions of outrage, pleas for mercy, and, on occasion, threats and offers of bribes. In both types of agency, therefore, supervisors at headquarters worry whether their far-flung cadres are honest, fair-minded, and whether they are working at all. Hence supervisors often subject both police and inspectors to informal numerical quotas of enforcement actions and to detailed reporting requirements.[2]

Police and inspectorates face a common set of basic problems, which can be summarized under the rubrics of effectiveness, efficiency, and enforcement style.

Effectiveness

Regulatory inspectors and police both are paid to prevent bad things from happening. But police and regulatory inspectors are called upon to prevent the most unpreventable kinds of offenses — offenses that are too unpredictable or invisible, perpetrated by offenders who are too irresponsible, desperate, elusive, or crazy to be deterred by the threat of private lawsuits and heavy damage awards. The world to be controlled is huge and constantly changing. Bad things can happen any time, anywhere (often in hidden places), and in more ways than lawmakers, regulation-writers, or enforcement officials can anticipate. The best-funded corps of police or inspectors, accordingly, is unlikely to have an enforcement official in the right place at the right time, except in a minority of instances. Police catch but a small proportion of reported muggers, thieves, bullies, and child molesters. Regulatory inspectors can visit most potentially dangerous mines, factories, chemical dumps, and nursing homes a few times a year at best, and for only a few hours; yet the risk of a neglected safety precaution is present 24 hours a day, at least 300 days a year. Measured by the crimes, fights, accidents, and acts of injustice they fail to prevent, therefore, both police and regulatory inspectorates seem doomed to criticism for ineffectiveness. (Of course, the incidence of crime, harmful accidents and injustices probably would be significantly higher if there were *no* police and regulatory inspectors. It is difficult to measure, and hence easy to underestimate, their deterrent effects.)

Efficiency (Method of Detection)

Since enforcement staffs almost always seem inadequate to detect and deter all the hidden and unpredictable sources of harm, police departments and regulatory inspectorates both must decide how to deploy their personnel most efficiently. How can the most "value added" per enforcement official be obtained?

The problem can be viewed in terms of reactive versus proactive enforcement. In the reactive mode, in which police and inspectors respond to complaints, "civilians" tell the official enforcement system when and where it is most likely to find a violation. In many police departments, over 80 percent of encounters between patrolmen and citizens are citizen-initiated [see Reiss 1971; Bayley 1979; Black, 1973]. Regulatory agencies that enforce antidiscrimination laws and worker safety regulations often have similarly high levels of complaint-guided deployment. Responding to complaints, however, often diverts enforcement personnel to comparatively low-priority problems. An enormous amount of police time is taken up by service calls or "social work" activity. Complaints tend to draw occupational health and safety inspectors to unionized workplaces with comparatively good safety records, leaving inspectors less time for employers with the least-protected workers and for testing for invisible toxic particles in the air of the workplace, which are less likely to stimulate complaints.[3]

In proactive enforcement, on the other hand, police can be directed to patrol aggressively in locales with the highest crime rates; inspectors can concentrate on factories that history has shown to have been the most hazardous. Regulatory agencies and police departments, however, both find it difficult to concentrate as many resources on proactive enforcement as they wish or on the targets they would like to give highest priority. Legislators often pressure top enforcement officials to respond above all to the complaints of their constituents, or to concentrate, for political reasons, on particular areas or industries (such as those given prominence in the news media).

Proactive enforcement can also lead to criticism for excessive intrusiveness. To gain access to offenders and offenses not identified by complainants, police departments may resort to ''agressive patrol'' (stopping and questioning suspects), undercover work and entrapment, secret surveillance, surprise searches, use of informers, extraction of confessions, and other tactics that offend norms of privacy, due process, and fair play. For regulatory agencies, the logic of proactive enforcement suggests surprise inspections of suspect enterprises and special demands for more data, certifications and impact statements; the targeted enterprises may complain to political officials about having been harrassed and subjected to competitive disadvantage.

Finally, proactive enforcement can be inefficient if the agency does not have a good sense of where and how its personnel can provide the most ''value added.'' Intensive police patrol in some parts of the city, a Kansas City study showed, had no significant effect on crime rates. [see Kelling et al., 1974] Similarly, if the harms that might be prevented by regulatory action are not easily predictable, as not infrequently is the case, proactive enforcement can lead either to a mindless set of routine surveys of *all* regulated enterprises, or to mis-targeted selective inspections that can be justified only by citing programatically insignificant violations. Both police departments and inspectorates, therefore, share the problem of obtaining adequate information for efficient deployment and the optimum balance of reactive and proactive strategies.

Enforcement Style

When they encounter probable violations, police and inspectors alike make discretionary judgments. They must make on-the-spot assessments of the adequacy of their evidence (''Will an arrest . . . or regulatory citation . . . hold up in court?''). They make intuitive judgments about the virtues (and inconveniences) of initiating formal legal action against the putative violator, as against issuing an informal warning and extracting an agreement to comply with the law in the future.

Formal enforcement in both types of agency typically is slow, labor-intensive and subject to numerous procedural steps designed to protect the innocent, each step allowing the defendant further opportunities for delay and obfuscation. The prosecutor who handles the case, more distant and detached than the policeman or inspector, may agree to a more lenient outcome than the field-level law enforcer thinks justified. On the other hand, the penalties the courts impose will often seem counterproductive. A young man sent to prison cannot finish school, get a job, or pay child support, and may emerge even more antisocial. Similarly, prosecution of a business for regulatory violations, even if it results in the exaction of a fine or an order to remedy a particular rule violation, may not induce the enterprise to make truly significant improvements in its safety or environmental control or personnel program, and the litigation may induce it to be even more uncooperative. An informal "plea bargain," whereby the inspector agrees to suspend formal legal action, provided the enterprise makes some immediate improvements, will often seem more efficient, effective and flexible.

On the other hand, the policeman or inspector who grants "curbside probation" risks being accused of legal impropriety, favoritism, or corruption. The offender may prove to be unreliable or "unreformable" and may end up doing serious harm, to the extreme embarrassment of the field enforcement official and his superiors. To avoid this risk, it would seem most prudent for top enforcement officials to instruct field level personnel to initiate formal legal action whenever legally justified.

Not surprisingly, given these conflicting considerations, some police departments and some regulatory agencies lean toward legalistic strictness, at least for some kinds of violations and violators, while others are more prone to "make exceptions," more oriented toward informal conflict-resolution, conciliation, pressure and persuasion than toward law enforcement.[4] No simple theory explains variations in enforcement style. Clearly, shifts in a regulatory agency's political environment — from domination by liberals and environmentalist groups, say, to domination by probusiness political parties — can influence enforcement practices, either through forced changes in agency leadership or changes in statutory instructions, just as a newly elected mayor's emphasis on fighting crime might push a police department toward a more legalistic style. Some agencies and departments, however, are staffed by experienced personnel who resist external political direction. The attitudes of the set of offenders an enforcement officer deals with may be an equally important determinant of enforcement style, as indicated by Shover et al's finding that Department of Interior inspectors enforcing strip-mine restoration regulations against small, "rugged individualist" entrepreneurs in the mountains of Kentucky and Tennessee operate differently from inspectors in the same agency who deal with large corporate strip-miners on the flat, open plains of eastern Wyoming (where the costs of complying with regulations are far lower per ton). (See below chapter 6) The enforcers' disposition toward leniency or strictness presumably will also be affected by each particular agency's patterns of recruitment, training and supervision, as well as by the eloquence with which individual offenders argue their cases. [See Kagan, 1978]

The balance of this essay, however, is concerned not with explaining enforcement variations within or across regulatory agencies, but with identifying what is distinctive about that choice in regulatory inspectorates as compared with police departments. By emphasizing differences between regulators and police, some of the factors influencing regulatory enforcement practices may be highlighted.

Differences

Social Function: Protecting the Status Quo versus Redistribution

Police departments were established in the nineteenth century in large part to protect institutions of private property from the threat posed by the "dispossessed" masses of burgeoning urban centers. Of course, police departments are also deeply concerned with ordinary peacekeeping and other "noneconomic" matters, such as traffic and crowd control. But much of a police department's daily business still entails the enforcement of laws against various forms of theft and trespass, the legal bulwarks of any system of property. A major social function of police departments thus is to protect the *status quo* in the distribution of property, privilege and power — or at least to prevent ad hoc individual efforts to change it incrementally by force or stealth.

Regulatory inspectors, in contrast, can be viewed as the instruments of a conscious political effort to change the status quo, to *redistribute* property, privilege, and power. In the terminology of welfare economics, the accidents, illnesses, injustices, and environmental degradations that stem from modern technologies and business practices are "externalities" — concomitants of doing business whose costs, due to market imperfections, are escaped by the business firms that produce them and are borne instead by workers, consumers, or the populace as a whole. Protective regulation aims to compel businesses to "internalize" such costs, to make expenditures that would prevent such social harms. In economic terms, forcing a manufacturing firm to spend more on machine guards and ventilation systems is a compulsory redistribution of income from the employer to the workers, who get more health or safety as an added "fringe benefit." Mandatory pollution controls redistribute wealth: the manufacturer's compulsory expenditures on abatement methods presumably relieve the factory's neighbors of some costs of pollution (e.g. reducing their cleaning, and medical bills) and add to the value of their homes. Pure food laws and housing codes are designed to compel food processors and landlords to spend more on sanitation and maintenance; and even if customers and tenants end up paying for the additional costs, they are getting something — more safety, peace of mind, amenities, etc. — that they formerly lacked the knowledge or power to demand. Put in terms of redistribution of power, protective regulation is designed to give workers, tenants, consumers, and environmentalists a greater say — through legally binding regulatory requirements — over how business managers use their property and the economic power that flows from it. Much regulatory legislation of the 1960s and 1970s was accompanied by populist rhetoric that made this redistributive theme explicit. [See Weaver, 1977; Levin, 1979; Wilson, 1980]

The extent to which the hoped for redistributive effects actually occur is of course problematic. Some critics presume that regulatory agencies gradually (if not initially) will be co-opted or captured by regulated enterprises and used for their own self-protective purposes. While this often has occurred in economic regulation, and sometimes in protective regulation,[5] it seems far less true of the intensified protective regulatory programs of the 1960s and 1970s, many of which were consciously structured to prevent capture by the regulated industry [Bardach and Kagan, 1982: Ch. 2] and that are closely monitored by proregulation advocacy organizations. Although compliance is always far from perfect, the billions of dollars spent during the 1970s on compliance with pollution control, auto safety, and worker safety and health regulations,[6] as well as the substantial sums recovered for complainants by consumer fraud and employment discrimination agencies, suggest that some "redistribution" can occur[7] and may even have far-reaching effects on corporate behavior.

Nevertheless, the redistributive thrust of regulatory legislation means that the regulator's basic function, unlike the police officer's, is not to use the law to "hold the fort" and quell outbursts of anarchy, but to change or encourage new systematic practices. Regulators must compel large expenditures of money on safety and pollution control equipment, better record keeping systems and quality assurance staffs, new modes of selling and communicating with the public, new testing and monitoring procedures.[8] Regulators must bring about changes in attitudes about what business practices are acceptable. They must induce shifts in the distribution of power, in corporate decision making, and in responsibility for preventing harms. In seeking these goals, moreover, regulatory officials must take on the most economically and politically powerful elements in civil society.

The Nature of Offenders

Policemen Police Individuals; Inspectors Police Business Organizations and Their Agents. Police officers sometimes do police business organizations, especially if one views narcotics networks, gambling organizations, burglary rings, and so on as businesses. But enforcement against "organized crime" is often concentrated in specialized strike forces, vice and narcotics squads — the more businesslike the offender, the more likely it will not be policed by ordinary patrol units. And when "decriminalization" of liquor distribution and gambling has occurred, the job of policing liquor licensees and casinos has been handed over to a specialized regulatory agency and a staff of inspectors [Skolnick, 1978]. Criminal violations by corporations — stock fraud, price-fixing, bribery, etc. — also are not the province of the men in blue but of specialized "white collar crime" investigators in the Securities and Exchange Commission, the Department of Justice and the Federal Bureau of Investigation.

Most criminal violations — car thefts, assaults, disturbances of the peace, and so on — are committed by individuals, acting on their own. Most patrol officers and police detectives, therefore, police individuals. The lawbreakers they encounter, moreover, tend to be of low social status — lower working class, racial minorities, welfare recipients, juveniles and derelicts, if not outright "criminals" — and certainly of a lower social status than the police officer. Indeed, one source of antagonism to police is that some officers, occupationally accustomed to interaction with socially deviant persons of low status, tend to treat *all* minorities and young people in a somewhat suspicious or disdainful manner.

Regulatory inspectors, in contrast, police "legitimate businesses." In looking for or discussing possible violations, they deal with white collar types who hold well-defined positions in established enterprises — entrepreneurs, managers, pollution control engineers, personnel officers, and so on. More often than not, such individuals are older, better paid and better educated than the inspector and also more knowledgeable about the practices, technologies, and hazards of the particular inspection site. They resent having to stop what they are doing to talk to an inspector when he drops in. They complain of being "treated like a criminal" if the inspector fails to display an appropriate amount of deference to their station and expertise.

The police officer derives authority not only from his official position as representative of the law but also from his uniform, the gun at his hip, and his power to use force. The regulatory inspector — except in the situations where *he* has the authority of greater expertise — has no such additional supports. He is much more likely than the police officer, therefore, to emphasize interpersonal diplomacy and to present himself as an impersonal, sometimes even unwilling, bearer of legal instructions from higher authorities — "Sorry, sir, but this is what the 'regs' require." (Interestingly, police officers seem most likely to adopt this posture when handing out traffic tickets, a function that is especially "regulatory" in nature.)

"All Bad" versus "Largely Good" Offenders.   The burglars, drunks, heroin peddlers, and other criminal offenders encountered by police officers are rarely engaged in what are thought to be socially useful occupations. In the case of regulated businesses, however, their offenses, even if irresponsible or socially harmful in and of themselves, are more likely to be viewed as negligent, non-malicious side-effects of socially useful activities. Air pollution from a coal burning electric utility and cotton dust in a textile plant are inherent by-products of important manufacturing processes. A plant manager might consciously increase the risk of product-contamination in postponing the cleaning of a food-processing machine, but he does not intend an accident to occur in the same sense as a mugger or purse-snatcher intends to harm his victim.

To be sure, regulatory officials do encounter firms that are thoroughgoing "bad apples." For some firms, fraud is a primary way of doing business. Some enterprises show repeated and deliberate disregard for safety or environmental rules. Some slum landlords *are* "slumlords." Some employers are outright racists. But such "bad apples," according to regulatory officials, generally make up a small proportion of the population of enterprises they police. Most often, therefore, a business enterprise that violates a regulatory prohibition will not be perceived as "all bad." Its "bad" conduct will often appear to the inspector to be the product of negligence or ignorance, not malice, and as a small proportion of its activities, dwarfed by the good.

Police officers, while viewing many lawbreakers as incorrigible, see others as essentially decent human beings who have "gone wrong" under the pressure of financial circumstances, momentary passion, or bad associates. The latter are often treated as good candidates for reform or rehabilitation. A warning rather than arrest and punishment might be deemed sufficient to put the individual back on the right track, to resume or to develop a role as a useful member of the community. Because regulatory inspectors most often deal with "legitimate businesses," this rehabilitative ideal is all the more prominent. Correction of the violation will seem more appropriate than retribution. Even if the inspector does recommend prosecution, judges, faced with an offending firm's credible-sounding promise to correct a violation and institute a preventive program, often decline to impose a heavy fine. Why deprive the enterprise of money that could be used to install pollution abatement or safety equipment? All the more reason, then, for the inspector to "back off" from formal prosecution — just as a police officer, recognizing the judicial propensity toward leniency in sentencing mothers of small children, men who hold decent jobs, boys from "good homes," and first offenders in general, may be less inclined to initiate formal prosecution in such cases.

Offenders Who Fight or Flee versus Offenders Who Litigate.   Partly because he must deal so often with angry or irrational individual offenders at the bottom of the social order, the police officer must always be wary of physical resistance or attack. (Among other reasons for antipolice violence may be that the police officer symbolizes the defense of the established order of property and privilege against the urges and frustrations of sometimes desperate have-nots; that the police often are called to intervene in highly emotional fights; and that police intervention in cases involving serious felonies threatens to result in the terrifying penalty of extended incarceration.)[9] Police officers, accordingly, must be organized to respond to each others' calls for assistance, night or day, and to use lethal weapons when necessary. They must be prepared to give chase to suspects or known offenders who flee. Police departments invest in sophisticated communications devices and quasimilitary plans to help bind dispersed field officers into a mutually reinforcing system when necessary.

Regulatory inspectors, policing a very different population, rarely have deep concerns about violent resistance or attack. Regulated corporations do not flee. Inspectors do not worry about rushing to each others' aid, and rarely are they linked to each other and their supervisors by two-way radio. The inspector typically faces the regulated enterprise on his own. Businessmen and corporations resist the law not by physical measures but by doctoring the records, making sophisticated excuses, raising legal defenses in court, mounting political counterattacks on the agency or its regulations, or by complaining to the inspector's bureaucratic superiors. Unlike many young or poorly educated criminal suspects, representatives of regulated enterprises can speak the language of the legal system, or can hire lawyers who speak it even better. They are not easily intimidated or threatened into informing on their superiors or fellow lawbreakers.

In consequence, an inspector, as compared to a policeman, experiences strong cultural pressures to be respectful of the legal rights and personal dignity of those he polices. He must be more cautious about making charges, requesting information, or demanding action that is not clearly specified in the written law. The police officer, dealing with individuals who may fight or flee, must be primarily attentive to the interpersonal dynamics of the situation, the personal character of the individuals involved, and only secondarily to the specific content of potentially relevant rules of law. The inspector, dealing with organizations prepared for legal resistance, runs the risk of being attuned to legally stipulated requirements rather than to the realities of the situation.

Sanctioning Individuals versus Sanctioning Organizations. If, as a consequence of differences in social status, regulatory inspectors are inclined to act respectfully toward the population they police and to forego formal legal action, the fact that they are issuing "only" economic sanctions against economic units creates countervailing dispositions.

Because offenders the police officer deals with may be violent, or inclined to flee, the police officer has the power to arrest offenders and take them to jail. For most misdemeanors, a night in jail before appearing in court is the only real sanction imposed by the legal system, and it is one that can be imposed unilaterally by the officer.

Regulatory inspectors have no powers of arrest. A regulated business corporation is unlikely to flee the jurisdiction between being charged and its trial date. Except for rare emergency situations, an inspector typically initiates formal legal action by writing up a citation (the equivalent of a traffic summons or "ticket"), not by imposing any immediate sanction. (As suggested above, this is yet another reason why inspectors, unlike police officers, don't have to worry about physical resistance).

In some regulatory programs, inspectors can impose summary sanctions when violations pose an imminent hazard to the public, such as the power of the Federal Aviation Administration to ground a plane, a Mine Safety and Health Administration inspector's authority to close a mine, and a food and drug inspector's power to "embargo" batches of food that might be dangerously contaminated. Ordinarily, however, the inspector will first seek bureaucratic clearance; the regulated company will get enough notice to take the preventive action itself or argue to the inspector's superiors that it is unnecessary. And in any case, such summary sanctions are exceptional. The typical consequence of a violation detected by a regulatory inspector is a written citation containing an explicit or implicit order to correct the violation. In some agencies, such as the Occupational Safety and Health Administration, citations of serious violations carry an automatic fine, but in most regulatory programs a violator often can avert a fine by promptly remedying the violation.

The differences in severity of sanction imply different attitudes toward their use. In the criminal process, both the immediate sanction (arrest) and the ultimate judicially approved sanction (such as incarceration) have clear and emotionally compelling human consequences — the offender is forcibly taken from his home or neighborhood, deprived of contact with family and work, and exposed to the fears, degradations, and anxieties of imprisonment. No police officer can escape awareness that, however justified he may feel his action to be, to arrest someone and expose him to extended incarceration is to impose a real, deeply personal punishment.

By contrast, the sanction triggered by a regulatory inspector's action typically is not a personal penalty imposed on an individual but an impersonal cost imposed on an organization. A regulatory fine is paid not by the responsible foreman or plant manager but by the corporate treasury.[10] A regulatory order for remedial action (the installation of a safety guard, the repair of a pollution control device) usually will add only incrementally to the operating or capital budget of the business enterprise and to the costs paid by its customers. To the inspector, "only money," not freedom, is at stake. Regulated enterprises, in fact, often abide by regulatory demands they feel are unjustified simply because they wish to avoid the delay, expense, and antagonism associated with fighting the agency in court over a relatively minor expense — much as motorists often pay a traffic ticket rather than undergo the cost and inconvenience of contesting it. Consequently, although inspectors, for reasons noted earlier, may be reluctant to take the ultimate step of initiating formal prosecution, the impersonal monetary nature of regulatory sanctions would seem to reduce any compunctions inspectors might have against taking the *first* step of citing clear regulatory violations and pushing for their prompt correction. (Some characteristics of regulatory violations, however, to be discussed below, encourage inspectors to "overlook" certain kinds of violations).

Occasionally, of course, regulatory sanctions and orders are very costly, even for a substantial business. In the mid-1970s, compliance with pollution control and occupational health regulations absorbed at least 30 percent of annual capital expenditures in the steel foundry industry [See Miske, 1979]. Product recalls ordered by regulatory agencies have had devastating effects on sales of an enterprise's entire product line. Moreover, even corporate executives sometimes take regulatory citations personally, as blots on their personal integrity or reputation. When regulatory citations and orders threaten heavy costs or are regarded as unfair, enterprises may be more inclined to contest regulatory citations and orders, and front-line enforcement officials may be more open to arguments for leniency, although systematic data on this point are lacking.[11]

Because the police officers, exposed to potentially hostile or desperate offenders, are armed with guns and truncheons and have the power of arrest, the possibility (and fear) of police abuse of power looms large in the public's mind. Innocent persons can be killed or wrongfully incarcerated by an officer's mistake or malice. Much academic, judicial, administrative, and political attention is devoted, accordingly, to preventing violations of suspects' rights and police misuse of force. In recent decades, police departments have promulgated detailed regulations on the use of force by officers. Police officers know they can be sued, that their arrests can be overturned in court, and that they can be called onto the carpet by internal review boards investigating citizen complaints. Police may not always abide by the essential tenets of due process and the presumption of innocence, but they can hardly avoid being forcefully and regularly reminded of them.

In contrast, since regulatory inspectors need not be armed, and abuse of power on their part leads "only" to higher costs for regulated enterprises (which are regarded as highly capable of mounting legal defenses), regulatory enforcement is far less pervaded by the specter of harming the innocent. To the contrary, inspectors in many agencies are exposed to academic, journalistic, and political criticism primarily for being too solicitous of regulated enterprises (thus jeopardizing the health or rights of "innocent" individuals). Regulatory rhetoric, dominated by horror stories about recalcitrant firms and flagrant violations, emphasizes the need for regulatory "toughness," as if to build counterweights to the cultural tendencies for inspectors to defer to the expertise and status of corporate officials. [Bardach and Kagan, 1982: Ch. 7] This is just the opposite of the institutional controls on policing, which try to compel concern for suspects' rights to counteract cultural tendencies toward police disdain for "the criminal element," social deviants and low status individuals. These cross-cutting tendencies, however, are always variable in intensity, and predicting which will predominate in general is problematic.

The Nature of Offenses

Transient Versus Continuing Violations.   Ordinary "street crimes" — robberies, assaults, vandalism — are momentary events. They are perpetrated quickly, in as private a place as possible. The offender quickly flees the scene. A police officer only rarely can catch the offender in the act, "red-handed." Restricted, by and large, to patrolling public places, the best a police force can do is to hope to deter offenses by walking beats and driving random routes in squad cars, or to catch offenders by responding quickly to complaints and getting a good description of the offender from victims and witnesses. Proving a case against a suspect often is problematic. The police officer, and after him the prosecutor, must be able to link the particular suspect to the crime by a firm chain of evidence (witness identification, physical evidence in the possession of the suspect, etc.). The officer must be able to evaluate suspects' protestations of mistaken identity and other alibis, and reconstruct the "correct" version of the past event from conflicting present testimony.[12]

Regulatory inspectors are less often concerned with transient violations or with searching for a suspect. Some regulatory enforcement officials, like police detectives, are compelled to gather evidence about past events to determine if a suspect has violated the law. Fire marshals and workplace safety officials engage in post-accident investigations. Consumer fraud investigators, given conflicting accounts of what the salesman or home repair contractor actually promised, engage in an essentially retrospective, adjudicatory task, as do antidiscrimination officials trying to determine the real reason (employer prejudice, as the complainant alleged, or the complainant's deficiencies) for a firm's failure to promote a black or female employee. Most of the regulations enforced by field inspectors, however, are *preventive* in nature. They mandate fixed physical facilities, guards, pollution control devices, sanitary conditions, and warning labels. The regulations compel regulated enterprises to keep records showing compliance with quality control requirements — maintenance of trucks and aircraft according to a fixed schedule, regular cleaning of meat-packing equipment, etc. The obligations, moreover, are imposed on the business organization as a whole; an inspector need not find the particular employee responsible for following them.

In consequence, regulatory violations are often continuing and easily observable. If the landlord hasn't fixed the broken water heater or toilet, the effects are obvious until repaired, there for the inspector as well as for the tenant to see. The same continuing, transparent character adheres to a smokestack without a properly operating scrubber, to unrestored strip-mined land, or failure to have contracted for the "validation" of employment tests that tend to exclude minorities from hiring or promotion.

The inspector, moreover, unlike the police officer, is authorized to search for violations in private places. Without a warrant, he can walk through the factory or nursing home and "search" through quality control records and maintenance logs.[13]

With evidence of violations thus preserved and accessible, and with the identity of the corporate violator apparent, the inspector, unlike the police officer, needn't rush to the scene at a moment's notice, or attempt to reconstruct past events by finding and interviewing witnesses. He often can take photographs of the offense — the grease spill on the floor of the auto assembly plant, the hole in the tenement apartment wall. He calculates ratios from records — patients to staff in a nursing home, proportions of minority employees at different levels of the corporate workforce — and any violation is preserved in fixed columns of numbers. The regulatory enforcement official in a licensing or permit-type program is in an even stronger position in terms of evidentiary problems; sitting at his desk, he compares the application (for an air pollution permit, a new pesticide marketing certificate, etc.) with the requirements in the regulations. If the permit official is unsure of the facts, he can always ask the applicant to produce more documentation, additional tests, design changes, or impact data. The burden of proof, in effect, is cast upon the "suspect," not the law enforcers.

One consequence of this facility of proof is that regulatory enforcement officials have far less incentive than police officers to violate legal rules in order to obtain evidence. They have little need to use force or deception to extract confessions, to browbeat witnesses, to pay off informers, or to penetrate the suspect organization by disguising their identities, tapping its phones or reading its mail.

There are exceptions, of course. Companies may be suspected of turning off their pollution control equipment at night, or of doctoring their records, or of lying about their reasons for failing to fulfill a compliance schedule, and this may give rise to more aggressive and intrusive regulatory enforcement efforts. Dow Chemical Company, for example, complained of the Environmental Protection Agency's aerial reconnaissance and photographs of its Midland, Michigan plant in search of pollution violations. Many agencies engage in surprise inspections on the theory that some violations could be covered up if a day's notice were given — an unguarded or polluting machine could be put out of service temporarily, false entries might be made in the maintenance log. Antidiscrimination agencies have sometimes used undercover investigators (such as white/black pairs) to apply for jobs or housing to see if blacks are turned down without reason.

But, again, these are exceptional measures. Regulatory agencies have shown little interest in secretly infiltrating business organizations, or in posing as customers or suppliers in order to gain access.[14] The usual regulatory response to fears of deception is to change the rules — to surround a transitory wrongful act with regulations that facilitate its detection. If it is feared that factories discharge pollutants illegally at night, they are required to install monitoring devices and maintain records, signed by the foreman for each shift, continuously showing all emissions. If it is hard to prove individual acts of discrimination, employers are compelled to file affirmative action plans requiring specific ratios of minorities, to provide detailed explanations for personnel actions, and to record good faith efforts to recruit minorities.

The enduring quality of many regulatory violations also means that the inspector can engage in extended personal contact with the violator. The police officer, too, can sometimes take time to talk with a juvenile delinquent or a husband who has assaulted his wife, or try to talk a fugitive into giving himself up, but most of his conversations with offenders are short and curt. But extended and repeated conversations with offenders are a major part of many a regulatory inspector's workday. Inspectors in some agencies use their opportunity for conversation to act as consultants rather than cops, that is, as experts who diagnose risks, persuade regulated enterprises why they should eliminate them, and provide information about how best to avoid further regulatory problems.

To some regulatory officials and many outside critics, the opportunity for extensive interaction with violators raises the fear of co-optation. Sophisticated businessmen and engineers, it is assumed, will dupe the unsophisticated inspector, persuade him to accept promises rather than performance, or draw him into greater concern for the firm's problems than for the rights of those whom the regulations are supposed to protect. Extended interaction with wealthy organizations also carries the risk of corruption. Many inspectors, from this perspective, are in the same corruptible position as police officers who have repeated contact with ongoing criminal organizations such as gambling dens, brothels, and narcotics rings.

Whether corruption actually occurs, of course, either in the case of vice squad members or inspectors, depends on many other factors. When regulatory violations are continuing and visible to complainants, for example, as in the case of many violations of worker safety rules, corruption is much less likely than when violations are quickly hidden, as in the case of some building code violations.

Nevertheless, ongoing contact with offenders and the attendant opportunity for corruption is a special concern of almost all regulation enforcement chiefs. They sometimes rotate inspectors from area to area, so as to curtail opportunities for close relationships, or instruct inspectors to avoid "consultation," or interrogate inspectors who issue fewer citations than average. These measures, however, also limit opportunities for inspectors to elicit cooperation from regulated businessmen through informal persuasion, advice-giving, and so on.

The Moral Ambiguity of Regulatory Offenses. With respect to many violations encountered by police, there is a social consensus that the actions in question are evil — *malum in se* — and deserve punishment. There are few recognized circumstances that will "excuse" robbery, aggravated assault, or arson. Coming face-to-face with physically harmed or psychologically traumatized victims, police officers are forcefully reminded, day after day, of the moral bases of the criminal law and the culpability of the offender.

This is not true with respect to criminal offenses such as marijuana possession, disturbing the peace, gambling, and prostitution. Such activities are generally regarded as *malum prohibitum*. They are forbidden for utilitarian reasons or for less widely-held moral reasons, and their enforcement is more controversial.

Many regulatory offenses share this controversial quality. It is not at all clear how "bad" they are. While most people would agree that pollution is bad, and that the factory that does *nothing* to control its emissions is bad, there is disagreement about what precise level is bad for public health and, given escalating costs of abatement, what level of control should be required. Many other regulatory issues too, present a fundamental conflict between a "natural rights"-based morality that values absolute protection and a utilitarian morality that values economic efficiency as well as safety.

In addition, criminal law reflects a relatively uncontroversial assignment of responsibility for harmful acts. For most people, the burglar is to blame, not the homeowner who failed to install a burglar alarm, even if the homeowner is affluent and the burglar grew up in a ghetto. There are exceptions, to be sure, especially for juveniles, and sometimes there are impulses to blame a victim who is perceived to have been provocative or irresponsible. And where it seems that the law violator "couldn't help it" because of ignorance of the law or because it "really wasn't his fault," police and prosecutors are less inclined to enforce the law strictly.

A great many regulatory offenses have this character. Workplace accidents are often caused, wholly or in part, by worker carelessness. Accidents in the home are often caused when consumers misuse a product, ignore warning labels, or neglect maintenance instructions. Many consumer deception complaints stem from sales practices that would deceive only the most ignorant or gullible consumer. Many a broken plumbing fixture or teetering bannister in an apartment house is "caused" only secondarily by the landlord's failure to fix it and primarily by the actions of irresponsible tenants or destructive kids.

Yet regulation often attempts to prevent harm by assigning all legal responsibility to the business firm involved, on the theory that *it* is best able to afford (or be coerced into) preventive actions. The regulations mandate safety devices and warning labels that would make a workplace, product, sales practice or apartment safe for even the negligent or irresponsible worker, consumer or tenant. When a regulatory inspector encounters a violation of this kind of regulation, punishment will often conflict with his own sense of where responsibility for preventing harms properly should lie. Absent powerful bureaucratic and social pressures to "go by the book," the inspector will be tempted to react the same "forgiving" way a police officer often does when an individual has violated the law "but it really wasn't his fault."

Most regulatory rules, moreover, do not embody traditional, *malum in se* norms that we learn from childhood. They were promulgated rather recently in distant capitals and published in closely-spaced official documents. Inspectors, therefore, will often encounter violators who are truly ignorant of some of the rules. Thus although many regulatory laws call for strict liability, regardless of the violating enterprise's lack of unlawful intent, inspectors often will have a normal inclination, on moral grounds, to forgive first offenses.

The moral ambiguity of many regulatory offenses is exacerbated by the ex ante, preventive nature of the rules. Police officers usually enforce the law only when serious harm has actually occurred to an identifiable victim (an assault, a theft, etc.) or when there seems to be a clear and present danger of such a harm. Indeed, their actions are most suspect when they act in a wholly preventative manner, when they "hassle" an individual or disperse a group of teenagers simply because they are suspicious that those individuals might do something wrong later on. The enforcement of laws against loitering and drug possession is justified — and harshly criticized — on the basis of its preventive, essentially "regulatory" character.

The regulatory inspector continually encounters violations that only *might* lead to real harm. Regulations, as noted above, often require fixed facilities, records, and maintenance schedules whose violation is easily detectable and provable. But these facilities and records are only presumed *correlates* of the desired outcome, such as safety, and the correlations inevitably are far from perfect. A nursing home may fall short of the specified patient-staff ratio, or square feet per patient rule. Something may be missing from a nurse's charts. But if the management and staff are essentially dedicated and concerned, any particular violation will probably be irrelevant to the real standard of care. In many other sites, too, the inspector often will encounter rule violations — failures to have certain devices, keep certain records, and so on — where the particular combination of operating personnel, managerial attitudes, technological processes, and alternative back-up systems make any risk of harm resulting from the violation seem remote indeed. There is no identifiable victim, and not even a probable one. The violation will not seem "wrong". And the inspector will encounter still more cases in which it will simply be unclear whether the failure to comply creates a significant risk of harm, but in which a technically sophisticated corporate engineer will make a plausible but hard-to-evaluate argument that the risk is negligible (and that the expense of correcting the violation, accordingly, would simply be wasted money).[15]

Flexibility versus Strict Enforcement Revisited. The moral ambiguity surrounding many regulatory violations, borne of the propensity of regulation-writers to pile up multiple layers of preventive requirements, guarantees that the citations the inspector issues will often be resented. The recipient will complain that although he violated the rule, no real danger or injustice was created under the circumstances and hence to impose a fine or compel expenditures on compliance would be unjust. Resentment among the regulated, moreover, undercuts regulatory effectiveness. Resentful enterprises are more likely to tie agencies up in legalistic appeals and lobby to curtail the agency's funding. In subsequent dealings with inspectors, they are more likely to withhold information and cooperation, both of which are essential to an effective regulatory program.

The logical solution would be a flexible enforcement style — demanding penalties and strict compliance when violations present serious risks, dealing more leniently with less serious violations. We expect such a flexible approach from police officers in order-maintenance situations; that is, we hope that they will arrest individuals who threaten serious harm to life or property and charge them with disturbing the peace, trespass, or assault, but that the officer will simply "cool off" less threatening situations without making an arrest, even though technical violations of the same laws might have occurred. For both inspectors and police officers, however, the decisions involved in such a flexible enforcement style entail the possibility of two serious kinds of mistakes; the enforcement official might (1) underestimate the seriousness of the situation of the offender's degree of irresponsibility, thus committing the error of *undue leniency*; or (2) overestimate the seriousness of the situation or risk of harm and commit the error of unnecessary or *excessive strictness*.

The problem typically takes different forms, however, for inspectors than it does for police officers. The police officer typically must make his judgment on the spot. An "undue leniency error" in dealing with a potentially violent offender can result in immediate harm to other people or to the officer himself. On the other hand, an "excessive strictness error" — arresting, searching, or using force against a person who turns out to be innocent or a harmless minor offender — is not likely to be costly to the officer himself, nor is it likely, given the lower class status of most such individuals, to evoke much serious public criticism of the department. This imbalance of consequences, as William K. Muir, Jr. has pointed out, impels many younger officers toward a posture of suspiciousness and aggressive toughness in uncertain situations. [Muir, 1977]

For regulatory inspectors, the possibility of error of either kind may be higher. Unlike a barroom argument or domestic fight to which a police officer is called, in which the threatened harm is imminent, for inspectors the harm threatened by a regulatory violation will often be remote and highly uncertain, such as an increased risk (of what degree?) of environmentally caused disease or of an accident some time in the future. Whether an enterprise's failure to adhere to a pollution abatement schedule, to repair window screens to keep flies out of a cannery, or to install extra fire exits in a factory, as required by regulation, will *significantly* increase the probability of ecocatastrophe, food poisoning, or death from fire is almost always a debatable issue.

In addition, for inspectors the adverse consequences of the two kinds of error probably are more equally balanced, or more variable from case to case. Because inspectors deal with articulate, well-represented businesses, inspectors' errors of excessive strictness can lead, as noted, to curtailment of cooperation, litigation, complaints about the inspector to higher officials, and political attacks on the agency for "overregulation." This, of course, would suggest the desirability, from the inspectors standpoint, of "leaning" toward leniency.

On the other hand, for some inspectorates, undue leniency errors are equally if not more dreadful. If an inspector is induced by technically sophisticated corporate engineers to accept as adequate that which is really dangerous, the result can be large-scale disaster — accidents in which workers are killed, vehicles crash, people are poisoned, fires erupt out of control — for which the agency will often be blamed. (In contrast, police are rarely blamed for the depredations of a killer or a string of burglaries.) Short of disaster, even if the inspector invariably exercises good judgment, regulatory violations that are "let go" might be detected by disgruntled employees, citizen watchdog groups, or investigative journalists, who can publicly accuse the inspector of "being in bed with the company," or of indifference to the rights of the people. Regulated businesses can complain bitterly to politicians that regulators have violated canons of equal application of the law by giving "breaks" to competitors. Consequently, where in the recent past there has been a calamitous accident, revelation of serious harm or scandal, or where proregulation interest groups are well organized and watchful for signs of laxity, agencies sometimes treat undue leniency as the type of error most devoutly to be avoided. To that end, they may try to "program" their inspectors to cite each and every violation that they spot, regardless of seriousness, and to avoid bargaining with representatives of regulated enterprises. [See Bardach and Kagan, 1982; 72–77, 203–4]

Such legalistic tactics, however, ignore two striking advantages regulatory agencies have (over police acting in order-maintenance situations) in dealing with situations of uncertainty: (1) *time* to gather more information, and (2) offenders that typically are not mobile individuals but stable, organized entities. Because the harm threatened by a regulatory violation so often is not instantaneous, and the situations the inspector deals with are not fleeting, emotional, and explosive, the inspector, when uncertain about a violation's seriousness, can engage in further dialogue with executives, engineers, and ordinary employees in the regulated enterprise. He can ask them to support their contentions about the adequacy of existing controls. Because regulated enterprises, unlike many criminal law violators, act not out of rage, drunkenness, or psychopathology but in terms of rational calculation and concern for good will, they often can be bargained with — induced to agree to study a possible problem, provide more information, or monitor alternative precautions — in return for the inspector's agreement to delay enforcement against non-emergency violations. Because regulated businesses operate in fixed locations, they know the inspector can return to check on fulfillment of pledges, and that he can respond to unjustified excuses by intensifying the level of surveillance, expanding demands for information, or initiating a well-publicized prosecution.

Towards Professionalization of Regulatory Enforcement

The idea of "professionalization," as applied to law enforcers as well as to lawyers and doctors, represents a plea for greater autonomy from outsiders — legislators, judges, lay groups, etc. — who attempt to set standards for the "professional's" behavior. Professionalization implies the grant of a certain amount of discretion to the practitioner to use his or her own judgment, rooted in expertise and experience, to determine what would be best in the particular case. External controls also are unnecessary, the argument runs, because a profession develops and enforces its own public-regarding standards.

With respect to police departments, professionalization originally implied more selective, merit-based recruitment, training in crime detection and an ideology that stressed the policeman's role as "officer of the law"; all this helped justify the demand that police departments should be freed from patronage ties to and interference from local political party leaders and municipal politicians. In recent decades, in response to the advent of more intensive judicial controls, and criticism by minority groups, a more "professional" police force has come to mean one in which officers are trained to respect due process rights, deal with family fights and unruly crowds in more sophisticated ways, and accept departmental regulations restricting use of firearms. Such "internal" controls presumably would make detailed external control by the judiciary and civilian review boards less necessary.

From their inception, many regulatory inspectorates reflected the Progressive Era ideal of government by experts dedicated to the public interest and insulated from political influence at the level of day-to-day enforcement decisions. This ideal of government by specialized experts helps explain why each new set of regulatory laws gave rise to a separate enforcement agency. In practice, however, achievement of the professional ideal, especially its internal "expertise" component, was spotty. Some agencies required inspectors to have considerable prior on-the-job experience in a particular industry, but other agencies did not. Inspectors in many municipal agencies have been straightforward political patronage appointees. Most state and federal inspectorates have been staffed primarily by individuals who have passed a very general civil service examination.

At the same time, the political autonomy aspect of the ideal of regulation by "professionals" gradually came under attack. Regulatory rulemaking and enforcement decisions, it was realized, cannot simply flow from the application of technical knowledge; inevitably they entail political value judgments, such as how much to weigh safety versus economic productivity and costs. Moreover, the conventional wisdom came to hold that in making such judgments, regulatory officials are dominated by regulated industries. Thus in the 1960s and 1970s, external legal controls on regulation tended to supplant the professional ideal. Legislatures enacted much more detailed regulatory statutes, imposing strict deadlines and objectives for regulators to attain. Citizen groups were guaranteed greater participatory rights in rulemaking and enforcement decisions, both of which were made subject to closer scrutiny by judges (and more recently, with respect to rulemaking, by governmental economists applying cost-benefit tests). The emphasis shifted, in short, from granting regulators discretion to act according to their own sense of responsibility to making them more strictly accountable to outside reviewers and critics. Regulatory enforcement officials, not surprisingly, began to complain of feeling more "regulated" themselves, more closely bound by legal constraints, more concerned about defending themselves in court.

It is too late in the evolution of American inspectorates to expect any complete return to the professional model, or to imagine that political preferences could or should be excluded from enforcement policy. Nevertheless, the attempt to control regulatory enforcement primarily by external legal requirements is deeply troublesome insofar as it induces in both inspectors and the regulated an attitude of legal defensiveness, a concern for adequate documentation rather than substantive achievement, and a degree of rule-bound rigidity. One might expect, therefore, a gradual effort on the part of regulatory officials to regain more control by pushing for the professionalization of regulatory inspectorates.

A complete specification or even a full outline of what more professionalized inspectorates would be like is beyond the scope of this essay.[16] A few remarks based on the comparison with police departments might be suggestive, however. Clearly one aspect of professionalism would be a more careful recruitment and training of inspectors. Many agencies have begun to insist on better educated, technically trained inspectors, California's food and drug agency, for example, requires of new inspectors a master's degree in public health, biomedical engineering, or food technology. Greater technical expertise would seem to enable an inspector to deal more effectively with the problem of determining whether a regulatory violation in fact poses a substantial risk of harm. In dealing with technical experts in the regulated enterprise, a more "expert" inspector would not only have more confidence to reject weak arguments for leniency, but also to accept good arguments. Still, the training of most regulatory inspectors falls short of the intensive and more rounded education currently given police officers, which includes instruction in criminology, sociology of the relevant community, and realistic simulations of conflict situations. Inspectors, while taught the legal rules and, in some agencies, the latest data and techniques for assessing risks, rarely are given intensive or systematic training in the equivalent of "police-community relations," that is, in interpersonal relations with complainants and businessmen; in the economics of the regulated industry; in the organizational dynamics, strengths and weaknesses of different kinds of business firms; in standards for exercising discretion; in cultivating allies, such as technical experts, within regulated firms (which would be the equivalent of police cultivation of informants by "working the beat"); or in alternatives to enforcement.

The development of more sophisticated training of inspectors and of professionalism in general would be spurred, as in the case of "police science," by the development of a more general body of literature concerning regulatory enforcement, both practical and critical, empirical and normative. Such a development might be encouraged by the formation of a Society of Regulatory Enforcement, drawing its members from a variety of agencies and from regulated enterprises as well, and the publication of a periodical magazine or journal reporting on training methods, enforcement techniques, and targetting strategies, along with research findings and normative debates.

The idea of professionalism in regulatory enforcement might also reflect the fundamental differences between regulatory enforcement and policing discussed earlier. Police officers, we saw, often deal with explosive or emotional situations, with offenses that stem from desperation, rage, or pathology. Putting aside service functions and traffic control, police deal with a predominantly lower class population of individuals, in situations in which normal social controls, restraints of conscience, or concerns for preserving reputation and property have broken down. The organizations they police, such as narcotics networks, are literally beyond the law, with little incentive to comply with it. Police deal, in short, with the virtually ungovernable. Policing essentially involves the use of force (or the threat of force) to bring order to anarchy, to pacify the warring, or punish the undeterrable.

The business enterprises that regulatory inspectors deal with, even the worst of them, live in a much less anarchic world. They are organized entities with property to protect, customers and good will to retain. They are embedded in a web of market considerations and liability laws that, however imperfect, impose some constraints and compel rational response to long term as well as immediate incentives. The basic task of regulation, therefore, is not pacification or punishment but, to use a dictionary definition, "to adjust" behavior — to change incentive structures, to plug gaps in existing control systems, to bring hidden risks or externalized harms to a higher level of salience on the plant manager's crowded agenda. The professional inspector, from this perspective, would be trained to blend the threat of legal enforcement and adverse publicity with the analysis of defects in the regulated enterprises' procedures and policies. The inspector's primary objective would be to use the threat of sanctions to bargain for systematic organizational changes.

Professionalized inspectorates, in this sense, like more professionalized police departments, would be much more expensive for governments to recruit, train, and retain. A staff of lower-paid bureaucrats, programmed to apply checklists by rote, would be much cheaper, and in an era of budgetary restrictions is politically more attractive. A more professionalized inspectorate would require greater trust from business, proregulation advocacy groups, legislators, the news media, and the public at large; winning such trust, in programs surrounded by sharp disagreements on appropriate goals and standards, is highly problematic. (Recall the higher level of consensus behind most criminal law, which might explain higher levels of support for police discretion.) Nevertheless, the promise of more professional inspectorates to provide enforcement that would be both more effective and more reasonable cannot easily be ignored. The evolution of police professionalism, and the acceptance of the idea of guiding rather than eliminating police discretion, suggests that regulatory inspectorates in the United States may gradually evolve in the same direction.

Notes

1. The research was supported by the Twentieth Century Fund, and was conducted in 1977–1980. A complete account of the methods and findings is in Bardach and Kagan (1982).
2. On "activity" quotas for police see Rubinstein (1973).
3. See Draft Final Report of the Interagency Task Force on Workplace Safety and Health. December 1978. For similar effects in other agencies, see Mayhew (1968) Vladeck, 1980: 160; Feller et al., 1977: 13, 27–52, 55.

4. The classic study of enforcement style variations in police departments is Wilson, 1968. See also Wilson, 1967. On variation in regulatory agencies, see Bardach and Kagan, 1982.
5. It is always essential to distinguish programs of protective regulation (health, safety, pollution, etc.) from so-called economic regulation concerned with restrictions on market entry (as in the case of railroads, occupational licensing, airlines, gambling casinos) and with regulation of rates or charges. The latter is always and sometimes explicitly concerned with "the health of the industry." That is not to deny that *protective* regulation, too, is susceptible to cooptation, but the politics and enforcement patterns in the two types of regulation tend to differ markedly.
6. See, e.g., Council on Environmental Quality, 1979; DeFina, 1978; Kosters (1978).
7. Some redistribution caused by strict protective regulation, it should be noted, is from marginal firms in an industry to dominant ones, or from one industry to another, as in the case of EPA regulations requiring scrubbers on all coalburning power plants, which shift demand from low-sulfur western coal to high-sulfur eastern coal. See Paul R. Portney, (1982). On the benefits of regulation to larger firms vis-a-vis competitors, see Clarkson et al. (1979).
8. The redistributive aspect of protective regulation may seem less prominent over time, after most firms have complied with *basic* regulatory requirements (such as installation of pollution abatement equipment, establishment of elaborate safety-oriented quality control or equipment maintenance routines, establishment of nondiscriminatory personnel policies, etc.). In such cases, the inspector's task is more to prevent deterioration of such routines toward to status quo ante, i.e., to ensure that compulsory redistribution is not "taken back." Regulatory inspection also will seem less redistributive when the regulations basically serve as a redundant "fail safe" system for redistributive precautions already established primarily in response to liability law — Federal Aviation Administration inspection of commercial aircraft is one example; another is FDA inspection of manufacturing plants for intravenous solutions.
9. Egon Bittner has suggested that the legitimate, situational use of force is the *defining* characteristic of police work, and that particular law enforcement and peacekeeping tasks are assigned to the police precisely because force may be required. See Bittner, 1970; and 1974.
10. The situation is different when inspectors deal with small proprietors or landlords who must pay fines and compliance costs "out of their own pocket" and may have difficulty passing compliance costs on to customers. Not surprisingly, regulatory agencies more often use conciliatory enforcement tactics or adopt strategies of benign neglect vis-a-vis small business.
11. In some agencies enforcement officials tend to avoid the effort, expense, and delay of contested matters by restricting enforcement efforts to routine, "easy to settle" matters, while avoiding the novel demand or the high cost-of-compliance case that probably would evoke resistance. Conversely, studies of antitrust enforcement by the Department of Justice and by the Federal Trade Commission show that ambitious enforcement officials seek out the "big case" that might create "new law." Similar reactions by ambitious inspectors might be prevalent. See Posner, (1972) (on the

enforcement of unfair trade practice laws by the FTC); Silbey, 1981. See also, Weaver, 1977; Katzman, 1980.

12.   The police officer's task is different, of course, if he attempts to catch the offender in the act by undercover work or wire-tapping, but these are techniques used most often to investigate ongoing illegitimate businesses that engage in repetitive offenses, such as narcotics sales, gambling operations, prostitution, etc. Not all offenses patrolmen deal with are transitory. The loud party or streetcorner assemblage that disturbs the peace may go on for some time. Encountering a group of underage drinkers in a bar or a double-parked truck blocking a street, a police officer has little difficulty discerning who is responsible. Even so, such violations last but a few hours at most, and if the police come tomorrow rather than today the evidence will have vanished.

13.   The Supreme Court ruled in 1978 that employers may insist that the OSHA inspector obtain a warrant for routine (noncomplaint-triggered) inspections, but the standard for obtaining a warrant is weak. More importantly, regulated businesses rarely demand a warrant, for fear of alienating the inspector. *Marshall v. Barlows, Inc.*, 436 U.S. 307 (1978).

14.   For an account of one regulatory official's qualms about having instigated undercover investigation, see Schrag, (1971).

15.   Many criminal laws that police enforce also are prophylactic in nature, such as an ordinance prohibiting drinking alcoholic beverages in a public park, or riding a bicycle on the sidewalk, or establishing an evening curfew for juveniles, as well as laws restricting the possession of firearms and prohibiting bars from serving alcoholic beverages to minors. A violation of such ordinances often entails no immediate harm, danger or disturbance of the peace; the activities are prohibited because they might do so. When police spend time enforcing such laws — and they often do — their activity seems much more "regulatory" in nature, and their job is more like that of an inspector. It is noteworthy that police tend to be discriminating in the enforcement of such laws, overlooking some violations when no significant harm or disturbance is threatened, or informally chastising rather than arresting most violators. See Davis (1975).

16.   For other preliminary discussions of professionalism in regulatory enforcement, see Bardach and Kagan, 1982: ch. 5, 6, and 11; Danaceau, 1982, Danaceau, 1981.

17.   Police departments, too, as Kenneth Culp Davis has emphasized, also tend to be woefully weak in articulating and enforcing internal rules concerning the exercise of discretion. See Davis, 1975.

References

Bardach, Eugene and Robert A. Kagan (1982). *Going by the Book: The Problem of Regulatory Unreasonableness*. Philadelphia : Temple University Press.

Bayley, David H. (1979). Police Function, Structure and Control in Western Europe and North America: Comparative and Historical Studies in Morris and Tonry, *Crime and Justice*, Vol. 1.

Bittner, Egon (1970). *The Functions of the Police in Modern Society.* Washington, D.C.: U.S. Government Printing Office.

———. (1974), Florence Nightingale in Pursuit of Willie Sutton: A Theory of the Police in Herbert Jacob (ed.), *The Potential for Reform of Criminal Justice.* Beverly Hills: Sage Publications.

Black, Donald J. (1973). The Mobilization of Law, 2 *Journal of Legal Studies* 125.

Council on Environmental Quality (1979). *Tenth Annual Report.* Washington, D.C.: Government Printing Office.

Clarkson, Kenneth W. et al. (1979). Regulating Chrysler Out of Business, *Regulation* 44 (Sept.–Oct.).

Danaceau, Paul (1982). Developing Successful Enforcement Programs, in Bardach and Kagan (eds.). *Social Regulation: Strategies for Reform.* San Francisco: Institute for Contemporary Studies.

———. (1981). *Making Inspection Work: Three Case Studies.* Washington, D.C.: U.S. Regulatory Council.

Davis, Kenneth C. (1975). *Police Discretion.* St. Paul: West Publishing Co.

Draft Final Report (1978). *Making Prevention Pay.* Washington, D.C.: Interagency Task Force on Workplace Safety and Health.

Feller, Irwin et al. (1977). Economic and Legal Aspects of Federal, State and Local Regulations Concerning the Production and Sale of Ground Beef. Vol. 3, College Park: Pennsylvania State University, Center for the Study of Science Policy, pp. 13, 27–52, 55.

Kagan, Robert A. (1978). *Regulatory Justice. Implementing a Wage-Price Freeze.* New York: Russell Sage.

Katzmann, Robert A. (1980). *Regulatory Bureaucracy: The Federal Trade Commission and Antitrust Policy.* Cambridge: MIT Press.

Kelling, George L. et al. (1974). *The Kansas City Preventive Patrol Experiment: A Technical Report.* Washington, D.C.: The Police Foundation.

Kosters, Marvin (1979). Counting the Costs. *Regulation* (July–Aug.).

Levin, Michael (1979). Politics and Polarity: the Limits of OSHA Reform. *Regulation* 33 (Nov.–Dec.).

Mayhew, Leon (1968). *Law and Equal Opporunity.* Cambridge: Harvard University Press.

Miske, J. (1979). Capital Formation and 10-5-1. *Foundry Management and Technology.* (April).

Muir, William K., Jr. (1977). *Police: Streetcorner Politicians.* Chicago: University of Chicago Press.

Portney, Paul R. (1982). How Not to Create a Job. *Regulation* (Nov./Dec.).

Posner, Richard (1972). The Behavior of Regulatory Agencies, 1 *Journal of Legal Studies* 305.

Reiss, Albert J., Jr. (1971). *The Police and the Public.* New Haven: Yale University Press.

Rubinstein, Jonathan (1973). *City Police.* New York: Farrar, Strauss and Giroux.

Rumbaut, Ruben G. and Egon Bittner (1979). Changing Conceptions of the Police Role, in Morris and Tonry (eds.) *Crime and Justice: An Annual Review of Research,* Vol. 1. Chicago: University of Chicago Press.

Schrag, Philip (1971). "On Her Majesty's Secret Service: Protecting the Consumer in New York City. 80 *Yale Law Journal* 1529.

Silbey, Susan S. (1981). Case Processing: Consumer Protection in an Attorney General's Office 15. *Law and Society Review* 849.

Skolnick, Jerome H. (1978). *House of Cards*. Boston: Little-Brown.

Vladeck, Bruce (1980). *Unloving Care: The Nursing Home Tragedy*. New York: Basic Books.

Weaver, Paul H. (1978). Regulation, Social Policy and Class Conflict. 50 *The Public Interest* 45.

Weaver, Suzanne (1977). *Decision to Prosecute: Organization and Public Policy in the Antitrust Division*. Cambridge: MIT Press.

Wilson, James Q. (1967). The Police and the Delinquent in Two Cities, in Wheeler (ed.) *Controlling Delinquents*. New York: John Wiley and Sons.

———— (1968). Varieties of Police Behavior: The Management of Law and Order in Eight Communities. Cambridge: Harvard University Press.

———— (1980). *The Politics of Regulation*. New York: Basic Books.

Weidenbaum, Murray and Robert DeFina (1978). The Cost of Federal Regulation of Economic Activity. Washington, D.C.: American Enterprise Institute.

II Enforcement Practice: Inspection, Compliance, and Sanctions

4 The "Criminology of the Corporation" and Regulatory Enforcement Strategies

Robert A. Kagan and John T. Scholz

When legislators, regulators, academics, and businessmen talk about the problems of regulatory enforcement, they usually make reference to the motives, attitudes, and capabilities of "typical" business managers and regulated firms. In their comments and in the public debate on regulation, we discern three somewhat different popularly-held "images" of the business corporation.[1] Each of these images, in turn, "explains" why regulatory violations occur. Stated most simply, the three images and the corresponding theories of noncompliance are as follows:

In the first image, business firms are pictured as *amoral calculators*. Motivated entirely by profit-seeking, they carefully and competently assess opportunities and risks. They disobey the law when the anticipated fine and probability of being caught are small in relation to the profits to be garnered through disobedience. Non-compliance stems from *economic calculation*.

The second image pictures the business firm as a political *citizen*, ordinarily inclined to comply with the law, partly because of belief in the rule of law, partly as a matter of long-term self-interest. That commitment, however, is contingent. Business mana-

This essay is a modified version of a paper which first appeared in Jahrbuch für Rechtssoziologie und Rechtstheorie, Vol 7, (1980).

gers have strong views as to proper public policy and business conduct. At least some law breaking stems from *principled disagreement* with regulations or orders they regard as arbitrary or unreasonable.

In the third image, the business firm is seen as inclined to obey the law but as a potentially fallible or *organizationally incompetent* entity. Many violations of regulations are attributed to *organizational failure* — corporate managers fail to oversee subordinates adequately, to calculate risks intelligently, to establish organizational mechanisms that keep all operatives abreast of and attentive to the growing dictates of the law.

Each of these images and theories of deviant behavior suggests a somewhat different regulatory enforcement strategy.

If regulated businesses are seen as keen-eyed *amoral calculators,* the regulatory agency should emphasize aggressive inspection of all firms and promptly impose severe legal penalties for any violations, lest the firm be tempted to try to "get away with more." The goal, in short, is *deterrence.* The governmental inspector, accordingly, should be a strict *policeman,* indifferent to businessmen's manipulative excuses.

If regulated business firms are viewed as *political citizens,* responding to the perceived reasonableness or unreasonableness of regulatory orders, the regulatory inspectors should be, in many cases, not a strict policeman but more of a *politician.* He should be concerned with *persuading* the regulated firm of the rationality of the regulation in question. But he also should be willing to suspend enforcement, to compromise, to seek amendments to the regulations. In short, he should be responsive to the "citizen's" complaints, ready to *adapt the law* to legitimate business problems created by strict enforcement.

If regulated business firms are thought to be prone to *incompetence* and regulatory violations due to organizational failures, the regulatory inspector should serve in large part as a *consultant.* His responsibility would be to analyze informational gaps and organizational weaknesses in the regulated firm, and to *educate* businessmen concerning feasible technologies and management systems that would best ensure compliance in the future.

There is no inherent reason to choose among these three "theories" once and for all, for they are not mutually exclusive. In fact, regulatory officials who confront violators day after day often combine these three images and enforcement strategies. If allowed discretion, they make case-by-case judgments about the reason a specific violation occurred and about the motives and capabilities of the firm's managers. One study of the British Factory Inspectorate, for example, found enforcement files filled with such inspectors' characterizations of firms as "good," "bad," "cooperative," "putting production first," or "regards legal requirements as trivialities" [see Carson, 1970:394 and Hawkins, forthcoming].

Housing code inspectors in Boston, according to a participant-observer, differentiate between violations they attribute to deliberate noncompliance by the landlord, to landlord negligence, or to the acts of slovenly or destructive tenants[2] [see Nivola, 1976: 130]. Reflecting this judgmental approach, regulatory inspectors in some agencies respond to most first-instance violations by issuing warnings or by negotiating agreements for remedial measures, rather than by initiating prosecutions or imposing other legal penalties. Punitive, deterrence-oriented sanctions are sought only if and when the inspector comes to doubt the good faith of the regulated firm, that is, when the firm clearly appears to be acting like a wholly amoral calculator.[3]

Sometimes, however, lawmakers or top enforcement officials compel inspectors to act on the basis of a single theory of noncompliance and to adopt a single enforcement strategy for all cases. As we will discuss in more detail below, legislation and pressure from citizen advocacy groups has forced some agencies in the United States to treat all violators as if they were amoral calculators, that is, to enforce the law strictly and impose or seek legal sanctions for all violations, regardless of the violator's motives and regardless of the seriousness of the violation. Consequently, the *dominant* theory of noncompliance adopted by regulatory policy makers, deliberately or implicitly, has real effects on enforcement practices. In the following sections, we will (1) spell out each of the three popular theories of noncompliance in greater detail; (2) note how they have been incorporated in regulatory enforcement processes; (3) discuss their empirical strengths and weaknesses; and (4) examine the adverse consequence of their misplaced application.[4]

The Corporation as Amoral Calculator, the Regulator as Policeman

Conventional wisdom explains the criminal activities of individuals in terms of a pleasure-pain calculus — the law is disobeyed when the gain derived from the crime exceeds the potential pain of being caught and punished. A number of contemporary criminologists, using economic models that downplay sociological or psychological factors, contend that increasing the probability of detection and the certainty of incarceration measurably deters ordinary street crime [Wilson and Boland, 1978; Tullock, 1974; Zimring and Hawkins, 1973; Wilson, 1975]. Similarly, today's most widely accepted model of corporate criminality portrays the business firm as an amoral, profit-seeking organization whose actions are motivated wholly by rational calculation of costs and opportunities. In this Hobbesian view of the firm-in-society, businessmen, driven by the norms and pressures of the marketplace, will break the law unless the anticipated legal penalties (the expected legal sanctions *discounted* by the probability of delaying or avoiding them) exceed the additional profits the firm could make by evading the law or spending the money needed for compliance in a more lucrative way.[5]

From this standpoint, any leniency shown to regulated firms by enforcement officials is foolish, if not a sign of corruption. When consumer activist Ralph Nader sponsored a study of the Food and Drug Administration (FDA), the author noted:

> It became the practice of the [FDA] . . . to hold hundreds of meetings each year with representatives of industry to discuss . . . cooperative methods . . . to ensure that the provisions of the law were not violated. . . . If the Justice Department held regular meetings with the Mafia suggesting that it knew of gambling . . . which if not stopped would lead to a raid of the premises, it would be following a procedure not unlike that used by the FDA to convince the food industry to obey the law [Turner, 1970:121].

The conclusion was that the FDA must earn a reputation as a businesslike, rapidly moving "cop" [Turner, 1970:40]. Regulatory reforms and proposals during the last decade, reflecting this attitude, have focused on strengthening the deterrent effect of enforcement activities by increasing the certainty and severity of legal sanctions. Suspicious of regulated firms' ability to "capture" enforcement officials, reformers prevailed on the federal government in the early 1970s to take over or strictly supervise state enforcement of legal standards governing worker safety and health, air pollution, nursing homes, blood collection, and numerous other regulatory programs. Statutes and regulations were enacted prescribing specific nationwide rules, sometimes denying enforcement officials any discretion to grant exceptions or take costs of compliance into account [Currie, 1976:1107, 1134; Seskin, 1978]. Inspectors in some programs were legally prohibited from making appointments for inspections in advance[6] and instructed to issue citations for or write up *every* regulatory violation they saw (as opposed to merely issuing warnings for "first instance," less serious violations).[7] In some programs, monetary fines for violations have been mandatory, thus limiting the discretion of agency officials and judges to suspend fines in cases where businesses undertook (or could be induced to make) a good faith effort to comply.[8] Many statutes have increased the authorized level of fines to up to $25,000 *per day* for continuing violations.[9] To reduce legal delays, agencies have been granted more powers to impose fines and issue summary orders without first having to seek a court order.[10] Citizen complainants have been authorized to bring lawsuits to compel enforcement officials to issue regulations and prosecute violations more vigorously.[11]

Interviews with inspectors and regulated firms confirm that such laws have produced marked changes in enforcement procedures. Bargaining between inspectors and business managers has been sharply reduced in many programs. The protests of corporate managers about technological or financial impediments to compliance are treated with extreme skepticism or as irrelevant. The inspector is more of a "policeman," making no independent judgments about a violation's degree of seriousness or "how bad" the firm's management really is.

Limits of the "Amoral Calculator" Theory

There is an essential truth, of course, at (or near) the heart of the corporation-as-amoral-calculator theory: businesses *are* motivated to increase profits, hence they often will be tempted to violate the law if they perceive the opportunity for gain. But temptation is not necessarily translated into action. A majority of business firms, some studies indicate, do not violate even those regulations that frequently are violated by other businesses [Lane, 1977; Ball, 1960: 598]. This seems to be the case even when possibilities of detection and punishment are obviously slim [Kagan, 1978]. When there are firms in the same industry in the same city, with ostensibly equal opportunities for gain and equal risks of detection, some violate regulations frequently and some do not.[12] The profitability of businesses, too, seems to be a weak predictor of level of compliance [Lane, 1977]. Thus the "amoral calculator" theory, with its exclusive focus on legal penalties, does not adequately explain observed compliance, or predict *which* firms will violate regulations. It also fails to explain a number of anomalies we discovered in our interviews, such as small steel foundries that expended what for them amounted to considerable financial resources ($40,000) defending themselves in court against charges that involved trivial fines and compliance costs; or foundry managers who readily complied with air pollution regulations requiring substantial investments, but bitterly resisted orders of the Occupational Safety and Health Administration (OSHA) that would cost far less to comply with. These anomalies suggest that *managerial attitudes* toward the particular regulation or agency in question — rather than (or in addition to) purely economic calculations — are important in explaining corporate noncompliance. This, of course, is a basic contention of the corporation-as-political-citizen theory.

The amoral calculator theory also espouses a truncated view of the social setting of the business firm and of the "costs" to corporations of regulatory violations. It encourages an unduly stark image of the world, in which regulatory enforcement activities alone must protect society from irresponsible corporate behavior. It takes no cognizance of the pressures for responsible behavior exerted on business corporations by the market, customers, trade associations, insurance companies, sellers of safety devices, labor unions, and professionals on corporate staffs. There are far more "inspectors" than those who work for regulatory agencies. For many major corporations, the adverse publicity associated with any conviction for a serious regulatory offense often has a far more serious financial impact than the largest legal fine.[13] Consequently, the monetary amount of statutory penalties and the frequency of inspection — variables emphasized by the amoral calculator theory — will be inadequate predictors of compliance or noncompliance.

A final limit on the explanatory power of the corporation-as-amoral-calculator theory is suggested by the enormously expensive corporate blunders one can read about in the newspapers almost every month. If corporations decide whether or not to break the law only after careful and cold-blooded calculation, why do the obvious risks of severe penalties and liability awards fail to prevent events such as the following?

> Firestone Tire and Rubber Corporation was forced by the National Highway Traffic Safety Administration to recall an estimated 7.5 million steel-belted tires because of safety-rule violations that increased the risk of blow-outs. The defects apparently stemmed, at least in part, from changes made during the course of production, without stopping to re-conduct road tests. The recall, it is estimated, will cost Firestone $230 million[14] [Wall Street Journal, Nov. 29, 1978].

> A construction scaffold collapsed on a huge cooling tower being built by Research-Cottrell, Inc. in West Virginia, killing 51 workmen. Research-Cottrell is a large, sophisticated firm,; it had built 15 towers previously, using the same techniques, without any similar incidents. According to OSHA investigation, the tragedy was caused by improper testing of the concrete holding the scaffolding, which violated not only OSHA rules but official company policy as well. Research-Cottrell faces OSHA civil penalties of $105,000, possible criminal prosecution, and millions of dollars in claims by the survivors of the workmen [*Wall Street Journal*, Nov. 27, 1978].

In these incidents, the company — or rather, some middle- or lower-level officials in them — clearly miscalculated the risks associated with failure to comply fully with safety regulations, even though it was probably official company policy to comply fully with those regulations because of the financial liabilities involved.

Limits of the Regulator-As-Policeman Strategy

The "amoral calculator" image of the corporation, we noted, has led in many programs to an emphasis on strict enforcement of uniform and highly specific legal standards, backed by severe penalties. In many respects this approach has produced marked social change. Billions of dollars have been spent on air and water pollution control equipment, safety tests and warning labels, and have produced measurable results. But these changes have been enormously costly. We interviewed numerous "professionals" in business corporations responsible for regulatory compliance — environmental engineers, industrial hygienists, safety engineers, quality control engineers, and the like. Their most prevalent complaint — one that is confirmed by a growing body of research and scholarly analysis — is that the legalistic enforcement strategies of recent years frequently require unnecessary and wasteful expenditures.

Highly specific legal rules governing production processes and facilities may well facilitate enforcement. But in view of the almost infinite variety of production processes in a large country, general rules often make little sense if applied rigidly to all particular cases[15] [Dunlop, 1976: 27]. When all businesses are regarded as inherently "bad apples," and inspectors are denied discretion to make exceptions or grant extensions of time, rigidity or legalism becomes built into the system. OSHA has been criticized for requiring installation of protective devices prescribed in the rules regardless of the degree of actual risk posed to workers under the particular circumstances[16] [President's Interagency Task Force, 1978; Northrup et al., 1978]. Corporate environmental engineers often complain about receiving fines for minor violations resulting from unavoidable breakdowns in pollution control equipment. Others note that they have been forced to install prescribed abatement equipment that is technologically inappropriate for their particular plant, or that is unduly costly in relation to the minimal environmental improvements it would yield. These complaints often appear to be well-founded[17] [U.S. Small Business Administration, 1975; Ackerman et al., 1974]. In the aggregate, these individual instances of legalistic enforcement generate wasteful and unnecessary expenditures for the economy as a whole. "Progress" is purchased at a needlessly high price.

The counterproductive tendencies of legalistic enforcement may be of equal importance. One problem pointed out by businessmen we interviewed is that legalism diverts regulators from their presumed purposes.[18] When inspectors act like policemen with their eyes cast only on their manual of regulations, they fail to see hazards that are truly serious but that had not been anticipated by the regulation-writers and explicitly condemned by the rules. Safety engineers in some factories complained that rule-oriented OSHA inspectors forced the regulated companies to divert energies and funds from abatement of hazards that the safety engineers thought most important, and to spend money and time on the correction of rule violations that were in fact less important from a safety standpoint [Northrup et al., 1978: 44–46, 228–233].

A second and perhaps more important counterproductive tendency is the *stimulation of opposition* and the *destruction of cooperation*. While it is certainly true that business firms will respond to threats of unavoidable and severe sanctions, one response may be legalistic contestation and political counterattack. When inspectors are instructed to treat all business officials as if they were amoral calculators whose arguments about technological or financial factors are to be mistrusted or disregarded, business officials who think of themselves as trying hard to do "the right thing" are understandably offended. When inspectors insist on conducting time-consuming inspections without appointment and write up all violations, regardless of importance, business officials often respond by raising legalistic defenses. Experienced enforcement officials in the California Division of Occupational Safety and Health, like those in some other agencies, observe that since a more legalistic enforcement policy was instituted, there has been a great increase in the number of administrative appeals and court cases. Inspectors, accordingly, must spend much more time preparing formal reports "that will stand up in court" rather than visiting more workplaces and discussing violations and abatement measures with employers. By the same process, legalistic enforcement diminishes opportunities for cooperation. "We tried in the old days to help employers find *solutions,*" one inspector supervisor told us, "but federal law now requires us to be very legalistic."[19] One major steel company, embroiled in conflicts with OSHA, replaced the trained safety engineer who had headed its accident-prevention program with a lawyer. According to interviews with company and agency officials, a petroleum refinery in California abandoned its policy of granting air pollution inspectors free access to certain operating data after one inspector, mistrustful of the data, stalked into the restricted-entry refinery "control room" and physically seized records without permission.

Finally, legalistic enforcement may motivate regulated firms to organize politically and attack the agency at the legislative level. The steel foundry industry, for example, composed primarily of small firms weakly organized for political action, formed a political action committee, hired lobbyists and challenged OSHA in the Supreme Court because of the depth of members' outrage at OSHA's legalistic enforcement practices. Such events, which are symptomatic of a wider "regulatory backlash" in the political arena, suggest that indiscriminate reliance on the "amoral calculator" theory and a legalistic enforcement strategy can jeopardize the agency's legal mandate, its funding, and its very existence.

Corporation as Citizen, Regulator as Politician

Certain sociological perspectives on deviant behavior, such as "labeling theory," suggest that the actions of lawmaking and law enforcement officials, no less than the character of individual offenders, are a primary source of deviant behavior [Lemert, 1976: ix; Nettler, 1974; Sykes, 1978]. Imposition of "middle-class" moral standards on minority groups and harassment by prejudiced policemen are asserted to be causes of crime in and of themselves. The labeling of a youngster as a "delinquent" can cause increased resentment and hostility. Contact with biased and unsympathetic law enforcement officials can lead to increased levels of criminal activity rather than deterrring it [Reiss, 1972: 58; Piliavin and Briar, 1964; Klemke, 1978]. Noncompliance is attributed to expressive (rather than instrumental) "rebellion" against laws or enforcement actions perceived to be illegitimate by individuals or by a "deviant subculture"[20] [Cohen, 1955; Wolfgang and Ferracuti, 1967; Sutherland, 1939]. At bottom, the theory assumes that governmental disrespect for citizens, or arbitrary refusal to take their concerns into account in the enforcement process, weakens respect for compliance with the law.

One could imagine a similar explanation of at least some business noncompliance with regulations. Corporations that are generally disposed to obey the law may adopt a strategy of selective noncompliance when regulations and enforcement officials treat them arbitrarily or impose unreasonable burdens. Corporate officials we interviewed, and many scholarly studies as well, repeatedly referred to instances of governmental arbitrariness: ill-conceived and conflicting regulations; officious and poorly trained government inspectors, unreasonable paperwork requirements; bureaucratic delay; governmental indifference to the disruption or inefficiencies in productive processes caused by literal enforcement of regulations.[21] Businessmen refer indignantly to regulatory officials who impugn the credibility of corporate data provided in support of criticisms of the technical underpinnings of proposed regulations. They refer equally indignantly to inspectors who treat them "as if we were criminals."[22] They ask why they should waste time and money complying with regulations that might seem to make sense in theory but that are impractical or unduly costly in particular cases.

There is some scholarly evidence that the perception of "unreasonableness" in fact increases the probability of regulatory noncompliance. One study showed that landlords subject to inflexible rules violated rent control regulations more frequently than landlords subject to rules that took their "rate of return" into account in setting rents. The rate of violation did not vary between landlords who thought rent control was necessary in general and those who did not; the differences corresponded instead to perceived "reasonableness" of specific implementing regulations [Ball, 1960]. Similarly, a study of World War II price-control regulations in the Chicago area showed that violations were not correlated with the sales or profit levels of regulated firms, but that violations tended to occur when the rules started to produce acute shortages of essential raw materials or supplies, i.e., when unreasonably rigid regulations led to disruption of basic business functions [Katona, 1945: 141; Clinard, 1946]. Our interviews with business executives revealed similar reactions. For example, the corporate workplace safety director in one large company, which has an excellent safety record in most of its factories, told us that he encourages plant managers to delay compliance with OSHA's regulatory orders that they think are unreasonable, at least until all appeals are exhausted.

If the corporation-as-citizen theory holds that regulatory "unreasonableness" is a significant cause of regulatory violations, it also implies that "reasonable" regulations and enforcement practices will produce compliance, without the ever-present threat of immediate punishment. While this assumption is intuitively implausible to those who view business corporations as amoral, short-run profit-maximizers, many government regulatory officials we interviewed insist that "voluntary compliance," as they call it, is a major factor in all successful regulatory programs. "Enforcement officials have long recognized," wrote two FDA officials, "that at least 95 percent of compliance comes voluntarily and that this is the major source of consumer protection"[23] [Delmore and Stone, 1970: 123]. In England, a thorough study of the Factory Inspectorate concluded:

> Whilst inspectors regard the threat of legal sanctions in the background as important, in practice they find that in most cases advice and persuasion achieve more than duress. They have learned from experience that recourse to legal sanctions is only one means of achieving the objectives of safety legislation, and it is rarely the most apt or the most effective [Robens, 1972: 63].

It is important to underscore "the threat of legal sanctions in the background" in the theory of voluntary compliance. It is not *entirely* voluntary. Indeed, compliance perhaps would dissipate if there were virtually *no* threat of regulatory enforcement or if firms believed their competitors were regularly violating the law with impunity and were thereby gaining a competitive edge.[24] Nevertheless, there do seem to be substantial inducements to regulatory compliance other than the immediate threat of regulatory penalties. One factor is that many of the harms regulations seek to prevent also expose businesses to costly private liability suits. "Loss control representatives" from liability insurance companies constantly advise business firms of the latest preventative practices. Another inducement to compliance is moral in nature. While we have seen no polls on the subject, it is plausible to believe that well-educated, upper-middle-class corporate officials, with their private concerns about social stability and their institutional concern for an orderly business environment, tend to be strong adherents of the basic principle of law-abidingness. Executives we interviewed seemed to believe, for the most part, that their company should obey legitimately enacted laws, even if corporate expenses are increased, and work through normal political or judicial channels to get the regulations amended, if need be. In addition, most major corporations have a growing staff of in-house professionals who work directly with regulatory officials and share their values at least in part. This "new class" of corporate professionals includes industrial hygienists, safety engineers, biologists, toxicologists, pollution control engineers, and the like. Corporate professionals of this kind whom we interviewed tell us that they regularly cite regulatory goals and rules to enhance their own influence vis à vis production officials.[25] Increasingly, one sees newspaper and magazine advertising proclaiming a corporation's achievements in pollution control, energy-saving, equal employment practices, consumer protection, and the like. This trend illustrates the prevalent corporate concern for maintaining a reputation as a "good corporate citizen." Such a reputation presumably helps retain the loyalty of employees,[26] stockholders, customers,[27] and banks, and also helps smooth relationships with the multitude of government agencies whose approval is needed for new ventures. The other side of the coin is that widely publicized exposés of irresponsible behavior, such as Ralph Nader's attack on safety defects in the Chevrolet Corvair, can have a drastic effect on sales — and hence reinforce private efforts to ensure compliance.

These inducements to compliance do not guarantee perfect compliance. Adherents of the corporation-as-citizen theory must acknowledge the existence of "bad apples" and the periodic failure of these controls even with respect to "good apples." Most important, the theory holds that the inclination to obey the law is contingent: it depends on the reasonableness of the legal requirement. In many regulatory fields, the substantive content of "responsible" business behavior is subject to dispute. As Thomas Schelling has observed, the decision facing the regulated business firm often is not "should we do the right thing," but "what is the right thing to do?" [Schelling, 1974] Should affirmative action programs favor minority groups over more senior or more qualified whites in recruitment and promotion? How much should consumers or investors be asked to pay for relatively small increments of pollution reduction or worker safety improvements in the corporation's factories?

From this perspective, regulatory enforcement is not a mechanical act of coercing amoral actors to obey unequivocal laws. Rather it should be a continuing effort, undertaken in particular corporate settings, amidst conflicting scientific claims and normative values, to ascertain and elicit adherence to the business procedures most likely to advance the public interest. In dealing with "corporate citizens," regulators must function as politicians. That is, they must be willing to compromise among values, to adjust regulations to changing circumstances when strict enforcement would involve unexpected or unreasonable costs. On the other hand, like good politicians, they must provide leadership in developing and persuading businesses to adopt socially acceptable solutions.

That does not mean, of course, that strict enforcement and legal sanctions are unnecessary or inappropriate. Punishment and deterrence of *unjustifiable* violations are essential even under a "cooperative" enforcement strategy. Rather, the inspector-as-politician strategy calls for *discriminating* as opposed to *legalistic* rule enforcement. The inspector must attempt to detect and punish the "bad apples" without unnecessarily penalizing or offending the "good citizen," to distinguish the legitimate excuse from the evasive maneuver.

Many regulatory agencies do act on the assumption that winning cooperation is a primary method of implementing the law — and hence that business firms, as "citizens," can be induced rather than coerced into compliance. Officials in a federal price control agency met regularly with industry groups and rapidly transformed their complaints into amendments of regulations, on the assumption that voluntary compliance could be achieved only if the regulations were perceived as fair and equitable [see Kagan, 1978]. The Bureau of Motor Carrier Safety of the California Highway Patrol, which deliberately avoids a legalistic enforcement style, attempts to build consensus for its truck safety regulations by providing a forum in which trucking associations, unions, insurance companies, and safety council members meet to work out proposed regulations.[28] A California Food and Drug Division official complained that the absence of a trade association among the state's 5,000 small bakeries made the establishment and enforcement of bakery sanitation standards more difficult.[29]

To prevent legalistic enforcement, the FDA has created a flexible range of responses to violations uncovered by their inspectors, from notices that merely point out minor violations, to "regulatory letters" ordering the firm to correct the violation and report back to the agency, to criminal prosecution if the company is unresponsive, and immediate court-ordered seizures if the product hazard is deemed imminently hazardous. FDA inspectors' reports receive numerous reviews before more coercive action is taken. On the theory that few serious violations could be covered up if the inspectors make appointments in advance, California truck safety inspectors agree to come back at a different time if the terminal superintendent is busy at the moment they first come. Housing inspectors in some cities use their discretion to cite or not cite violations to bargain with landlords for better maintenance: the inspector wins cooperation and establishes himself as "reasonable" by giving to landlords more time to repair minor defects, on condition that the landlord will take prompt action to repair violations that are really dangerous to tenants [see Mileski, 1971; Nivola, 1976].

Another enforcement strategy that logically flows from the corporation-as-citizen theory involves "delegation" of many specific regulatory standards to responsible persons in the regulated firm itself. Most large corporations already have active quality control, worker safety, and environmental affairs departments that regulate internally the same activities that government agencies attempt to regulate from the outside. These units, for the most part, possess or are capable of generating the information and expertise needed to anticipate and prevent the kinds of catastrophes regulators have tried to control by rules written from afar. In many cases, therefore, the agency can leave specific precautionary measures to the firm's judgment. Agency officials insist that the company establish internal regulations and inspection systems, set performance goals, and so on. The agency's task then is to monitor company performance on a spot-check basis. The locomotive safety inspection programs established early in this century followed this strategy, which has been quite successful [see Scharfman, 1970, vol. 1: 270–273, vol. 4: 75–77; U.S. Office of Technology Assessment, 1970]. More recently, California Occupational Safety and Health officials have contracted with certain companies to allow union-management safety committees to plan and implement safety standards in lieu of regular government inspections and automatic enforcement of government regulations.[30] Proposals have been made to cut back intensive government inspection of meat-packing where companies establish qualified quality assurance programs [see Grumbly, 1982]. By requiring pharmaceutical companies to hire certified personnel to direct premarket clearance experiments for new drugs, the FDA has strengthened the professionalization and intracorporate power of company researchers while reducing, at least in theory, the need for close and legalistic governmental supervision.

Limits of the Corporation-As-Political Citizen Theory

If it is true that business corporations may be moved, as a matter of principle, to violate regulatory rules or orders they regard as arbitrary and unreasonable, it is also true that many firms violate laws *not* out of any defensible principle, but because they think they can get away with it. Examples of truly unscrupulous "bad apples" abound[31] [see Schrag, 1971; Stone, 1975]. A single company may be a "good apple" on some issues and a "bad apple" on others. That limit would be acknowledged by proponents of the "citizen" theory: it purports to provide a *common* explanation for regulatory violations, not an *exhaustive* one. The theory, however, provides no basis for predicting when a firm will be a "good apple" that can readily be induced to comply if dealt with sympathetically and flexibly, and when a firm will act like a "bad apple," eager to take advantage of any "softness" on the part of enforcement officials.

Moreover, there is no bright line differentiating unreasonable from reasonable regulatory orders, and hence no clear distinction between "amoral" and "principled" violations. Businessmen justify a great many violations by attacking specific regulations or arguing that certain circumstances should be treated as extenuating. Some of these arguments are sincere, some constructed after the fact, and it is often hard to tell the difference.[32] On some issues, there are sharp differences from company to company concerning what is reasonable: officials in one firm may regard a set of risks as remote and regulations calling for their removal as arbitrary, but officials in another firm may place a higher priority on controlling remote risks and may find the same regulation perfectly acceptable.[33]

These variations in managerial attitudes and differences in attitudes toward risk make it difficult for regulators to pursue a "cooperative" enforcement strategy and to act as consensus-building politicians. The regulators may guess wrong. They may treat an "amoral calculator" as if he were a "good corporate citizen," granting extensions of time when he promises to come into compliance, only to find that he fails to keep his bargain. The resulting betrayal is an embarrassment for the inspector and a possible disaster for persons the regulation is designed to protect. It is asking a great deal to expect field inspectors to discern accurately whether the firms's managers are "good apples" acting in good faith or "bad apples" who are bluffing.[34] Similarly, it takes considerable technical knowledge and judgment for inspectors to decide whether or not an exception to the rules can be made in a particular case, when urged to do so by the regulated business, without unduly increasing the risk of harm. Experienced enforcement officials often speak of honest inspectors who were "taken in" by the perspective advanced by the managers of a regulated enterprise. Although the popular theory that regulators inevitably become the ideological captives of the regulated industry is clearly exaggerated and often untrue [see Weaver, 1978], there have been many agencies that demonstrably have become "too cooperative." Consequently, politicians and consumer protection groups often attack any instances of nonenforcement or bargaining as a sign of corruption. Thus it is often far *safer* for the inspector personally and for the agency politically to adhere to the rules strictly in all cases than to try to make discriminating case-by-case judgments about the businessman's character or about the risks and costs at stake.[35]

The Corporation as Incompetent, The Regulator as Consultant

Ordinary street crimes are committed, it is generally assumed, not only by amoral calculators and socially or politically disaffected citizens. Some crimes are committed by individuals who are in some sense socially or mentally disordered. Some offenders, it is said, are imperfectly socialized to normal concern for the feelings or rights of others. Some act out their impulses and aggressions compulsively [see Abrahamsen, 1960]. The behavior of such individuals seems indifferent to the threat of legal penalty or to appeals to conscience. For many of these offenders, law enforcement strategies emphasize efforts at rehabilitation: therapy, education, supervised probation, job training, and so forth.

Few observers attribute corporate law violations to psychological characteristics of business managers [but see Clinard, 1946]. But an analogy can be and often is drawn, at least implicitly: for the business corporation, disorganization is the equivalent of mental disorder. Just as individuals can fail to learn and internalize social norms, business firms can fail to develop organizational units responsible for studying and implementing regulatory requirements, responsible for checking the purely profit-oriented impulses of other corporate units and the indifference of individual employees. Just as some individual criminals seem totally oblivious to the harm they inflict on others, corporations with limited views of their social responsibility can fail to study or take seriously the human risks posed by their operations.[36] Just as individuals may violate driving laws or miss tax-report deadlines through simple inattention or preoccupation with personal problems, corporations may allow established precautionary routines to slip gradually into disuse.

Christopher Stone studied a number of major corporate scandals involving breach of legal duty, ranging from production of unsafe brakes on airplanes to marketing of unsafe drugs [Stone, 1975]. He concluded that a substantial number, although certainly not all, of these instances of corporate misconduct did not stem from amoral calculation or from principled disagreement with the law. The corporations' boards of directors, he was sure, would have sternly disapproved the conduct involved, had they been apprised of it in advance. The violations, therefore, seemed to stem from corporate mismanagement or what might be called "*dis*-organization." Managers were not told of and did not adequately monitor "short-cuts" taken by subordinates. Sometimes bad news and the illegal maneuvers taken to cure it were actively hidden from superiors. The production department did not understand the law the same way the general counsel's office did. Quality control or safety testing engineers were not given adequate authority to insist on attention to their concerns.[37] Similarly, the *Robens Report* on occupational safety and health law enforcement in Great Britain noted:

> Traditional concepts of criminal law are not readily applicable to the majority of [regulatory] infringements . . . Relatively few offenses are clear-cut, few arise from reckless indifference to the possibility of causing injury, few can be laid without qualification at the door of a particular individual. The typical infringement . . . arises rather through carelessness, oversight, lack of knowledge or means, inadequate supervision or sheet inefficiency. [Robens, 1972:82]

The idea that "law-abiding" corporate managers will fail from time to time to control all of their personnel would come as no surprise to organization theorists and academic students of corporate behavior. Anthony Downs has suggested a "Law of Imperfect Control: No one can fully order the behavior of a large organization" [Downs, 1967: 143–145; Landau and Stout, 1979]. Even with respect to primary production goals, it has been noted, corporations do not calculate their actions with perfect economic efficiency.[38] The division of labor and separation of functions characteristic of large organizations also limit the breadth of perception and the range of official responsibilities of specific organizational sub-units [see Schelling, 1974]. The plant manager in Texas is not personally responsible for the legal fines paid by the corporate treasury in New York, and may well have moved on to another job by the time the violation is proved [Stone, 1975]. Internal conflicts and the struggle for resources among different departments, and between management and labor, distort implementation of official policy [Selznick, 1957]. The pressures of time and multiple problems lead management to accept easily found compromise solutions rather than continuing to search for and implement optimal ones [see Cyert and March, 1963]. Cognitive overload, conflicting goals, and limited rationality presumably could also lead the firm to ignore or underestimate hazards. Changing circumstances — new personnel, sudden shortages in raw materials, and the like — could easily overpower routines which had been established to control risks.

The contribution of corporate ignorance, incompetence, inattention, and internal conflict to regulatory violations was frequently mentioned by both regulators and business executives whom we interviewed:

> An environmental engineer for a Georgia metal fabrication company said he noticed that one of the fans in the air pollution control "bag house" was vibrating excessively. Fearing this would lead to a breakdown and violation of pollution regulations, he went to tell the chief maintenance official about it. The maintenance man, his desk full of urgent "work orders" for repairs on a variety of production machines, responded, "Here's a wrench. *You* fix it!"

> Workers in an aluminum smelter refused to wear "air-conditioned" space-man type suits provided by management to protect them from heat and noise because they could not complete their tasks nearly as quickly when wearing them. They preferred to disregard these safety precautions and have more "rest time."[39]

It could be argued, of course, that corporations would be better managed and their internal control systems would be policed more carefully if enforcement agencies increased the threat of heavy legal penalties sufficiently. Many of our respondents acknowledged that corporate industrial hygienists and quality control engineers acquired more status and influence within the corporation when regulatory agencies turned to aggressive enforcement and harsher penalties. Nevertheless, as Christopher Stone argues, deterrence alone may not be effective. Judges are reluctant to impose very heavy legal penalties for violations that appear to stem from incompetence rather than willfulness. Given the dynamism and variety of productive processes, specific legal regulations will often fail to anticipate and proscribe the most serious risks to the public; only a committed and alert management can maintain the spirit of concern, inquiry, and aspiration that is needed. Finally, as indicated above, formal prosecution and legalistic penalties are clumsy tools. They cut too broadly, seem unnecessarily punitive, and alienate potential allies inside corporations rather than winning their cooperation.

For these reasons, many regulatory agencies respond to specific cases of corporate incompetence — and to the expectation that incompetence will be a major cause of violations in general — by adopting a rather different enforcement strategy. The agency seeks to be an educational as well as a law enforcement body. It holds meetings and seminars for corporate officials to dramatize the extent of the regulatory problems and the latest abatement techniques.[40] Inspectors serve as *consultants* more often than as policemen. Upon finding a violation, legal penalties are not their first recourse. Instead, like private business consultants, they attempt to analyze the causes of the violation, to locate weaknesses in the company's control system, to point out cost-effective ways of complying with regulations. To note two examples:

> Auditors for the California agency that regulates debt collection agencies to prevent abusive collection techniques routinely suggest methods of correcting and preventing violations. Punitive action is instituted only if written assurance of compliance is not received by an agreed-upon date.[41]

> The FDA's Hazard Analysis Control Point Investigation Technique undertakes analysis of typical food and drug production processes to locate the most common sources of contamination and key indicators of potential breakdowns. Inspectors are then instructed to focus their investigations on these critical points (as opposed to routinely checking compliance with the FDA's almost endless list of general regulations). In effect, this is an enforcement program for evaluating and improving the *company's quality control system* for detecting critical problems [Hile, 1974: 101].

Regulatory violations, according to the corporation-as-incompetent theory, sometimes come about because corporate sub-groups prevent critical information from reaching top management, or because the corporation simply fails to generate systematic information about potential hazards and make it available to groups that would be endangered, such as workers, consumers of its products, or neighbors of its factories. Acting upon this assumption, some regulatory programs emphasize mandatory gathering and dissemination of information. For example:

> Employers are obligated to assemble and report to OSHA detailed records of accidents affecting employees. Some employers must establish medical programs to take regular samples of blood and urine from workers exposed to dangerous substances, such as lead, and to make the analysis available to the workers.

> Manufacturers are obligated to conduct inventories of all potentially harmful chemicals they use and of all discharges into the air and water. For certain sources of pollution, they must install detailed monitoring equipment, and make the records available to inspectors.

The chief value of such disclosure and reporting programs, undoubtedly, is not that they necessarily lead to action by the recipients of the reports — the public and the government — but that they force the corporation itself to focus on the measures and the risks they signify. The company must assign personnel to gather the statistics and report them. Top management acquires another tool for monitoring sub-units.

A related regulatory strategy, also based on the idea that violations stem from corporate inattention, is to force corporate managers to assign high-level officers or qualified professionals to establish and monitor compliance programs. The

FDA, for example, requires manufacturers of blood plasma products and intravenous solutions to appoint approved experts to oversee quality-assurance operations. California worker safety regulations require an employer to establish a safety training program for employees and to appoint a responsible management official to run it.[42] In some instances, agencies have required companies that have a record of irresponsibility to appoint officials who will be responsible for certain compliance programs, much as a court assigns a probation officer to watch over juvenile delinquents. The California Food and Drug Division settled a court case against one small manufacturer on condition that the company hire a recognized consultant to design and install a quality control system. The Securities and Exchange Commission has required some corporations that have violated regulations to establish audit committees, independent of management, to police certain corporate activities.

Limits of the Corporation-As-Incompetent Theory

Like the corporation-as-citizen theory, the idea that corporations often violate regulations through inadvertence and mismanagement is undoubtedly true, but of limited *predictive* value. It tells us neither when nor why or in what regulatory areas a corporation is likely to slip into incompetence. Nor does it distinguish, *in advance,* whether a firm is an amoral calculator or a well-meaning but ineffectual blunderer.

The problem of prediction engenders considerable risks for a consultative or educational enforcement strategy. If he is up against a truly "bad apple," the consultant-inspector can be duped into not penalizing intentional violations. Top corporate officials determined to break a law can readily circumvent mandatory corporate self-monitoring mechanisms. On the other hand, regulations imposing specified data collection or licensing procedures for key personnel on an entire industry, simply because a few firms have proved themselves incompetent, impose unnecessary costs on the competent firms. Conversely, the consultative approach may encourage complacency. The "capture theory" of regulatory agency behavior warns that close consultative relationships between agency and industrial experts may change the agency's motivation from "accelerating learning" to stabilizing competition in the industry.

The fear of charges of capture or corruption is, in fact, an important limit on consultative enforcement practices. Just as important, however, are the difficulties agencies face in hiring, training, and retaining technically competent and system-oriented "consultants" who could work with management. It is far easier for agencies, from inspectors up to top officials, to think of themselves as bureaucrats whose responsibility is simply to know the rule book and enforce the law.

Conclusion

> Scholars generally agree . . . that a theory of legal behavior must be multiple; legal
> acts work on the minds of subjects in various ways. . . . First, there are *sanctions* —
> threats and promises. Second, there is the influence, positive or negative, of the
> social world: the *peer group*. Third, there are internal values: *conscience* and related
> attitudes, the sense of what is and is not legitimate and what is or is not worthy to be
> obeyed [Friedman, 1975: 69].

> The interesting question is, which factors are the strongest? And which prevail in
> case of conflict? Nothing in the literature furnishes a satisfying answer. It is doubtful
> that a *general* answer exists [Friedman, 1975: 120].

Each of the popular theories of corporate legal behavior (or misbehavior) we
have described seems to capture an important aspect of reality. Many corporate
officials affirm that it is their company philosophy to comply with applicable
regulations as a matter of policy. They may adopt that policy as a matter of
civic-mindedness (Friedman's "conscience" factor). They also perceive significant social and hence economic pressures to comply or to maintain a reputation for
reliability or good citizenship. These pressures stem from customers, workers,
unions, trade associations, public interest groups, the press, and professionals on
their staffs. Yet there are always some firms that choose the illegal alternative
when meaningful sanctions seem remote and it is more profitable to violate the
law; most firms, perhaps, will make these calculations on *some* issues. At other
times businesses disobey or delay compliance with regulations because of a sincere
belief that the regulation is unreasonable ("not worthy to be obeyed," in Friedman's terms) as applied to their particular product or process. Still other violations
occur despite the wishes of company management; through inattention or carelessness, sub-group conflicts, and organizational failure to prevent or catch these
deviations, the peer group or organizational pressures for compliance break down.

One implication of the diverse sources of noncompliance is that indiscriminate
reliance on any single theory of noncompliance is likely to be wrong, and when
translated into an enforcement strategy, it is likely to be counterproductive. To treat
every firm as an amoral calculator, whereby any deviation from specific regulatory
rules is met by legal penalties, burdens the economy with unnecessary costs. It also
breeds legal and political opposition on the part of good corporate citizens who are
offended by being forced to meet unreasonable requirements and by the perceived
injustice of punishment pursuant to legalistic rule application. Conversely, if
regulators were always to act as responsive politicians or consultants, and always
withhold penalties, in hopes of convincing or teaching the company to do "the
right thing," the amoral calculators will take advantage of their flexibility. The
relevant question, therefore, both from the standpoint of explanatory or predictive

theory and from the standpoint of regulatory strategy, is not which theory to use, but *when* each is likely to be appropriate.

The difficulty, as we have seen, is that *none* of these theories, in and of themselves, has much predictive power. None of the theories, for example, fully suggests under what circumstances pressures for company policies of law abiding-ness or policies of internal vigilance are likely to break down. The "amoral calculator" theory directs attention to the frequency of inspection and legal sanctioning power of the agency. The "corporation as citizen" theory directs attention to the ability of the corporation's constituents — workers, customers, etc. — to detect and complain about violations. The "corporation-as-incompetent" theory directs attention to the existence, corporate position, and powers of indus-trial hygienists, quality control engineers, product safety testers, and environmen-tal scientists employed by the company. But which of these factors is most important? Similarly, if regulatory unreasonableness — or the perception of it — is a major source of noncompliance, when is it most likely to occur? Economic factors are undoubtedly important, such as the regulated firm's cost of compliance and the difficulty of passing those costs on to customers. But the perception of unreasonableness may stem not only from the economic impact of the law but also from the degree of corporate expertise on the subject matter of the regulation. We note, in that regard, that managers of smaller businesses seemed more likely to declare a regulatory requirement unreasonable when they, the businessmen, had some expertise on the subject (such as plant manager's knowledge of the risks that a procedure in his factory posed in terms of worker safety), than when they had no expertise on the subject (such as the effects of their factory's air pollution on community health).[43] What's more, the structure of the agency is probably a factor: agencies that regulate a large number of industries, as opposed to specializ-ing, often lack the expertise for discriminating judgments and hence their rules and actions more often are regarded as unreasonable than actions by industry-specific agencies. Which of these factors is most important, however, is not clarified by the popular theories of corporate noncompliance.

These dilemmas constitute an agenda of research questions suggested by our study, not answered by it. Our basic supposition at this point, however, is that the determinants of business noncompliance are so manifold that any comprehensive predictive theory will not quickly be discovered. For regulatory policy, this implies that the primary goal should be adaptability. Regulators should be alert to the possibility that violations may derive either from amoral calculation, princi-pled disagreement, or incompetence. Inspectors should be prepared to shift from strict policemen, to politician, to consultant and back again according to their analysis of the particular case.

There are substantial technical and political impediments to such an adaptive enforcement strategy, however. Because of the diversity of regulated business enterprises and complexity of regulations, enforcement officials often lack the technical knowledge to assess accurately the degree of risk that would be posed by relaxing the rules in a particular case. Nor is it always easy to gauge the competence and motives of corporate managers. Legislatures, prodded by consumer protection and environmental groups that mistrust both business and bureaucrats, often refuse to grant regulatory officials discretion. Even when they do, funding is not generous, which makes it difficult for most agencies to recruit, train, and retain inspectors sophisticated enough to serve as competent consultants *and* as tough-minded sifters of justified from unjustified excuses *and* as stern sanction-appliers when necessary. As long as accidents continue to occur — and the undesirability (if not the impossibility) of a risk-free society suggests they will — regulatory agencies can and will be blamed for failing to enforce the law vigorously enough. New and more inflexible regulations then will be promulgated. Inspectors who exercise discretion will risk being deceived by business, being blamed for accidents, and being suspected of corruption. Thus, the politics of security from hazards and the politics of organizational survival both favor a follow-the-rules enforcement strategy. For political reasons, too, the vision of the corporation as amoral calculator is likely to dominate the "criminology of the corporation" in modern Western society.

Notes

1. We use the terms *business firm* and *business corporation* interchangeably, primarily because most respondents did, although some "theories" seem especially applicable to the large corporation.
2. The propensity for regulatory enforcement officials informally to classify violations as "negligent" versus "deliberate," "excusable" or "not", has also been observed among consumer fraud investigators. See Silbey, 1978.
3. This pattern was followed in the agencies described in the studies cited in the two preceding footnotes, as well as by some agencies whose officials we interviewed, including the Motor Carrier Safety Unit of the California Highway Patrol and the pre-1972 California Divison of Industrial Safety.
4. In 1977, 1978 and 1979 we interviewed regulatory officials in a variety of agencies, as well as numerous managers of regulated business firms, concerning the consequences of stricter and more aggressive enforcement strategies.

    These interviews were undertaken as part of a study of the regulatory process directed by Professor Eugene Bardach, Graduate School of Public Policy and Professor Robert A. Kagan, Department of Political Science, University of California, Berkeley. See Eugene Bardach and Robert A. Kagan, *Going By the Book: The Problem of Regulatory Unreasonableness*. A Twentieth Century Fund Report. Philadelphia: Temple University Press, 1982. The Center for the Study of Law and Society in Berkeley provided office space and other assistance.

We (or our research assistants) conducted open-ended interviews of inspectors and higher enforcement officials of the federal Food and Drug Administration and the Occupational Safety and Health Administration. We also interviewed inspectors and directors of enforcement at a number of California state agencies: the Division of Occupational Safety and Health; the Food and Drug Division and Nursing Home Division in the Department of Health; the Bureau of Motor Carrier Safety in the California Highway Patrol; the Milk and Dairy Section of the Department of Agriculture; and the Bay Area Air Pollution Control District. We also interviewed municipal building and housing code inspectors and fire marshals in the city of Oakland, California. In several instances we or our research assistants accompanied inspectors on a daily round.

Secondly, we conducted open-ended interviews of executives and managers in companies regulated by each of the above agencies, concentrating on a limited number of firms in certain industries: steel foundries (4) and aluminum manufacturing companies (2) (with respect to workplace safety and health regulation and air pollution regulation); automobile assembly plants (2) (with respect to worker safety); blood banks and blood products manufacturers (2) (with respect to FDA regulation of "biologics"); petroleum refineries (3) (with respect to air pollution) trucking firms or trucking departments (3) (with respect to truck safety regulation); nursing homes (2) and dairy products manufacturers (2). In addition, we interviewed labor union officers in four companies and insurance company representatives from two insurance firms with respect to safety matters.

Third, we conducted a two-day workshop in May 1978, at the Graduate School of Public Policy at Berkeley in which we recorded round table discussions among enforcement officials from most of the above-mentioned agencies and a few representatives of regulated firms.

The sample of agencies and regulated businesses is not systematic. We cannot contend that their responses are "representative" in a scientific sense. Our goal, in this exploratory study, was not to compare a broad range of agencies and companies, but to concentrate on in-depth interviewing so as to discover attitudes and analyses by participants in the regulatory process that pointed to *significant problems,* as they experienced them, and which suggested directions for more systematic research.

5.   This view, it should be noted, is prevalent not only among regulators but among established businessmen, too, who are critical of the ethics of their "fly-by-night" competitors. See Lane, 1977.

6.   See, e.g., Federal Mine Health and Safety Act of 1969 (30 U.S.C., §§ 801f); California Assembly Bill 1600 (1973) (inspection of nursing homes).

7.   Interviews with supervisors and inspectors in California Division of Occupational Safety and Health, Bay Area Air Pollution Control District, U.S. Food and Drug Administration, California Department of Health Division for Nursing Home Inspections, and with regulated firms in each of these fields.

8.   See Continental Steel Corp., 30 *Occupational Safety and Health Review Commission Reports* 1410 (1974); California Labor Code, § 6428.

9. A $25,000 per day *criminal* fine is authorized, for example, in the 1970 federal Clean Air Act Amendments (with $50,000 a day for repeat offenders) and the federal Mine Safety Act. The 1977 Clean Air Act Amendments authorized *civil* penalties (which are easier for the agency to prove) of up to $25,000 a day, as did the Toxic Substances Control Act of 1976.

10. See e.g., California Labor Code, §§ 6325–6327 (summary orders to shut down dangerous workplaces); Bay Area Air Pollution Control District, Regulation No. 5 (summary orders to shut down pollution source); Federal Railroad Safety Act of 1970 (summary orders to reduce train speeds); Federal Hazardous Substances Labeling Act, as amended (5 U.S.C. § 1265 (1970)).

11. See § 304 of the 1977 Clean Air Act; *Environmental Defense Fund v. EPA,* 465 F2d 528 (D.C. Cir., 1972). The Occupational Safety and Health Act has similar provisions, 19 U.S.C. 662 (d). Nursing home advocacy groups have sued federal officials for inadequate enforcement of quality of care regulations and fire marshals have been held liable for failure to close down buildings with fire code violations.

12. There are three major petroleum refineries in the same county in California, each inspected for air pollution violations virtually every day. They have sharply different violation rates, according to enforcement officials we interviewed, and they display different patterns of interaction with the agency, ranging from cooperation to resistance. See also studies by Lane [1977] and Ball [1960].

13. For example, in 1978 the government ordered the Ford Motor Company to recall 1971 Pinto cars because a number of them had exploded in collisions, due to the gas tank being located too close to the rear of the car. Although that defect had been changed on all models in subsequent years, Ford sustained losses in sales of 1978 Pintos that cost far more than the recall itself.

14. One apparent reason Firestone officials did not conduct the full range of tests was that sales officials were concerned about bringing out the new line of tires to prevent continued incursions by foreign radial-tire manufacturers.

15. Professor John Dunlop, after having served as U.S. Secretary of Labor (a department that administers several major regulatory programs) observed: "Uniform, national rules . . . do not reflect the reality of the workplace" [Dunlop, 1976: 27].

16. In addition, OSHA has frequently demanded extensive redesign of manufacturing equipment even though much less expensive personal protective equipment for workers (respirators, ear plugs, etc.) would produce roughly equivalent worker protection.

17. Sometimes insensitive "technology-forcing" is not only unduly expensive but is actually counter-productive. In *Paccar, Inc. v. NHTSA,* 573 F.2d 632 (1978), the court struck down a National Highway Traffic Safety Administration (NHTSA) regulation requiring improved braking systems for trucks, because of evidence showing that the required new systems were not reliable and may in fact have increased the likelihood of truck accidents. The NHTSA apparently promulgated the regulation despite this evidence because it distrusted the arguments from industry and because it wanted a law to enforce in order to give industry an incentive to improve.

18. That legalistic rule-following tends to undermine "purposive" law enforcement is a recurrent theme in legal theory. For a recent and provocative restatement, see Nonet and Selznick [1978].

19. Workshop on "The Inspectorate," Graduate School of Public Policy, Berkeley, May 1978.

20. These theories and the works cited here have not escaped criticism from other criminologists. For a summary, see Sykes [1978].

21. On unreasonable reporting requirements, see U.S. Commission on Federal Paperwork, Final Summary Report (Washington, 1977). For an example of the harmful effects of bureaucratic delay, see Tucker [1978: 43], reporting such extensive delays in regulatory approval of new "biological" pest control techniques that some companies have abandoned development efforts.

22. The chief executive officer of an Alabama bank, after referring to the 24 separate federal sets of regulations and reporting requirements he had to comply with, was quoted as saying, "It's no crime to be a banker, but it might as well be" [LeMaistre, 1978: 26].

23. This theme was repeated by representatives of 15 regulatory agencies at a workshop on "The Inspectorate" at the University of California, Berkeley, May 1978.

24. Chester Bowles, head of the Office of Price Administration during World War II, reflected this view when he said that 20 percent of the population would automatically comply with any regulation, 5 percent would attempt to evade it, and the remaining 75 percent would go along with it as long as the 5 percent were caught and punished [Bowles, 1971].

    One study of the liquor industry noted that most firms believed that their competitors generally ignored the law. "The assumption that other participants have few scruples fosters the belief that survival in such an arena depends upon the adoption of the same attitude." Thus, weak enforcement, among other factors, weakened normative inducements to comply with liquor laws and even fostered attitudes supportive of ignoring the laws [see Denzin, 1977].

25. Several corporate safety managers told us that they could more readily obtain cooperation from supervisors and foremen for changes in plant safety activity when they could say, "That's the law." Similarly, a corporate director of transportation told us that federal truck safety regulations are a great asset to him in pushing for adequate maintenance, restrictions on driver hours, adherence to speed limits, and other useful activities which tend to get overlooked. See also, on this point, Schelling [1974].

26. The classic statement of the idea that "public service" serves as a motivational device is Barnard [1938: 147].

27. In Kreisberg's study of the steel industry during the Korean conflict, only the smaller, more marginal suppliers routinely charged "gray market" prices above those agreed upon by the industry to control wartime shortage-induced inflation. Firms with established reputations eschewed profiteering even though there was no agency to enforce the agreed price and no legal penalties for charging higher prices [Kreisberg, 1956]. For a persuasive analysis of the economic value of a reputation for honesty and, by implication, good citizenship, see Nelson [1976]. In these respects, the image

of the corporation as citizen tends to converge with the picture of the corporation as self-interested and amoral calculator. The amoral calculator that took long-term public relations and adverse publicity liabilities into account might be a good corporate citizen. Adherents of the amoral calculator image, however, tend to emphasize short-run calculations and strictly *legal* "costs"; that is the distinguishing feature of the "image."

28. In contrast, the California Air Resources Control Board (CARB), taken over in the mid-seventies by strong environmentalists, abolished an industry advisory committee that had served to provide technical advice to the board, and pushed local enforcement officials to increase formal enforcement. One result is increasingly political opposition, and some clear cases of legalistic opposition by industry, whose representatives often cite the technically flawed and unrealistic nature of CARB regulations.

29. Where trade associations do exist, they can be valuable allies for enforcement agencies that are not too mistrustful to work with them. The U.S. Department of Transportation adopted a plan whereby the standards for safety of cast aluminum wheels, used on racing and sports cars, were set by the Speed Equipment Manufacturers Association. The association assures compliance by denying its "seal of approval" to wheel manufacturers that do not establish adequate quality control programs and send castings to the association regularly for testing. Association inspectors — who are inevitably more knowledgeable, because more specialized, than governmental inspectors — visit the plants of members and make suggestions. The association "seal" is an invaluable sales aid, thus assuring high levels of membership in the association.

30. Air pollution control agencies recently have begun to make agreements with large industrial installations, such as refineries, whereby the company has more discretion over which pollution sources to concentrate on and which technologies to use, so long as improvement is shown; this is a departure from traditional techniques, under which the agency insisted on strict enforcement of uniform rules controlling every source and prescribing the control technology to use. See Maloney and Yandle [1980].

31. Recently, U.S. House of Representative documents revealed that a large chemical company failed to notify nearby residents that their health was endangered by toxic chemicals dumped into waste sites because the company feared incurring legal liability [*San Francisco Chronicle,* April 11, 1979, p.7; Galdston, 1979: 25]. Aluminum industry officials we interviewed are of the opinion that several American steel companies have been rather unscrupulous in resisting compliance with air pollution regulations.

32. Businessmen may also retrospectively justify or rationalize a violation they committed for purely economic reasons by convincing themselves that the law was unreasonable anyway. For a discussion of this tendency among juvenile law-breakers see Matza [1964] and Sykes and Matza [1957].

33. Corporate safety directors we interviewed, some of whom had worked for several companies, referred to clear differences among managements in the importance they placed on safety and their willingness to spend money to reduce risks.

34. An enforcement official responsible for regulating the quality of care in California

nursing homes told us that his inspectors are instructed to treat each inspection as a potential prosecution because a home can change from good to bad in a couple of weeks if personnel changes occur.

35.   The resulting "minimax" strategy — minimizing the maximum harm by treating all citizens as if they were potential criminals — is a common strategy among urban policemen. See Muir's [1977] insightful analysis.

36.   These views occasionally emerge in public discussion. The popular motion picture "The China Syndrome" portrays a near-disaster in a nuclear power generation station, aggravated by attempts of greedy company directors to suppress information about it. A prominent nuclear critic was quoted as criticizing the film in one respect: it showed the company's board chairman as "an ogre," although "it would have been more realistic to portray him as an idiot. It's incompetence rather than malevolence," *Newsweek,* April 16, 1979, p. 31.

37.   See also the corporate blunders noted in text accompanying notes 22–24, above.

38.   The classic analysis of organizational limits on corporate rationality is Cyert and March [1963]. See also Hedberg et al., [1976].

39.   The propensity of workers to decline to use protective equipment on machine guards provided by management, on grounds of convenience and efficiency of work, was a recurrent theme in our interviews. It is one reason OSHA mandates more expensive "engineering controls." See n. 16, above.

40.   For example, after new regulations have been formulated, the federal Food and Drug Administration issues interpretive press releases, prepares educational materials with compliance instructions for distribution through trade associations, conducts workshops with industry's leaders, sends speakers to trade association meetings, and publicizes regulations and new problems through several FDA publications. One state food and drug official we interviewed began new enforcement campaigns with workshops to plead with and threaten industry's leaders followed by a well-publicized and carefully documented prosecution of one major uncooperative firm.

41.   Ellen Worcester, "Policing Debt Collectors: A Case Study of the Enforcement Function," unpublished paper, in possession of the authors. In contrast, an FDA enforcement official told us, "We're a law enforcement agency, not a service agency. . . . If we go into a factory and see someone picking his nose while he is handling shrimp, we don't say, 'Gee, you ought to buy gloves for that guy.' We say, 'You have violated Section whatever of the act.'"

42.   This is not a new idea. An 1873 California law required every mine to employ a safety supervisor, who was made criminally responsible for accidents due to neglect of duty on his part. In 1876, San Francisco required the owners and operators of steam engines to appoint a licensed manager for each boiler [Eaves, 1910]. The Securities and Exchange Commission has for many years forced corporations that wish to sell shares to the public to hire certified public accountants to attest to the reliability of the financial information made public.

43.   By the same token, oil refinery pollution control engineers, who worked full time on the subject, were quite willing to dispute regulatory rules for specific pollutants, and the models of ambient air flow or the epidemiological studies on which the rules were based.

References

Abrahamsen, David (1960). *The Psychology of Crime*. New York: John Wiley.

Ackerman, Bruce, et al. (1974). *The Uncertain Search for Environmental Quality*. New York: The Free Press.

Ball, Harry (1960). Social Structure and Rent Control Violations, 65 *American Journal of Sociology* 598.

Bardach, Eugene and Robert Kagan (1982). *Going by the Book: The Problem of Regulatory Unreasonableness*. Philadelphia: Temple University Press.

Barnard, Chester (1938). *The Functions of the Executive*. Cambridge, Mass.: Harvard University Press.

Bowles, Chester (1971). *Promises to Keep*. New York: Harper & Row.

Clinard, Marshall (1946). Criminological Theories of Violations of Wartime Regulations, 11 *American Sociological Review* 285.

Cohen, Albert (1955). *Delinquent Boys*. New York: The Free Press.

Carson, W. G. (1970) White Collar Crime and Enforcement of the Factory Acts, 10 *British Journal of Criminology* 383.

Currie, David (1976). The Occupational Safety and Health Act, 1976 *American Bar Association Research Journal,* 1107.

Cyert, Richard and James March (1963). *A Behavioral Theory of the Firm*. Engelwood Cliffs, N.J.: Prentice Hall.

Delmore, Fred and Kermit Sloane (1970). FDA's Voluntary Compliance Program, quoted in Turner [1971].

Denzin, Norman K. (1977). Notes on the Criminogenic Hypothesis: A case study of the American liquor industry, 42 *American Sociological Review* 905.

Downs, Anthony (1967). *Inside Bureaucracy*. Boston: Little, Brown.

Dunlop, John (1976). The Limits of Legal Compulsion, 1976 *The Conference Board Record* (March): 27.

Eaves, Lucille (1910). *A History of California Labor Laws*. Berkeley: University of California Press.

Friedman, Lawrence M. (1975). *The Legal System*. New York: Russell Sage Foundation.

Galdston, Ken (1979). Hooker Chemical's Nightmarish Pollution Record, 1979 *Business and Society Review* (Summer) 25.

Geis, Gilbert, and Robert Meier (eds.) (1977). *White Collar Crime* (rev. ed.). New York: The Free Press.

Hawkins, Keith (forthcoming). *Environment and Enforcement: Regulation and the Social Definition of Pollution*. New York: Oxford University Press.

Hedberg, Bo et al. (1976). Camping on a Seesaw, 21 *Administrative Science Quarterly* 41.

Hile, Joseph (1974). Food and Drug Administration Inspections — A New Approach, *Food, Drug and Cosmetic Law Journal*. (Feb.) 101.

Grumbly, Thomas (1982). Self-Regulation: Private Vice and Public Virtue Revisited, in Bardach and Kagan (eds.) *Social Regulation: Strategies for Reform*. San Francisco: Institute for Contemporary Studies.

Kagan, Robert (1978). *Regulatory Justice: Implementing a Wage Price Freeze*. New York: Russell Sage Foundation.

Katona, George (1945). *Price Control and Business*. Bloomington, Ind.: Principia Press.

Klemke, Lloyd, (1978) "Does Apprehension for Shoplifting Amplify or Terminate Shoplifting Activity?" 12 *Law and Society Review* 395.

Kreisberg, Louis (1956). National Security and Conduct in the Steel Gray Market, 34 *Social Forces* 268.

Landau, Martin and Russell Stout (1979). To Manage is not to Control: or the Folly of Type II Errors, 39 *Public Administration Review* 148.

Lane, Robert (1977), Why Businessmen Violate the Law, in Geis and Meier [1977].

LeMaistre, G. A. (1978). A Plethora of Regulations: A Case of Too Many Cooks? 4 *National Law Journal* 26.

Lemert, Edwin (1976). *Human Deviance, Social Problems and Social Control*. New Jersey: Prentice-Hall.

McKie, James (ed.) (1974). *Social Responsibility and the Business Predicament*. Washington, D.C.: Brookings Institute.

Maloney, M. T., and Bruce Yandle (1980). Bubbles and Efficiency, 4 *Regulation* 49.

Matza, David (1964). *Delinquency and Drift*. New York: John Wiley.

Mileski, Maureen (1971). *Policing Slum Landlords*. Yale University Ph.D Dissertation.

Muir, William K. Jr. (1977). *Police: Streetcorner Politicians*. Chicago: University of Chicago Press.

Nelson, Robert (1976). The Economics of Honest Trade Practices, 24 *Journal of Industrial Economics* 281.

Nettler, Gwynn (1974). *Explaining Crime*. New York: McGraw-Hill.

Newsweek (April 16, 1979) p. 31.

Nivola, Pietro (1976). *Municipal Agency: A Study of Housing Inspectorial Service in Boston*. Harvard University Ph.D Dissertation.

Nonet, Philippe and Philip Selznick (1978). *Law and Society in Transition: Toward Responsive Law*. New York: Harper-Colophon.

Northrup, H. et al. (1978). *The Impact of OSHA*. Philadelphia: The Wharton School.

Piliavin, Irving and Scott Briar (1964). Police Encounters with Juveniles, 70 *American Journal of Sociology* 206.

Portney, Paul (ed.) (1978). *U.S. Environmental Policy*. Baltimore: Johns Hopkins University Press.

President's Interagency Task Force on Workplace Safety and Health (1978). *Making Prevention Pay*, Draft report.

Reiss, Albert Jr. (1972). *The Police and the Public*. New Haven: Yale University Press.

Robens, Lord (1972). *Report of the Committee on Safety and Health at Work*. London: Her Majesty's Stationery Office.

San Francisco Chronicle (April 7, 1979) p. 7.

Sharfman, I. L. (1970). *The Interstate Commerce Commission*, Parts 1–4. New York: Commonwealth Fund.

Schelling, Thomas (1974). Command and Control, in McKie [1974].

Schrag, Peter (1971). On Her Majesty's Secret Service: Protecting the Consumer in New York City, 80 *Yale Law Journal* 1529.

Selznick, Philip (1957). *Leadership in Administration*. Evanston, Illinois: Row, Peterson.

Seskin, Eugene (1978). Automobile Air Pollution Policy, in Portney [1978].

Silbey, Susan (1978). *Consumer Justice: The Massachusetts Attorney General's Office of Consumer Protection*. University of Chicago Ph.D Dissertation.

Stone, Christopher (1975). *Where the Law Ends: Social Control of Corporate Behavior*. New York: Harper Colophon.

Sutherland, E. H. (1939). *Principles of Criminology*. New York: Lippincott.

Sykes, Gresham (1978). *Criminology*. New York: Harcourt, Brace.

———— and David Matza (1957). Techniques of Neutralization: A Theory of Delinquency, 22 *American Sociological Review* 664.

Tucker, William (1978). Of Mites and Men, *Harper's* (August, 1978) p. 43.

Tullock, Gordon (1974). Does Punishment Deter Crime? 36 *The Public Interest* 103.

Turner, James (1971). *The Chemical Feast*. New York: Grossman Publishers.

U.S. Office of Technology Assessment (1970). *An Evaluation of Railroad Safety*. Washington, D.C.: U.S. Government Printing Office.

U.S. Small Business Administration (1975). *The Impact on Small Business Concerns of Governmental Regulations that Force Technological Change*. Washington D.C.: U.S. Government Printing Office.

Wall Street Journal, November 29, 1978; November 27, 1978, and April 9, 1979.

Weaver, Paul (1978). Regulation, Social Policy, and Class Conflict, 50 *The Public Interest* 45.

Wilson, James Q. and Barbara Boland (1978). The Effect of the Police on Crime, 12 *Law and Society Review* 367.

———— (1975). *Thinking About Crime*. New York: Basic Books.

Wolfgang, Marvin and F. Ferracuti (1967). *The Subculture of Violence*. London: Tavistock Publishing Co.

Zimring, Franklin and Gordon Hawkins (1973). *Deterrence: The Legal Threat in Crime Control*. Chicago: University of Chicago Press.

5 ENFORCEMENT OF OCCUPATIONAL SAFETY AND HEALTH REGULATIONS
A Comparison of Swedish and American Practices
Steven Kelman

At the beginning of the 1970s the attention government paid to safety and health at the workplace increased dramatically in many industrial countries.[1] In the United States this increased interest was symbolized by passage of the Occupational Safety and Health Act of 1970,[2] which created a new federal agency (the Occupational Safety and Health Administration, or OSHA) to promulgate and enforce regulations regarding safety and health conditions in the workplace. (Previously, occupational safety and health regulation had been undertaken almost exclusively at the state level.) In Sweden there had been some sort of central government involvement in occupational safety regulation since 1889, and the law creating a single agency with responsibility for such regulation (*Arbetarskyddsstyrelsen,* or Worker Protection Board, ASV) had been passed in 1949.[3] However, at the beginning of the 1970s the attention paid to occupational safety and health issues in Swedish politics increased substantially. ASV enjoyed large budget increases. Many new inspectors were hired. And the government began the lengthy process of preparing statutory changes as well, which eventually produced a revision of the 1949 statute in 1974 and the adoption of a new Work Environment Law in 1976.

In both the United States and Sweden, then, government became determined at the beginning of the 1970s to "get serious" about workplace safety and health. This paper seeks to contrast how this commitment to "get serious" was translated into different methods adopted in the two countries for enforcing safety and health regulations. Sweden and the United States were selected because, on the one hand, the two countries both enjoy similarly high standards of living and democratic forms of government, and, on the other hand, the political context for occupational safety and health regulation in the two countries differs dramatically. In terms of proportion of the labor force organized, unions in the United States are weaker than in any other democratic industrial country. Swedish unions are the strongest. The United States is the only one among democratic industrial nations with no mass-based socialist or communist party. The Swedish Social Democratic party, with close ties to the unions, is the most powerful such party and held power continuously from 1932 to 1976.

The expectation might be that these differences in political environment would produce a situation where workplace safety and health regulations were enforced with a light hand in the United States and an iron fist in Sweden. For the period of awakened interst in these issues in both countries at the beginning of the 1970s, not only was this prediction not borne out, but the opposite turns out to have been the case. In the United States the system adopted by the Occupational Safety and Health Act called for inspectors who found violations of regulations to fine employers immediately for the infractions. In Sweden penalties continued to be assessed not when a violation was first pointed out, but only after persistent failure to correct the problem. In the United States OSHA headquarters established an extensive apparatus to supervise inspector activities. In Sweden, until 1975 ASV had not a single official whose main job it was to supervise field activities, and even after this, the unit set up was modest in size and scope. Furthermore, in the United States, the director of each local inspection office closely supervises the work of each inspector. In Sweden little such supervision occurs. Given these counterintuitive findings, it becomes essential to attempt to see what explains them.

The empirical research on which this paper is based covers the period through 1976. This means that it does not include the sustained period of slow economic growth in both the United States and Sweden during the second half of the 1970s, or the period of nonsocialist rule in Sweden since 1976 and the accession of the Reagan administration in 1981. A few brief words about changes since 1976 will appear at the conclusion of the paper.

The General Context of Enforcement

In both the United States and Sweden, occupational safety and health regulations are enforced by a corps of inspectors who work out of field offices of the agency (called ''Area Offices'' in the United States and ''Districts'' in Sweden). The regulations are adopted centrally and made available to employers (and unions) so that firms will know what regulatory compliance requires. Inspectors visit plants to see to what extent plant conditions fulfill regulatory demands. The heart of any inspection, both in the United States and Sweden, consists of a walkaround of the plant, with employer and employee representatives present. The inspector looks at machines, takes air samples, and speaks with workers. (Measuring the extent of chemical contaminants or noise requires the special skills of an industrial hygienist, and if a plant has significant health as well as safety hazards, inspection by a person who has been trained only as a safety engineer will generally not suffice.) An inspection may last an hour in a tiny shop or several weeks (literally) in a large plant.

To investigate enforcement procedures in the United States and Sweden, enforcement materials (such as training manuals) were examined and agency-level officials interviewed. In addition, I visited two OSHA Area Offices located in the same region and conducted in-depth interviews with almost all inspectors in each office using a standard questionnaire. (These surveys are referred to as the ''In-Depth Inspectors' Survey.'') I also interviewed the Area Directors and other supervisory personnel, and examined office records. The In-Depth Inspectors' Survey was complemented by two surveys I conducted afterward at the national level, referred to as the ''National Area Directors' Survey'' and the ''National Inspectors' Survey.'' I selected a sample of OSHA Area Directors, interviewed them by telephone, and requested their assistance in administering a printed survey to their inspectors. Similar procedures were followed in Sweden.

The Enforcement Process: United States

Perhaps the best single word to describe the American enforcement process, in its various aspects, is *formal*. OSHA lays out inspection procedures in great detail. Inspections take the form of searches for violations. They result in formal citations (and penalties) for specific regulatory infractions. These citations are frequently formally contested by employers. If contested, OSHA must formally prove, in a court setting, that the violations did in fact occur. The process of enforcing the rules thus itself goes according to well-defined rules.

Inspection Procedures

In terms of inspection procedures, OSHA lays out the rules for its inspectors in voluminous detail in a 122-page *Field Operations Manual*.[4] The first step is an ''opening conference'' with the employer, where the inspector is instructed to inform the employer about the purpose and general plan of his inspection, and provides him with a copy of the Occupational Safety and Health Act. The inspector is also supposed to look at the accident log the statute requires employers to keep. By seeing what types of accidents there have been over the past years, an inspector is supposed to get a better idea of what hazards to look for.

For the heart of the inspection, the "walkaround," the statute prescribes that both employer and employee representatives be given an opportunity to accompany the inspector. Whether or not an employee representative accompanies the inspector, the inspector is told by the *Manual* to interview individual employees about hazards.[5] (The inspector might ask employees whether, say, certain work processes normally in operation have been turned off during the inspection.)

During the walkaround, the inspector takes written notes on violations observed. After the walkaround, he conducts a "closing conference" with the employer. Here the inspector is instructed to apprise the employer of what violations he believes he has found and to inform him that fines may be assessed for the violations. In connection with each possible violation, the inspector is supposed to ask the employer how long he believes it will take to abate the hazard and what it will cost. The inspector should also inform the employer of his right to contest any violations.[6]

Several days later, if the inspection uncovered violations, the employer receives a formal citation in the mail. The statute requires that a copy of the citation be "prominently posted" at the workplace.[7]

Two key elements of the OSHA enforcement system are routine imposition of monetary fines without trial and levying these fines the first time an inspector discovers a violation, whether or not the violation is subsequently corrected (so-called first-instance sanctions), or whether the employer had notice that the matter was a violation in the first place. If OSHA had to put an employer on trial before penalties could be imposed, this would make such imposition relatively uncommon, since trials consume lots of resources. To make imposition of fines a significant element of an enforcement program, a way must be found to routinize the punishment. The statute does this by in effect allowing inspectors to impose fines.[8]

Violations and Fines

The statute classifies violations as "nonserious," "serious," "failure to abate," "repeated," and "willful." (Unhappy with the implications of "nonserious," OSHA changed this category in 1976 to "other.") For nonserious violations, fines are discretionary and may go as high as $1,000 per violation. For serious violations, fines are compulsory and may also be as high as $1,000. Repeated and willful violations carry fines up to $10,000. An employer is fined for "failure to abate" when an inspector has previously cited for a violation of a regulation and the violation has not been corrected after the period permitted for abatement. The fine is up to $1,000 a day *for each day* the violation continues.

Citations list a date by which each violation must be corrected. The employer must send a letter to the Area Director informing him of steps taken to abate the violations uncovered.[9] Area offices can find out directly whether violations have been corrected by doing follow-up inspections. These are required for serious violations, discretionary in other cases. If no follow-up inspection is made, the Area Office must rely on employer abatement letters to monitor correction of violations.

The *Field Operations Manual* gives very detailed rules for determining the size of fines. (These procedures are summarized on a worksheet the inspector meticulously fills out for each violation on his citation.) Three criteria are laid down for determining the gravity of a nonserious violation: the probability of injury or disease occurring from the hazard, the severity of the resulting injury or illness were an accident to occur, and the extent to which the regulation is violated. For each criterion, the inspector is supposed to rate the violation in a category A, B, or C, in ascending order of seriousness. The three ratings are then averaged to produce an overall rating. The *Manual* then presents a penalty schedule for violations in the different categories. But the penalty assessment process is far from done, for these "unadjusted penalties" must then be adjusted for "good faith," size of the firm, and inspection history. (For example, a 20 percent reduction is automatically dispensed if this is the firm's first inspection.) All in all, "adjustments" may lower the unadjusted fine by as much as 50 percent.[10] The detail with which OSHA headquarters prescribes rules for inspector behavior is illustrated by the publication in 1976 of a list that took each chemical on OSHA's threshold limit value list and indicated how much the regulation had to be exceeded in order for a violation to be classified as serious. [OSHA, 1976: Chapter IX].

Although the statute allows penalties of up to $1,000 per violation for nonserious violations, it should be clear that the average penalty is considerably below that. For the period researched there were no fines at all attached to about two-thirds of non serious violations. For 1976, the average fine per violation was $37. The average fine per inspection was $188.[11]

Since OSHA inspections are intended as searches for violations, their purpose could be defeated were advance notice given, enabling an employer to, say, shut off work processes. The *Field Operations Manual* underlines the importance of not giving employers any advance notice.[12] (One industrial hygiene inspector I interviewed told me that he didn't even like the opening conference at the beginning of the inspection, because it gave employers a chance to turn off processes.)

OSHA's first-instance sanctions system means that even if an employer corrects a violation in front of the inspector's eyes, this cannot influence whether or not a fine is imposed, since the employer was supposed to be in compliance even before the inspector came. The *Field Operations Manual* notes that if, say, an employer instructs a foreman to make an immediate correction of a blocked aisle or a hazardously protruding object, "corrections shall be recorded to help judge good faith," but that, "although corrected, the apparent violation shall be the basis for a violation or proposed penalty."[13]

Citation and Appeal

OSHA citations are written so as merely to state what sections of the regulations have been violated. Both the gobbledegookish reference to the section of the *Code of Federal Regulations* that has been violated and a description in words (taken from the wording of the regulation) are given. Thus, a violation might read something like:

29 CFR 1926.500 (9) (c)   Failure to guard wall openings, from which
                           there is a drop of more than 4 feet —-openings 2 through
                           6 not guarded.

Any OSHA citation may be appealed. Appeals are first heard by an administrative law judge in the area where the business is located. Proceedings are oral and include cross-examination. OSHA is always represented by a lawyer, and the employer is usually represented by counsel. Burden of proof is on OSHA. A three-member review commission panel in Washington is the next step. It relies on the record developed earlier and on new briefs filed by the parties. Its decisions may in turn be appealed to the court of appeals and from there to the Supreme Court.

Since violations must be proved in order to mete out punishment, OSHA inspectors must be scrupulous about documentation. Inspectors in the In-Depth Inspectors' Survey reported that their supervisors' most common request after reviewing their last ten inspection reports was for documentation. This means taking photos ("I try to get in the employer or an employee representative so the employer can't say it was taken at another plant," one inspector noted) and employee statements. For a violation to exist, there must be worker exposre to the hazard, so if a particular machine is not running when the inspector comes through, the inspector must get a worker to say he normally uses it. Consideration of court challenge is the main explanation for a number of policies followed by many area offices. For example, most chemical exposure limits are expressed as eight-hour averages because exposure often varies widely over different phases of the process cycle, while other times a process is in operation only for a short period each day. Sometimes the inspector sees that exposure is relatively constant or observes that a process cycle is short enough to provide measurements of exposure peaks and troughs without sampling for a full eight hours. In such cases, eight-hour sampling merely increases the time an inspector must spend.

The problem is that if the regulations express a threshold limit value as an eight-hour average, an inspector who has not sampled the full period is open to legal challenge. Thus many area directors are wary about letting inspectors use their judgment on whether a full eight hours is necessary in a particular case, afraid of what will happen when lawyers question OSHA relentlessly about some 18 1/2 minute sampling gap. Four of fourteen area directors I surveyed while they participated in a training course responded that if an inspector had sampled for only six hours, they would insist that zero values be entered for the remaining two hours for the purpose of computing whether the threshold limit value had been exceeded. This means that in some cases where a threshold limit value has been exceeded, legal requirements prevent citation. In contrast, responses to the Swedish National District Chiefs' Survey showed that in half of the Districts, inspectors issued written inspection notices in health cases without doing any sampling at all. (This is not as arbitrary as it may sound. Frequently an experienced person can tell that for a certain type of operation, a threshold limit value will be exceeded where control measures are absent.)   In situations such as these, the issue in any citation appeal may be not whether a hazard exists but whether legal requirements have been followed. To take a bizarre Catch-22-type situation, determining non-compliance with threshold limit values requires sampling, often using devices attached to the employee's body, but such devices may hinder employee movement, leading an employer to claim that the sample was not representative of worker exposure.

Perhaps the most unfortunate results come when legal requirements actually interfere with compliance because they make regulations so hard to understand. There have been numerous complaints about the incomprehensibility of OSHA regulations, but one OSHA official pointed out that ''there is a limit as to how far we can go in paraphrasing or simplifying the language of the standards, because, as you well know, the standards are a legal document in addition to an engineering document. [U.S. House of Representatives, 1972]

Although OSHA inspectors may not legally give on-site consultation, there is no logical reason to believe that during an inspection they should not give employers advice, to the extent of their expertise, on how to correct violations. Yet in 1971 the OSHA legal office stated that if inspectors gave advice and an employer following the recommendations had not succeeded in correcting the problem, the citation could be thrown out in court.

Supervision of Inspectors

Supervision of individual OSHA inspectors by their managers and of OSHA Area Offices by OSHA headquarters is relatively intense. No citation leaves the office without being scrutinized by the Area Director or his assistant. OSHA has a management information system that collects large amounts of data from Area Offices. For each inspection, the inspector must fill out a report including information about where the inspection fits on OSHA's priority system, how many employees worked at the plant inspected, and so forth. [OSHA, 1975] A statistical assistant completes a citation log each week that reports information about every individual violation in each citation the area office issues. For each violation, there is listed the exact reference from the Code of Federal Regulations, whether the violation was serious or nonserious, the fine, and the abatement date.

This massive input gives rise to an equally massive output. Some printouts aggregate data for each inspector and allow comparisons among inspectors in one Area Office. Others aggregate data for each Area Office and allow comparisons among Offices. From the printouts one can determine how a given Area Office compares with others on such parameters as percentage of citations where a penalty was imposed, number of inspections with serious violations, average penalty per violation, division of inspections according to OSHA priorities, or average lapse time between the date of inspection and the mailing of a citation. Seven of the ten Area Directors in the National Area Directors' Survey stated that they used management information system data to evaluate the performance of their inspectors. The most common ways were to see how productive inspectors were, how many serious violations they assessed, and how much time they spent in the field as compared with in the office.

There are several units at OSHA headquarters involved in controlling the field. One unit scours Management Information System printouts looking for problems and reports on problems to the appropriate OSHA Regional Office which in turn contacts the Area Office. This unit also conducts periodic audits of Area Offices, which include on-the-spot visits and even accompanying inspectors on inspections. In 1976, as part of continuing efforts to tighten control of the field, a unit at headquarters began giving Area Offices lists of *specific firms* they should inspect, according to OSHA's hazard priorities.

The Enforcement Process: Sweden

The Swedish enforcement process contrasts markedly with the one adopted in America after passage of the Occupational Safety and Health Act. Routines for conducting inspections in Sweden are set out in considerably less detail than for

OSHA on six pages of a stencil entitled "Rules and Regulations for the Factory Inspectorate."[14] The inspection processes in the two countries are quite similar. One important difference is that in Sweden the inspector is assigned responsibility for a specific set of workplaces, which he gradually gets to know better. Important differences also result from the fact that the Swedish enforcement system allows neither the routine imposition of fines nor first-instance sanctions. It has, in fact, technically not been illegal to fail to comply with ASV regulations.[15] An employer is first served notice of a problem when an inspector after an inspection sends him a written inspection notice containing specific points where he is required to make changes. It is only if the employer refuses to comply with the points in a written inspection notice that he can be punished. Until 1974 the law allowed only the imposition of an order formally demanding that an employer comply or of a prohibition against using a machine until a violation was corrected. If an order or prohibition was violated, ASV handed the case to a district attorney for possible prosecution. In 1974 the law was changed to allow the imposition of a conditional fine in conjunction with an order or prohibition, assessed only if the employer does not correct the violation. The issuance of orders and prohibitions is taken up specially by a factory inspectorate council in each district (with labor and management representation) and is complicated enough so that it is not undertaken routinely. Only a tiny proportion of all inspections eventually result in some sort of formal legal action.

Inspection and Notice

Only a minority of inspections produce written notices. In many cases, the inspector simply gives oral suggestions for improvements during the closing conference, and these have no legal force. If a written inspection notice is sent, it gives, like an OSHA citation, specific abatement dates and requests the firm to send in abatement letters. Notices are sent in duplicate to the local union. In Sweden, unlike America, the question of giving advance notice of inspections is left up to the individual inspector. The course material used to train Swedish inspectors says that "there are advantages to giving advance notice of your visit. Then the employer can prepare himself, and the safety steward can have time to talk with fellow workers." [Lindstrom et al, 1975: 7] This course material also emphasizes that inspectors should try to create a relaxed attitude during the inspection. During the walkaround, the inspector is instructed, "You can talk about things that don't directly have to do with your mission, in order to create good rapport. Be sure to avoid controversial subjects." [Lindstrom et al, 1975: 9] And while an OSHA inspector is instructed to be taking notes constantly during his inspection to record violations, Swedish inspectors are warned that "to write too much during the walkaround can be impractical and irritating. While you're writing, the others will perhaps have nothing to do, or, even worse, will begin discussing some other problem, leaving you outside the discussion.''[21] [Lindstrom et al, 1975: 11]

Swedish inspectors, in their written inspection notices, are not supposed to refer to violations of regulations but instead to what steps should be taken: instead of talking about failure to guard a machine, a Swedish written inspection notice would say something like, ''A fixed guard should be installed to cover the unguarded transmission'' [Lindstrom et al, 1975: 13]. Inspectors are also instructed that it is poor psychology to spring anything in a written inspection notice that has not already been discussed with the employer in person: ''If upon further reflection at the office you think that the point you discussed was too vague, you can discuss this over the telephone and talk about it before sending the point in written form'' [Lindstrom et al, 1975: 10].

The dominant view within OSHA has been that regulations must be enforced according to the book. This leads to problems, as attested by stories about inspectors, rulers in hand, who allegedly require that 39-inch guardrails be replaced by 42-inch ones. The problem as OSHA headquarters sees it is that if more discretion were granted inspectors, they might run out of control. ''For the sake of uniformity we have to cite for whatever's in the book,'' one Area Director told me. ''If you start telling people to use their judgment, you start having 84 different opinions.'' In Sweden, the view traditionally was different. One of the reasons for the lack of immediate legal force for regulations has been that inspectors were supposed to use their discretion, not citing violations they felt unrelated to safety in the particular instance and requiring changes they felt were called for in other cases, even when these did not appear in any regulation.

In Sweden, as in the United States, formal legal actions against employers may be appealed. In the very small number of such formal legal actions that occur, appeals are not uncommon. They involve only submission of a letter by the appealing party and a reply by the District. There is no hearing or opportunity for oral examination, and no rules exist for where the burden of proof lies in deciding appeals. Lawyers are almost never involved.[16]

Supervision of Inspectors

Supervision is at best an insignificant part of the job of a Swedish District Chief. In response to a question in the Swedish National District Chiefs Survey, ''Is there anyone in the District who reads an inspector's written inspection notices before they are sent out?'' four of the eight District Chiefs responded straight out that nobody did. In response to the question, "Is there someone who checks whether an inspector follows up the written inspection notices he has sent out?" all eight responded that there was nobody who did. In response to the question, "Is there anyone who checks whether an inspector sends out written inspection notices with sufficient frequency?" seven of the eight District Chiefs replied that nobody did. Instead of supervising, District Chiefs spend their time on public relations and on doing inspections of their own. (All but one of the eight District Chiefs reported that he had workplaces of his own assigned to him, usually the largest in the District. American Area Directors do not conduct inspections themselves.) One of the most dramatic contrasts in the In-Depth Inspectors' Survey concerned a question about what supervisors looked for in deciding whether an inspector was performing well. Only 16 percent of the American group (6 of 39) replied that they did not know what their bosses were looking for, and another 8 percent said they did not know for sure but made guesses. Of the Swedish inspectors, however, an astonishing 78 percent (14 of 18) responded that they did not know what their boss' standards were.

In Sweden, districts send some statistics into headquarters, but these have not been used for field control purposes. Once-monthly statistics were compiled in a district, and they were available to the district chief for possible use in evaluating inspectors. ASV did not process them. The only way a District Chief could compare performance with another district would have been to look at an ASV annual report where the data appeared. Five of eight chiefs surveyed in the National District Chiefs' Survey said they did not use the monthly statistics in any way.[17]

Statistical reporting, constantly driven to new levels of refinement by OSHA, has been streamlined even further in Sweden to give inspectors more time to inspect. In 1977 both monthly reports on inspection activity and time reports began being sent in only for a district as a whole and no longer for individual inspectors. Furthermore, some items on monthly inspection activity reports were eliminated.[18]

Local-level differences in the extent of supervision are replicated at the national level. While OSHA headquarters devotes major attention to supervision of the field, ASV headquarters devotes hardly any. There is no unit of ASV responsible exclusively for field supervision. Staff in the Office of Standards Development are available to answer questions from the field about difficult compliance problems. Until 1975 field control was the direct responsibility of the Chief of Standards Development, who lacked time for the task.[19] Occasional memos for the field were prepared, and there was an annual meeting of District Chiefs to discuss problems. In 1975 the Bureau of Field Coordination was established, which at the end of 1976 had two employees. There was no intention of radically increasing field supervision.[20]

Enforcement and Nongovernmental Agents

An important difference between the enforcement process for occupational safety and health regulations in Sweden and the United States involves the role of nongovernmental agents in enforcement. In Sweden in the 1970s plant-level safety stewards (appointed by the local union) and joint labor-management safety committees came to play a crucial role, alongside inspectors, in the enforcement process.

The appointment of plant level safety stewards and safety committees was first encouraged through a 1942 agreement between the national union and employer federations on occupational safety and health. Safety committees had by no means been unique to Sweden. (Many large American firms have had safety committees.) In Sweden unions had also sometimes selected a safety steward, frequently a shop-level union official who also held other union positions, to represent employees in making demands to management. The 1942 agreement required that safety stewards be appointed at all workplaces with ten or more employees and that safety committees be appointed at workplaces with more than one hundred employees. Following the 1942 agreement, safety stewards and safety committees were appointed around the land, but for the next twenty-five years, they maintained what one today might call a "low profile." (In the less discreet vernacular of the time, "nobody seemed to care" about them.) One problem was that most safety stewards did not know much about what made workplaces unsafe or unhealthy. The 1942 agreement had established the Joint Industrial Safety Council designed to educate safety stewards, but its efforts reached only a modest proportion of the target group.

We will return to the role of safety stewards below in explaining the observed differences between the Swedish and American enforcement processes.

Inspector Attitudes: United States and Sweden

Dramatic differences in inspector attitudes in the two countries parallel the differences between the way the inspection systems have been organized. The American enforcement system set up after 1970 was designed to be enforcement-minded, while the Swedish system was cooperation-minded. One of the seven-point scale questions in the In-depth and National surveys was directly designed to tap enforcement-mindedness versus cooperation-mindedness. At one pole of the scale was the statement, "It's better for OSHA to be a tough enforcer of the regulations, even at the risk of being considered punitive," and at the other end the statement, "It's better for OSHA to seek to persuade employers to comply with regulations voluntarily, even at the risk of being considered soft." The mean replies (table 5-1) illustrate the enforcement-mindedness of the Americans and the cooperation-mindedness of the Swedes.

Some of the comments Swedish inspectors made to me during the in-depth interviews illustrate their cooperation-mindedness:

> Our role is to get employers and employees to come closer to each other. I try to reconcile the parties during the inspection. The first time around I don't try to enforce every point, so as to get our relationship functioning as smoothly as possible.

> Sometimes we don't try to enforce every point. Then there's a danger that the safety steward will get unhappy. At that point, you have to reason with the safety steward, talk about common sense. We prefer to help employers and employees come to a common agreement, because then we've helped their feelings of dignity. We shouldn't dominate too much, but listen and steer their opinions in the right direction.

> I think we can give in on an issue, even if it makes the workplace more hazardous, in order to preserve cooperation. I don't want to destroy cooperation for good.

The overwhelming majority of the OSHA inspectors questioned in the In-Depth Inspectors' Survey felt that first-instance sanctions were necessary. Responding to an open-ended question about their attitude toward ''the penalty-imposing side of your job,'' 63 percent of respondents (24 of 38) answered that such sanctions were a necessary part of OSHA compliance activities. Those favoring these sanctions did so overwhelmingly because they thought there would be little compliance otherwise. ''Teeth are the only way to impress management with the seriousness of the situation.'' one inspector said. If first-instance sanctions disappeared, replied another, ''OSHA would flop — we might as well write it off the books.'' If the inspectors had no power to impose penalties, ''They'd laugh at you when you came into the plant,'' a third stated. ''It's the only means of enforcing the law,'' said a fourth. ''It's the only arm that we have,'' replied another.

Sense of Mission

One way to promote good inspector performance is to infuse organizational members with a sense of mission [See Selznick, 1957] A sense of mission is easier to infuse the clearer and more operationalizable the organization's goals are. The OSHA enforcement system, with its emphasis on detecting violations and fining employers, gives inspectors an operational goal that makes, by and large, for good morale. They know what they are supposed to do; most are go-getters about it, and a few are gung-ho. This gives the American inspectors an advantage over their Swedish counterparts, whose job is more unclear.

Considerable crusaderism, and hints of hostility to private industry on the part of some American inspectors, were revealed in responses to a question in the

In-Depth Inspectors Survey about whether inspectors would be willing to leave their present job for a safety or health-related job in private industry, were such a job offered them at the same salary (or, if not, how much higher the salary would have to be for them to accept the offer). A full 38 percent of the American respondents (15 of 38) volunteered that they would not want to go into industry under any circumstances and gave a reason directly related to what they were able to accomplish protecting workers at their current OSHA jobs.[21] "This job is on behalf of the mass of people out there who have to be made to feel that someone cares," stated one inspector grandiloquently. Another 23 percent of respondents (9 of 40) gave a specific cash figure that would attract them to a job in industry, but this was typically double their current salaries. These cash figures were often accompanied by explanations that stressed what one could accomplish in OSHA or by criticism of industry.[22] By contrast, *none* of the Swedish inspectors, asked the same questions, expressed either hostility towards private industry or many traces of crusaderism. Only one of the 11 respondents expressed much of an interest in a private sector job, but the others, who wished to stay, mentioned reasons such as the greater independence they had at their present jobs, fears that the workload would be heavier in the private sector, and happiness over civil service fringe benefits or job security. (Two respondents stated that higher pay in the private sector made little difference since marginal tax rates were so high.)

There is a cost to infusing OSHA inspectors with a sense of mission. Many American inspectors, armed with their goal of finding violations, often appear to be steamrollers. In the National Area Directors Survey I asked whether the operations of their offices had changed at all during the 1975 recession, as far as their penalty or citation policies were concerned. Six of the nine Area Directors replied there had been no change. Only six of the 22 inspectors questioned in the In-depth Inspectors Survey said they were less likely to cite a given violation as serious in a small firm than a large one. Twenty-one of the 26 respondents in the In-depth Inspectors Survey replied that they took no account when a firm threatened to shut down because they couldn't afford to pay for changes required by the regulations. Responses were peppered with comments such as "call their bluff," "they always say it and never do," and "they're just trying to scare you."[23] ASV inspectors were less rigid. Only six of 15 replied that they took no account of threats to shut down. Three respondents said they would not require the firm to make the changes, as long as no serious hazard was involved. Four respondents said they would require the change sometime in the future, but not immediately. Two more said they wouldn't take any account of such claims, but only because they worked in Stockholm where they were many jobs available, and that in areas with fewer jobs things would be different.

Inspectors' sense of organizational mission was measured by a seven-point scale question in the In-depth Inspectors Survey, where the two poles were

"OSHA has made a big contribution towards improving safety and health at the workplace" and "OSHA has hardly made any contribution to improving safety and health at the workplace." The mean response of the American inspectors was a notably one-sided 2.3, indicating a high sense of mission. On another seven-point scale question, where the two extremes were, "I have a feeling that, as a result of my work, many deaths and serious injuries in factories are being avoided," the mean response was 2.4. Interestingly, the mean response of Swedish inspectors on both questions was somewhat higher (2.6 and 3.0 respectively) indicating that these inspectors were less enthusiastic about the result of their efforts.

Explaining the Differences

Before occupational safety and health became a more important issue at the beginning of the 1970s, inspectors in both countries proceeded similarly. They encouraged compliance by offering employers normative rewards (praise for doing as they should). Fines were almost never used. One problem with this method was that real friendship ties could hardly be expected to grow on the basis of contact as infrequent as that between inspector and employer. In both Sweden and America, inspectors would find the same violations on later visits.

Policymakers drew lessons from past failures in developing new strategies. When policymakers choose among alternative control systems, they do so in the context of assumptions and experiences they have as members of their society. They begin with assumptions about how likely it is that individuals subject to a law will comply simply because the law expresses the authority of government. In neither America nor Sweden were occupational safety and health policymakers content with existing levels of compliance. There are, nonetheless, degrees of pessimism about baseline levels of obedience to the law. Out of the Swedish tradition, where a democratic system replaced one of elite rule only in the twentieth century, grows the notion that people ought to defer to the wishes of those in authority. Out of the American liberal tradition grows the notion that it is legitimate for people to define and pursue their own goals, independent of what the state thinks is best for them.

Contemporary Swedish society, like many European societies, emerged from a history of brutally sharp distinctions between ruler and ruled.[24] The Swedish word *överhet* is a generic term for those on top of society, seen as an undifferentiated presence by those at the bottom. The word has no equivalent in English. It translates literally as "those over us" and consisted of those — kings, aristocrats, bishops — born to rule over others. The inclusiveness of the word suggests a fusing of all sources of social power — political, economic, and religious — into a single elite before which ordinary people stand both in awe and in fear and trembling.

The American tradition is different from the Swedish. The early colonists came to America at a time when the first modern challenge to hereditary rule was taking place in England. This period of challenge to traditional rulers was also a period of ferment in political philosophy. The writings of Hobbes and, somewhat later, Locke represented a radical break with the classical tradition. For both, the starting point was a state of nature where there existed no political community but only individuals defining and pursuing personal goals as they pleased.

Some who came to America were influenced by the legitimization of individual pursuit of goals in the new philosophy. But the liberal tradition in America went deeper than ideas contained in books. For, as a new nation starting afresh, American reality corresponded to the Lockean model. This is the essential message of interpretations of the American experience beginning with Tocqueville's *Democracy in America* and running through Louis Hartz's *The Liberal Tradition in America* or Seymour Martin Lipset's *The First New Nation*. In America the starting point was individuals defining personal goals — deciding themselves what occupation to pursue and what religious faith to follow. And in contrast to Europe, though unequal classes certainly existed, nobody had been born to rule.

Out of the American liberal tradition grew dominant values about relationships between people and leaders quite different from those arising from the *överhet* tradition. In Sweden it was legitimate for rulers to define goals that people should seek and expect that people defer to those wishes. In America it was legitimate for people to define and pursue their own goals — to assert themselves — and deference to wishes of leaders was not emphasized.

But the forces of individual interest, once legitimized, are not easily controlled; there always exists the danger that people encouraged to be self-assertive will fail to see the distinction between doing so when this does no impermissible harm to others and doing so when such harm is done. The traditional problem of European states with established rulers has been to tame those rulers and let people breathe; that of America with its liberal tradition has been to tame the unruly so that other people can breathe.

If policymakers are pessimistic about predispositions to compliance, they are more likely to use punishments than rewards to induce compliance, since those not predisposed to obey the law will generally not be considered deserving of reward. Such assumptions also make the use of normative inducements of any kind less likely since those predisposed to noncompliance will probably be regarded as unlikely participants in a small group that may induce compliance. Edmund Burke saw the destruction of deference and other normative means of compliance as the essential evil of liberalism. The use of coercive legal punishment becomes required because other institutions of control can no longer be mobilized. Without deference or other normative means, "laws are to be supported only by their own terrors," Burke warned. "In the groves of their academy," he wrote of the liberal philosophers, "at the end of every vista, you see nothing but the gallows". [Burke, 1960: 388]

The *överhet* tradition in Sweden left in its wake more than a set of dominant values about relations between rulers and ruled. The challenge to the *överhet* state also produced political institutions that encouraged accommodation among contending groups.

The political challenge to the *överhet* state from the land-owning peasantry and the middle and working classes whose strength grew with industrialization came in the century following adoption of the constitution of 1809. The way the rulers responded to the challenge was crucial for the form Swedish political institutions were to take in the twentieth century. The constitution set up a system where neither king nor estates monopolized political power. Laws could be passed only with approval by both (although the estates had exclusive power to set taxes). Initially the king was the dominant figure. The estates met only once every five years. The votes of three of the four estates were necessary for parliamentary approval of proposals. Two of the four (nobles and clergy) were pillars of the *överhet* system, and in the early years of the new regime, many state officials sat in the estate of burghers and the permanent secretary for the estate of peasants was appointed by the king. And although the constitution divided the legislative power, it placed executive power in the "king alone." The king appointed the cabinet, and it was responsible only to him. Executive decrees, which did not need parliamentary approval, could be used to get around parliamentary participation in legislation. The king also sat on the highest court.

The cabinet attempted several methods to subdue Parliament. Ministers began actively participating in parliamentary debates, and in 1880 the king for the first time chose a prime minister from the peasant party, although no other party members were put into the cabinet (and when the prime minister resigned, the other ministers, loyal to the king, stayed on). A key feature of the reaction was the decision to establish commissions consisting of members of the cabinet or high bureaucracy on the one side and of the legislature on the other, as a means of influencing the legislature to accept the royal viewpoint. The idea was that within the small-group setting of a commission, legislators would be most likely to defer to nobles in the group and that commission members would then return to the legislature and fight for the pact agreed to.

By the turn of the century, the commission institution was established as a procedure for formulating new laws. It has remained so to this day. The initial reaction of the traditional rulers to the challenge from below, then, was to set up commissions where it was hoped deferent values would be more salient. Early success produced continued reliance on this form, but gradually the institution changed character. It became not only a forum for magnifying the salience of dominant values but also one for negotiation and compromise. Accommodationist institutions were psychologically appropriate for the transition from the *överhet* state as well, since individuals in such a society, taught to defer to the wishes of the rulers, are used to adjusting their wishes to those of others.

Out of Swedish tradition then grew a tendency to deal with conflict by establishing small groups of representatives for the various parties to work out agreements. Another result of this tradition was a belief among modern organizational leaders that they ought to educate members to the beliefs of their leaders. In America it became common to arrange proceedings modeled on adversary trials.

Except on Robinson Crusoe's island, individuals, even self-assertive ones, associate with each other. Such associations are often cooperative. People enter voluntary exchanges or they become friends. However, the interests of self-assertive individuals may also collide. When the collision is unilateral — that is, when it involves one party harming another rather than reciprocal harm occurring — no assurance exists that any procedure for conflict resolution will be developed at all. Self-assertive victims will be relatively quick to demand that their interests be taken into consideration, compared with deferent victims, while self-assertive victimizers, like the proverbial mule who must be hit on the head with a two-by-four to get his attention, will be relatively resistant to altering their behavior.

The relative American preference for adversary institutions is seen in the prominent role that courts play in America compared with other Western societies. The adversary trial is psychologically most congruent with self-assertive values because it allows each party to plant his flag where he stands and articulate his position without budging. While the individual in an *överhet* society is used to adjusting his wishes to those of others and thus is psychologically prepared for negotiations, the individual in a liberal society is used to pursuing his interests without interference. An adversary trial allows disputes to be resolved without violence, while still permitting people to beat their drums.

Furthermore, since liberal political philosophy does not regard government as natural, the question of why men should obey rulers is key. Hobbes despaired of the possibility of governing self-assertive men by means short of a Leviathan state. Locke was more hopeful, believing that liberal men would obey a government deriving authority from their consent. But Locke saw consent as being preconditioned on government impartiality. Thus arose a second reason for the relative propensity to choose adversary trials to deal with conflict: they were a potent source of legitimacy for the leaders who were to make decisions after the parties presented their cases.

American policymakers, then, when they look at the society around them, not only start off with more pessimistic assumptions about predispositions to compliance but also see a greater tendency to use the legal system to regulate human interactions. Swedish policymakers, on the other hand, not only start off with less pessimistic assumptions about predispositions to compliance but also see a society making far greater use of small groups to regulate human interactions. Thus, it is not surprising (though it is obviously not foreordained) that American policymakers chose an occupational safety and health compliance system based on punishments meted out through the legal system when they were dissatisfied with existing levels of compliance. Nor is it surprising that Swedish policymakers chose to use normative inducements, with legal punishments only as a backup.

When it was concluded in America that previous occupational safety and health enforcement methods were not working well enough, enforcement was made more punitive. In Sweden, in contrast, the role of the plant-level safety steward was revitalized. The first document of the new concern with occupational safety and health in Sweden, the joint union-Social Democratic program *A Better Work Environment* (1969), made no mention of new legal sanctions for violation of safety and health regulations. Instead the document talked exclusively about giving safety stewards new responsibilities and establishing a special fund to support their education. [LO-SAP, 1969] And the very first new piece of safety and health legislation passed in 1971 was a law adding a surcharge to employer workmen's compensation premiums to set up a work environment fund that would arrange for such training. From late 1974 through late 1976, the tremendous task of organizing courses for safety stewards at all but the tiniest workplaces was undertaken.

Safety stewards were now going to be the entering wedge at the plant level for the concern with safety and health among national leaders, and placed at the center of efforts to achieve compliance. This role as entering wedge applied both to employers and to fellow workers. The old view of the safety steward as a person encouraging safety consciousness among workers did not completely die. But in the new view this role extended beyond encouraging the avoidance of unsafe acts to increasing the salience of safety and health such that workers would be unhappy about unsafe conditions. If many complained or even quit, a new inducement, originating in changed worker preferences, would be created for employers to comply with regulations. Safety stewards would also be able to monitor compliance on an ongoing basis.

The most dramatic expression of the new role of the safety steward appeared in the revision to the Worker Protection Act in 1974. It allowed safety stewards to stop work temporarily until an inspector could arrive, in situations with an "imminent and serious danger for employee life or health."[25] Since its inception, this provision of the law has been used around a hundred times per year.[26] Its significance is largely symbolic, since few employers want to see work continued if an imminent danger exists. But the symbolism is significant: it proclaims the safety steward to be a person with an important monitoring role.

The revised *Instruction for Safety Stewards* issued as part of a new labor-management agreement in 1976 codified the new conception of the steward's role. Although the old instruction from 1942 had referred to the task of the safety steward as being to learn about the functioning of safety devices already installed, the new instruction stated that safety stewards should "monitor whether safety devices and other hygiene features are present, are in good condition, and are being used." Safety stewards should not only request that safety and health regulations be complied with but they should "participate in following up whether measures have led to the desired result." [LO/SAF, 1976: 42]

The safety committee would also be used for providing normative inducements for employers. This required that management sit on the committee. The commentary to the 1967 labor-management occupational safety and health agreement stated that it was important that "the very top management of the firm" sit on the safety committee. [LO/SAF, 1967: 38–39] The 1976 agreement was even more specific and also provided that foremen join the committee. [LO/SAF, 1976: 26]

A Note on Changes Since 1976

There have been important changes in the economic and political environment in both the United States and Sweden since the period covered by this research. In Sweden a persistent economic crisis has undoubtedly contributed to a lessened national attention to occupational safety and health issues. Furthermore, labor-management tension over these issues has increased somewhat, compared with the picture of broad ability to reach agreement over occupational safety and health questions that emerged from my research covering the period through 1976. Actually, given the country's serious economic crisis and the political instability resulting from the overthrow, after over four decades, of Social Democratic rule, the increased tensions in the specific area of occupational safety and health have been relatively mild. But overall labor-management battles have grown significantly, and the question I raised in the conclusion of my book, *Regulating America, Regulating Sweden,* about whether the successes at reaching agreement over a potentially contentious issue that the Swedes had achieved in the occupational safety and health area were a "last hurrah" for an older Swedish social system, remains very much unanswered. The enforcement system described here still continues basically the same; the new Work Environment Law that went into effect in 1978 made less difference in the enforcement system than some had predicted, perhaps at least partly because of the economic situation.[27]

As for the United States, OSHA's enforcement methods have made it the target of business hostility ever since the agency opened up shop. Frequent attempts were made to modify the system by statute or through the appropriations or authorization processes.

The Reagan administration has produced a major change of direction for OSHA, as well as for other "social" regulatory agencies. As far as enforcement is concerned, this change has been marked by statements by the new OSHA leadership that inspectors should not regard themselves as "cops" or adversaries to businessmen and that they should seek cooperation at the workplace. During the first year of the Reagan administration, the percentage of citations contested by employers declined from 23 percent to 9 percent.[28]

This change should not, I think, be seen as a move towards the Swedish system. As noted earlier, before occupational safety and health became a serious issue in the United States, state enforcement proceeded by the "voluntary compliance" model. The "cooperation-minded" policies of the Reagan-era OSHA may well simply represent a downgrading of the seriousness with which compliance with occupational safety and health regulations is regarded. (In fiscal year 1981 the number of OSHA inspections declined from about 63,000 to about 57,000.[29] The difficult task of achieving high levels of regulatory compliance without extensive use of sanctions may remain an elusive one for the United States.

Notes

1. The material in this chapter is adapted from Kelman, 1978; 1981.
2. Occupational Safety and Health Act of 1970, 84 Stat. 1590.
3. SFS 1949:1. A word on abbreviations and terminology. Organizationally, Swedish occupational safety and health inspectors work for the *Yrkesinspektion* or Factory Inspectorate, which in turn is under the direction of the Worker Protection Board. The combined name for the Worker Protection Board and the Factory Inspectorate is *Arbetarskyddsverket*, a name that only came into use a few years ago. I will henceforth simply use the abbreviation ASV to refer to the combined agency, although this abbreviation is not normally used in Sweden itself.
4. Occupational Safety and Health Administration, *Field Operations Manual,* rev. ed. Washington, D.C., 1974. This was the manual used during the period covered by the research for this study.
5. [4], chap. V-8
6. [4], chap. V-14
7. [2], Section 9(b).
8. The idea that an inspector can act as "prosecutor, judge, and jury" by both inspecting and imposing fines is contrary to most people's sense of justice, and therefore the statute constructs an elegant fiction, namely that OSHA may only "propose" penalties. The statute established a quasi-judicial body, independent of the agency, called the Occupational Safety and Health Review Commission, and technically only the

Commission can impose penalties. If the employer is cited by OSHA for a violation and OSHA "proposes" penalties, these penalties "shall be deemed a final order of the Commission" if they are not appealed (Occupational Safety and Health Act, Section 10(a). For this reason, fines are always referred to in OSHA jargon as "proposed penalties." The term *fines* will nevertheless be used here.

9. [4], chap. XII-5. For violations with an abatement period greater than thirty days, regular progress reports must be sent in to the Area Director.

10. [4], chaps. XII-33, 34. The penalty system underwent some changes in 1977.

11. OSHA Inspection Figures, 5 *Job Safety and Health* (April, 1977) p. 3. Statutory changes adopted by Congress after the period being researched prohibited fines for non-serious violations if there were less than ten such violations.

12. [4], chap. V-1.

13. [4], chap. V-9.

14. ASV, *Arbetsordning for yrkesinspektionen*. Stockholm, June 1974.

15. The Swedish word for ASV regulations, *anvisningar,* is the same as the one used for instructions on a package for how to bake a cake, and has the implication of advice or pointers.

16. Interview with Goran Lindh, ASV.

17. One said he looked at the number of inspections inspectors had done, another said that he paid attention only if an inspector's statistics "cried out," and a third said he did look but gave no further specification.

18. Interview with Artur Norr, ASV.

19. Interview with Arne Westlin, ASV.

20. Interview with Norr.

21. This includes three respondents who said they would take industry jobs "only if I could accomplish as much" as with OSHA.

22. That left 23 percent who replied that they wouldn't leave OSHA because there was less job security in the private sector and 15 percent who said they wanted to stay with OSHA because it provided the best opportunities for professional growth, in terms of experiencing many different types of hazard situations. (Of the six respondents who gave this answer, four, all of them quite young, added that they would well consider leaving once they had gotten this experience.) The rest of the respondents gave diverse reasons for not wishing to leave.

23. One respondent said that in such cases he will bend if it is a question of a small hazard, and another that if it is a noise case he will allow the firm to abate the hazard using personal protective equipment. Three respondents said that such cases were a matter for the Area Director, and that firms with economic hardships could take the matter up with him.

24. The following material, as well as that on the development of adversary institutions below, is adapted from Kelman, 1981: Ch. 4 which contains a much more detailed discussion.

25. Arbetarskyddslagen, Section 40(b).

26. See "Hundra stopp 1975 — och paragrafen anvands mycket mer," *Arbetarskydd* (May, 1976).

27. Some labor groups had criticized the Swedish system for being too ''cooperation-minded'' and urged stronger sanctions, although not a system going as far as the American system.
28. These statistics come from unpublished data gathered by OSHA. To be more precise they compare FY 1980 (October 1979–September, 1980) with FY 1981– (October, 1980–September, 1981).
29. Ibid.

Table 5-1. American and Swedish Inspector Attitudes on "Better to be Tough" vs. "Better to Persuade" (Seven-Point Scale Mean Response)

American Inspectors	(In-depth Survey)	3.4 (N = 40)
Swedish Inspectors	(In-depth Survey)	5.1 (N = 18)
American Inspectors	(National Survey)	4.2 (N = 78)
Swedish Inspectors	(National Survey)	4.8 (N = 73)

Note: Responses less than 4 are "tough," greater than 4 are "soft."
Source: In-depth Inspectors Survey and National Inspector Survey.

References

Burke, Edmund (1960). Reflections on the Revolution in France, in Bate (ed.) *Selected Writings of Edmund Burke*. New York: Modern Library.

Kelman, Steven (1978). Regulating Job Safety and Health: A Comparison of the U.S. Occupational Safety and Health Administration and the Swedish Worker Protection Board. Ph.D Diss, Harvard University.

——— (1981). *Regulating American, Regulating Sweden: A Comparative Study of Occupational Safety and Health Policy*. Cambridge: MIT Press.

Lindstrom, Ture et al (1975). *Inspektionsmetodik och yrkesskadeutredning*. Stockholm: Stencil.

LO/SAF (1967). *Arbetarskydd och foretagshalsovard*. Stockholm: Arbetarskyddsnamnden.

LO/SAF (1976). *Arbetsmiljoavtalet*. Stockholm: Tiden.

LO/SAP (1969). *En Battre arbetsmiljo*. Stockholm: Prisma

OSHA (1975), Office of Management Data Systems, *OSHA Management Information System Field Reporting Manual*. Washington, D.C.

OSHA (1976). *Industrial Hygiene Field Operations Manual*. Washington, D.C.

Selznick, Philip (1957). *Leadership in Administration*. Evanston, Ill.: Row, Peterson.

U.S. House of Representatives (March 1972). *Occupational Safety and Health Act of 1970 Oversight and Proposed Amendments*. Hearings before the Select Subcommittee on Labor of the Committee on Education and Labor. 92nd Cong., 2d sess.

6 REGIONAL VARIATION IN REGULATORY LAW ENFORCEMENT
The Surface Mining Control and Reclamation Act of 1977

Neal Shover
John Lynxwiler
Stephen Groce
Donald Clelland

Systematic empirical examination of regulatory bureaucracies and practices has been expanding rapidly in recent years. Social scientists and policy makers now can anticipate a steady output of work on which to base their future endeavors. Thus far, however, investigators have employed a relatively restricted set of theoretical interpretations of these processes, largely to the neglect of other potentially useful approaches. Existing theoretical approaches appear to cluster in two areas. On the one hand, we have a body of work that examines regulatory agencies as formal organizations, subject to the same kinds of problems and constraints as any other type of political bureaucracy. Work of this type generally adopts a holistic interpretation and probes issues related to organizational development, operating procedures and change [e.g., Kagan, 1978; Wilson, 1980]. On the other hand, another body of literature deals with the exercise of discretion by regulatory personnel, usually employing field-level personnel as the unit of analysis [e.g., Hawkins, 1980; Kagan, 1980]. Both approaches are important

The study on which this paper is based was supported by Grant #80-IJ-CX-0017 from the National Institute of Justice. Points of view or opinions in this paper are those of the authors, and do not necessarily reflect the official position or policies of the Department of Justice.

121

enterprises and promise to improve our understanding of the workings of regulatory bureaucracies.

An apparent shortcoming of current theoretical work on regulatory processes, however, is a general inattention to variation within regulatory bureaucracies. This approach falls between the poles of holistic analysis of regulatory bureaucracies and microsociological analyses of field-level operations. Studies at this middle level of analysis could demonstrate how local problems or structural arrangements within the same organization may produce substantial and important differences in the exercise of the regulatory mandate. This chapter is intended as a contribution to the development of such an understanding. We present a description, analysis, and interpretation of the development of two distinctive enforcement styles in two geographical regions of a newly created agency, the federal Office of Surface Mining Reclamation and Enforcement (OSM).[1]

Contexts and Enforcement Styles

Regulatory enforcement activity is a means of controlling or "policing" behavior. Consequently, there are some natural parallels between the work activities of regulators and the police. In both cases the controllers are faced with the problem of applying legal rules to specific cases. Typically, strict or literal enforcement of rules is impossible because they have ambiguous boundaries and referents, are subject to conflicting interpretations, or because the volume and complexity of violative activities exceeds enforcement resources. Thus, the manner in which law is interpreted or socially constructed is dependent on a variety of social factors.

Research on the police has given us an embryonic understanding of the ways departments differ across communities and the contexts that call forth certain types of organizational, i.e., structural, responses [see Reiss and Bordua, 1967; Gardiner, 1969; Manning, 1977; 1980; Wilson, 1978]. There is a lesson here for studies of regulatory law enforcement: regulatory bureaucracies and operations are tied, in ways yet to be determined, to the characteristics of the "communities" (social matrix) in which they operate. Thus, regulatory personnel, like police officers, are not entirely free to work out idiosyncratic styles of enforcement behavior. Rather, the contexts in which they operate play an important part in their "selection" of dominant organizational enforcement styles. Similarly, students of the regulatory process have begun to search for the apparent sources of structural and procedural variation, not only across agencies but within them as well [see Nivola, 1978]. The research reported here is a continuation of the latter efforts.

Just as analyses of police officers and departments suggest that dominant or typical approaches to enforcement cluster in distinctive types or styles [Wilson,

1968], so observers of the regulatory process have distinguished, albeit in a somewhat more speculative fashion, different types of regulatory law enforcement [see Thomas, 1980; Hawkins, 1980; Kagan, 1980; Kagan and Scholz, above, chapter 4]. Despite the fact that much of this work focuses on the individual inspector as the unit of analysis, the resulting theoretical insights would seem to be applicable to programmatic variation within regulatory bureaucracies.

Running through many of the analyses of regulatory enforcement is a distinction between two styles, which are designated by varying labels. One enforcement style is characteristic of inspectors who approach their work very much like police officers. Their orientation and approach is punitive. This "rule-oriented" approach reflects the belief that strict, uniform enforcement deters violators and potential violators. Insofar as possible, rule-oriented inspectors issue citations for every violation they observe during inspections. Correspondingly, they minimize the use of enforcement strategies such as consultation and bargaining. In sum, this style of enforcement is *legalistic*.

In contrast, however, other inspectors employ a *conciliatory,* "results-oriented" enforcement style. Flexible in their approach, they emphasize responsiveness, forbearance, and the transmission of information. Primary reliance on the strict, uniform application of formal sanctions is considered less effective than negotiation as a method for securing compliance. Conciliatory inspectors may employ trade offs, gaming tactics, and cajoling to obtain compliance from violators and potential violators.

It is important to recognize some potential limitations of these largely ad hoc formulations of enforcement styles. Fundamentally, they are hypothetical, ideal, and global constructs and the nature and strength of their covariation is unknown. They are not unidimensional in that they comprise several different dimensions of enforcement behavior. Consequently, in the absence of additional research, there is little reason to assume the two are entirely mutually exclusive or polar types. Stated differently, the constituent dimensions of the respective types may vary independently of one another and produce mixed types. If this is true, then extant regulatory programs or personnel could be classified on the basis of which type seems to predominate. Nevertheless, despite the qualifications, these theoretical constructs clearly build upon real differences in the enforcement behavior of field-level regulatory personnel.

Our study of OSM proceeded against this backdrop of theoretical literature on styles of police and regulatory law enforcement. Following some prefatory remarks the remainder of this chapter: (1) documents the existence of relatively different enforcement styles, legalistic and conciliatory, in two of OSM's five regional offices, and (2) employs earlier theoretical analyses of regulatory bureaucracies and behavior to account for these styles.

Background

The Office of Surface Mining

Culminating two decades of controversy and debate, on August 3, 1977 President Jimmy Carter signed the Surface Mining Control and Reclamation Act [SMCRA Public Law 95–87; Shover, 1980]. The act created an Office of Surface Mining Reclamation and Enforcement in the Interior Department and empowered it to promulgate regulations for the conduct of surface coal mining in the United States. During an interim period of approximately four years, OSM was to enforce these regulations while the states were given the opportunity to submit proposed laws and regulations, at least as rigorous, for OSM's approval. Those states that established approved programs of their own eventually would acquire primary responsibility ("primacy") for the regulation of surface coal mining within their borders. OSM would continue to be the primary regulatory authority only in states that failed to submit or to receive approval of their own programs.

OSM's formal organizational structure consisted of five regional offices that provided coverage of the states.[2] The formal structure of each regional office paralleled the formal structure of the headquarters, and each regional director was responsible to the Washington director. Within this formal structure, each regional director was granted considerable autonomy to operate as he saw fit. The analysis in this paper focuses on two of the regions, which we have called Region East and Region West.

We employed a variety of research methodologies in our investigation of the development and impact of the Office of Surface Mining,[3] and drew upon three principal data sources. First, extended interviews with regulatory personnel and mining company officials were conducted to examine the various issues, attitudes, and social processes surrounding OSM's regulatory efforts. Both initial and follow-up interviews were analyzed for regional variation in inspection and enforcement at the field level. Additionally, by analyzing secondary data we were able to examine alternative definitions of OSM and its operations both on national and regional levels. Finally, assuming again that a strategy of using several methodologies is to be preferred over reliance on a single one, we constructed a questionnaire for field-level OSM inspectors. The questionnaire responses enabled us to validate through quantitative analysis some of the relationships suggested both in earlier interviews and our review of the relevant literature.

American Coal Production

There are three principal coalfields in the United States: Appalachia, the Midwest, and the West. The thickness of coal seams, coal quality, production problems, and production costs vary across these three regions. Historically, nearly two-thirds of all coal produced in America was mined in Appalachia. However, this percentage has been declining and projections suggest that by 1985 it will drop to 34–43 percent of the total. The same projections indicate that Western coal production will increase anywhere from 250 to 600 percent, and its market share may increase from less than 20 percent to 32–43 percent of total U.S. production [President's Coal Commission, 1980: 94].

Surface coal mining began shifting to the West some 20 years ago. In the ensuing years nearly all the major coal companies have been purchased by oil companies which now are operating, or planning, very large mines. The major reason for the growing importance of Western coal is the rapid ascendance of surface mining. In 1960, surface mined coal represented approximately 30 percent of total U.S. coal production. By 1977 the share of total production accounted for by surface mining had increased to 61 percent, and is projected to grow even larger in the years to come [President's Coal Commission, 1980: 83]. The relative importance of underground mining has declined steadily as mining costs have risen and more efficient surface mining machinery has been introduced. Most of the new mines opened recently or expected to open in the future are surface mines [National Research Council, 1981]. Coal production in the West is characterized by enormous surface mines that provide low-heat-content, low-sulfur coal to electric utilities under long-term contracts. By far the largest mines are in the West, especially in Wyoming and Montana. In sum, the locus of American coal production has been shifting from underground to surface, and from Appalachia to the West. These trends are expected to continue into the foreseeable future.

Surface Mining Regulation

In Appalachia, coal is surface mined on relatively steep mountain slopes, in narrow valleys, and under a heavy average annual rainfall. There, much of the surface mined coal is produced by numerous small firms [Clelland et al., 1981]. Historically, the combination of inhospitable terrain, heavy rainfall, thin coal seams, thick overburden, low coal prices, and lax state regulation resulted in serious environmental and property damage in parts of the region [see Caudill, 1971; Brauson, 1974]. Among some Appalachian coal operators, indifference or hostility toward state regulatory programs and personnel was quite common. "Wildcatting" — mining coal without a permit — has been a problem (how large, it is impossible to say) in some areas of Appalachia. The abuses of surface mining in Appalachia provided much of the impetus for passage of federal surface mining legislation. Our Region East is located in the heart of the Appalachian coal fields.

In Region West, terrain is level or rolling, coal seams are many times thicker than in Appalachia and the overburden is thinner and easier to move and store.

Moreover, average annual rainfall is much less than in the East. Another important difference between regions is the pattern of ownership. Unlike Appalachia, where most of the coal is owned by industry or other private parties, the bulk of Western coal is owned by the federal government. Other large portions are owned by the railroads and by tribes of Native Americans.

Because so much Western coal is owned by the federal government, companies mining there have been accustomed to a federal regulatory presence over the past decade. As a rule, Western mines employ regulatory ''professionals'' who function as in-house ''inspectors'' and are responsible for tracking the operation's compliance with regulatory programs. Also, state regulatory authorities and programs have enjoyed a reputation for honesty and stringency superior to their Appalachian counterparts. Wildcat mining never has been a problem in the West.

Contrasts in Regional Enforcement Activities

A variety of data suggest that OSM personnel in Regions East and West developed somewhat different approaches to, or styles of, enforcement. This finding is supported by official statistics on OSM's enforcement activities and also by interview and questionnaire data.

Statistical Data

Although SMCRA was signed into law in August 1977, funding for the new OSM was not approved until eight months later. An initial force of inspectors was among the first group of employees hired, but it was several months before the inspection and enforcement program began operating smoothly in both the regions. Due to regional inconsistencies in record-keeping in the early months, we chose the 12-month period from July 1, 1979 through June 30, 1980 to examine OSM's inspection and enforcement performance in the two regions. By late 1980 most of the Western states had acquired primacy and OSM's enforcement activities were curtailed sharply.

The SMCRA provides for a system of mandatory enforcement for OSM and its regulatory personnel. The act explicitly requires inspectors to write a notice of violation for every regulatory infraction they observe on a mine site. Further, it requires them to issue a cessation order (an order to cease all mining) under two conditions: (1) when they observe a violation that causes or creates the threat of imminent danger to the health or safety of the public, or significant environmental harm, or (2) when an operator fails to abate, within the specified time period, a condition for which he previously received a notice of violation (P.L. 95–87, §

521). Using OSM records we were able to determine the number of notices of violation (NOVs) and cessation orders (COs) for both Region East and Region West during the period from mid-1979 until mid-1980.

In 1981 there were 6,689 "inspectable units" in Region East but only 161 comparable units in Region West [OSM, 1981]. (Comparable, reliable statistics for earlier years are not available.) Given the substantial difference in these numbers, it would be expected that Region East inspectors would issue many more NOVs and COs than inspectors in Region West. This is, in fact, what happened. During the specified time period, Region East issued 3,254 NOVs and 901 COs while Region West issued 88 and 5 respectively. However, these raw numbers on inspection activities must be converted into rates if they are to be used for purposes of comparison.

During 1979–1980 Region East employed 60 inspectors while Region West employed only seven.[4] Given this difference, and knowing nothing else about the two regions, we would expect that Region East inspectors would write a larger number of NOVs and COs. When we convert the number of NOVs and COs to rates (number per inspector), this difference remains: Region East inspectors issued 54.23 NOVs and 15.02 COs per inspector while Region West inspectors issued only 12.14 and 0.71, respectively.

Alternatively, we can calculate rates of enforcement activity by employing the amount of coal produced in the two regions as a base. Use of such a base measure can be defended as a surrogate measure of the total volume of earth that must be moved in mining operations. In turn, this serves as a reasonable measure of the total volume of mining activity that is potentially sanctionable. For the period of mid-1979 to mid-1980 the states in Region East produced 189.01 million short tons and the states in Region West produced 200.96 million short tons [U.S. Dept. of Energy, 1981; 1981a].[5] The rates of inspection and enforcement activity calculated for Regions East and West by these statistics indicate that inspectors in the former issued 17.22 NOVs and 4.77 COs per million short tons of coal produced during July 1979 through June 1980. At the same time, inspectors in Region West issued only 0.44 NOVs and 0.03 COs per million short tons of coal produced.

A final comparative measure of inspection activity in the two regions can be calculated using the total number of completed inspections. During the period in question, Region East inspectors completed 12,451 inspections and Region West inspectors completed 378 inspections. The resulting rates are 2.62 NOVs and 0.73 COs per ten inspections in Region East and 2.34 NOVs and 0.14 COs in Region West. On this measure, as on the others, there is a substantial difference in the level of inspection and enforcement activity in the two regions. Table 6-1 provides a summary of the various measures, including comparable statistics for all OSM regions.

In addition to the data contained in table 6-1, statistics on referrals for criminal prosecution show a marked regional difference. OSM is represented in the courts by solicitors (attorneys) who, although employed by the Department of the Interior, are independent of the agencies to which they are assigned. Between 1978 and 1982 solicitors in Region East referred 12 cases to U.S. attorneys for criminal prosecution while their counterparts in Region West did not refer any cases.

In view of their different histories and production problems, we may assume that a part of the reason for these differences in inspection and enforcement activity in Regions East and West is the natural result of real differences in the incidence and prevalence of sanctionable mining practices. Unfortunately, this interpretation only shifts the problem of understanding. We still need to determine how regulatory personnel interpret objective differences in mining practices and violations and how they convert these interpretations into distinctive enforcement policies and practices.

Interview and Questionnaire Data

As the foregoing statistical data suggest, a program of vigorous, rule-oriented enforcement took shape in Region East. There, as one inspector told us, OSM "started out . . . like a bunch of SS troops." Region East inspectors were imbued with a philosophy of firm, impartial enforcement and were encouraged to apply the regulations in a quite literal fashion. Another Region East inspector stated:

> [W]hen you put the hard hat on, and get out of the truck on that mine site you've got to be — you just, you're like a state cop out there. You've got to enforce the law. No more, or no less. . . . At least that's the way this office is run. That's the way they're all run in this district. And in this Region.

Because relatively little emphasis was placed on the need for and the desirability of discretion and flexibility, enforcement in Region East manifested important features of the legalistic style discussed earlier.

A different style of enforcement was developed in Region West. From the outset managers there viewed the SMCRA and the regulations as flexible resources. Whereas a rule-orientation was characteristic of Region East, a results-orientation toward enforcement was adopted in Region West. Vigorous, impartial rule enforcement was played down as a necessary or even desirable strategy.

> I think [the director of Region West] thought, and had, you know, I think. . . . I heard him speak one time in a citizen's group meeting and say: "Look, I understand in the East why they [OSM] 'hit the ground running,' but I'm not about to go to the Exxons and the Peabodys — that's who I deal with out here. I don't deal with jackleg

coal miners, you know. 'M.C. Coal Company,' you know, mining ten thousand tons a year. I deal with these multi-million dollar operations. So I'm going to be very cautious.''

In Region West relatively greater emphasis was placed on conciliatory enforcement and efforts to work accommodatingly with mine operators.

We reasoned that extant regional differences on inspectors' legalistic and conciliatory orientations would be reflected by regional variation in questionnaire responses. In the questionnaire we included two scales designed to measure these regional differences: a *legalistic scale* and a *conciliatory scale*.

We have produced the results of the questionnaire measures in table 6-2. (Readers should note that due to the low number of respondents in Region West the statistics must be interpreted with caution.) Consistent with expectations, Region East personnel scored substantially higher on the legalistic scale than did their counterparts in Region West (mean scores of 4.95 and 2.33 respectively). Contrary to our expectations, however, there was no appreciable difference between the two regions in inspectors' scores on the conciliatory scale (9.18 in Region East and 9.33 in Region West).

Although we are puzzled by the regions' comparable scores on the conciliatory scale, several possible explanations for this come to mind. First, we note that the three items that constitute the conciliatory scale deal, for the most part, with *consultation* and *education* of mine operators — there are no items that directly refer to inspectors' use of *negotiation* strategies of enforcement. Thus, the conciliatory scale lacks the same degree of face validity that is evident in the legalistic scale. Second, as we pointed out earlier, legalism and conciliation, as enforcement styles, probably do not appear in ''pure'' and mutually exclusive forms in the real world. If this is the case — and there is little research to aid us here — then our enigmatic findings may be more commonplace and representative of actual variation among inspectors and regulatory programs than existing theory allows. Third, because OSM was a *new* agency it may have been extremely difficult, especially in Region East where operators were poorly informed about the regulations, for personnel who implemented the program to emphasize excessively either of the two styles of enforcement. Put differently, inspectors charged with applying a new set of regulations may find it relatively difficult to avoid completely the use of some consultation and education as a routine part of their duties. There is, in fact, a good deal of interview data to suggest the validity of this interpretation. For example, a Region East inspector told us:

I've had some [mine sites] where I go out there and make the inspection, and find he's not even started on it yet, still buttoning up his last job. And he's not started on the area I intended to inspect. And that's a sterling opportunity to take him by the hand and go out there to the area that he's going to mine and say, ''Now, you're permitted [a mine permit] for a silt pond down here . . . and this is the way I want it constructed, just like the plans say. Now if you're going to have a problem with this, you know, need a board baffle in there and you want to change that to rock, it's easier to do. But, you know, these are things you need to be thinking about before you start in there and get yourself all sideways." He might have had some problems with his topsoil. "How are you going to pile your topsoil up above the highwall? That's ridiculous. I don't know who permitted it that way, but it's ridiculous." I said, "How are you going to get it up there?" He says, "There ain't no way." I said, "Well, that's something you need to change before you get out here and get sideways, you know. You're doing the work I've told you on your other jobs but, you know, get the permit changed so you can stay straight before you get wrong. Do it right the first time."

Fourth, it is possible that Region East inspectors, because they deal with a more heterogeneous group of operators than does Region West, had various categories of operators in mind when they responded to the questionnaire items. Fully aware, on the one hand, of a group of willful violators — "amoral calculators," in the words of Kagan and Scholz (see above, chapter 4) — they endorsed the highly legalistic approach to enforcement. On the other hand, because they also were aware of operators whose noncompliance resulted from ignorance or ineptitude — "organizational incompetents" (Kagan and Scholz, see above, chapter 4) — they scored high as well on the conciliatory scale. We believe the latter two interpretations probably are the major explanation for the two regions' equivalent scores on the conciliatory scale.

Analysis

Having sketched the different enforcement orientations developed in Regions East and West, our remaining task is to interpret and explain this occurrence. The data suggest the major determinants of regional variation can be grouped into regional differences in: (1) employees' experiences with and beliefs about coal operators and state regulatory programs; (2) the political and regulatory environment; and (3) the regulatory task.

Employees' Experiences and Beliefs

Managerial personnel in the two regions took their posts with an understanding of the historical differences in surface mining east and west. Those placed in Region East were fully cognizant of the historical record of lax regulation and operators' recalcitrance in Appalachia. Supervisors and managers in this region had prior experience of one kind or another with the Appalachian coal industry. A portion of their inspector corps had worked previously for state regulatory programs in Appalachia and had endured the frustrations of those experiences. A number of them saw their OSM employment as an opportunity to establish a regulatory program that would be taken seriously by the industry — something that, in their opinion, had not been true of the state programs in which they had labored. They operated under no illusions about the ease of their task. A certain resistance to any form of external interference was seen as almost second nature in some areas of Appalachia.

> It's attitude. I don't know whether it's — maybe environmental — you know, the way that a person is from childhood, raised up with a certain independence. The people in _____ County — and I admire them to a great extent . . . I admire them because they are a — in the mountains they are an independent, very independent-type people. They don't appreciate anyone — whether it is federal government, whether it's the county, the state, whoever, you know — they don't appreciate anyone coming up there and say "Now, you've got to do this." They look at it that you're encroaching on something that's none of your business. Their attitude is "This is my land. I'll do with it what I darn well please." And they'll go so far as to say "As long as it's not hurting anyone else, then why are you up here hassling me about?"

In addition to an awareness of this general antipathy toward external interference, supervisors and inspectors alike were aware of the existence of a group of operators considered to be "hard core nonconformists." Some of these operators had threatened or assaulted state inspectors in the past with relative impunity.

> [Y]ou've got [one kind of operator] that practically won't talk to you at all. They just . . . you don't, you really feel uncomfortable around them 'cause you don't know — you're afraid they're going over the edge any minute. They practically won't talk to you, and consider you to be a Communist and everything else. But I've been fortunate, I haven't had too many of these kind. Usually this — your wildcat category is where these kind of operators fall.

OSM's Region East personnel saw their task, in part, as one of curbing this segment of the industry and, generally, bringing the rule of law to the operation of the Appalachian surface mining industry.

Aware of the history of ineffective state regulation, they wanted to set an example of vigorous, effective enforcement for the states, that eventually would acquire primacy.

> [O]ur philosophy was: "worst case operators" first — ones the states wouldn't go on, you know. . . . We realized that because there had never been enforcement back here, and there was going to be mandatory enforcement by the states, that OSM literally had to lead the way, sort of show that this is what was going to be expected in the future when you get your turn — which is coming up. And you couldn't very well demand that of them [the states] if you didn't demand it of yourself, and at first take

on the worst. It's sort of like beating up the "bully on the block." Take on the bully on the block. Beat him up real good . . . and then half your problems are over because the word gets out.

Region East managers believed that aggressive, consistent enforcement, especially against known violators, would enhance the operators' perceptions of the *credibility* and *legitimacy* of OSM and its operations. Such enforcement activities, due primarily to communication among operators would eventually convince them that the OSM, unlike state authorities, would not simply "go away." A Region East manager told us:

> [E]ssentially, there's a big grape vine out there. I mean, I'm not a neophyte to the industry, not knowing there's a big grape vine. And if "Fred" tells "Joe" that "Gee, yes, the OSM visited me and here's what they told me." And, "Boy, they socked me a good one and I had to . . . and I've just been assessed a $27,000 fine. Oh, my God." And they do talk like that in bars. (They don't share enough information, I think, for reclamation techniques.)

In addition to their general suspicion of state regulators and segments of the coal industry, Region East personnel realized that many operators possessed limited literacy skills, and that their mine planning rarely extended beyond a few days or weeks. For such operators, a major task simply of informing and educating would be required. In short, OSM personnel began their work on the assumption that the job would be difficult, that state regulation had been ineffective or corrupt, that many operators would resist their actions, and that an aggressive enforcement program would be required if the operators were to take the program seriously. Only by vigorous, impartial, and consistent enforcement would the operators come to see the program as credible and legitimate, major objectives in Region East.

Although differences should not be overstated, on balance, personnel in Region West began their work with a different set of assumptions. They understood that western coal producers were accustomed to stringent regulation and perceived regulation itself as a legitimate governmental function. Consequently, Region West personnel did not anticipate a high level of operator resistance to their efforts. In the West, mines are extremely large and mining is based on production schedules made sometimes years in advance. Long-range planning is an integral part of the mining process and mine personnel do not present the problem of limited literacy encountered in portions of Appalachia. Furthermore, there is no evidence to suggest the existence of any significant level of operator defiance, either as an individual or cultural phenomenon in the West, as there has been in parts of Appalachia.

Region West personnel also assumed a higher overall level of good faith on the part of coal operators who, it was believed, were interested in mining in an environmentally sound way and also avoiding adverse publicity.

[M]ost of the mines out here are rather large mines. There are very few small ones. . . . For instance, we're talking about mines with several thousands of acres involved. As compared to mines back East that have less than one acre. Now the people that run these mines are large companies, mostly, and public opinion is very important to these outfits. And the attitudes, the working relationships we had with the operators here were much different than those relationships back in Appalachia. . . . The attitudes of the people here are a lot different . . . so you don't have the failure to abate situations that arise in the East.

The importance of examining differences in an inspectorate's shared beliefs about, or perceptions of, (1) prior levels of regulation, and (2) operators' resistance and their compliance capabilities should be obvious. We assume that an agency's personnel devise regulatory strategies, in part, on the basis of these collective perceptions (see above, Kagan and Scholz, chapter 4).

Evidence suggests that in some important respects personnel in Regions East and West have retained quite different beliefs about the coal industry and the adequacy of state-level regulation. In our mail questionnaire we asked several questions designed to assess inspectors' perceptions of the trustworthiness of coal operators and state regulatory authorities. Table 6-3 summarizes responses to three questions about these issues and areas. As can be seen, the results are consistent on all three measures: Region East inspectors generally are more suspicious of coal operators, perceive a higher level of willful noncompliance, and are more fearful of an erosion of industry compliance after the states acquire regulatory primacy.

Political Environment

The struggle to enact the SMCRA was bitter and protracted [see Shover, 1980]. Nowhere was the conflict more heated and intense than in the coal fields of Appalachia. The suspicions and antagonisms engendered during that battle did not abate when the act was passed. Rather, they persisted and were brought to bear in critical scrutiny of, and attacks on, OSM, especially by segments of the mining industry. One of the major constitutional challenges to the SMCRA originated in Appalachia — although not in Region East [see *Hodel v. Virginia Surface Mining and Reclamation Assoc., Inc., et al,* 452 U.S. 264 (1981)]. Generally, industry's criticism has been considerably more intense in Region East than in Region West.

Though few in number, the large, complex surface mines in Region West promise to alter drastically the nature of the national coal market.[6] Many Appalachian operators view these mines as an economic threat and have embraced a conspiratorial view of OSM and its relationship with the large mining companies. In the eyes of Appalachian operators, OSM was working in concert with western producers to eliminate eastern competition. As one Region East operator suggested: "They [Western coal producers] can't market their coal against our coal.

So, they use the federal government to put the clamps on us in order for them to build the market up for their coal''. Such beliefs are widespread among the smaller Appalachian coal producers [see Lynxwiler and Groce, 1981].

Historically, the coal industry has been a major source of government revenue in Appalachia. Coal operators were aware of their importance to state economies and frequently used the threat of relocation to states with less stringent regulation in order to maintain regulation at the lowest common denominator. This history of economic blackmail was a major rationale for enactment of SMCRA. After OSM began operations, the various states in Region East attacked it, fearful of the harm it could cause regional coal operators and, therefore, employment rates and tax revenues.

The picture has been different in Region West. While the Western states have attacked the federal regulatory presence, it has been in the context of the more generalized ''Sagebrush Rebellion.'' This movement by westerners and their elected state representatives casts the federal government in the role of a greedy, insensitive owner of large tracts of Western land that usurps the states' right to use and develop them for their own purposes. In this context, attacks on OSM lost much of their special focus.

Finally, in Region East OSM began operations against an historical backdrop of considerable indigenous citizen opposition to the excesses of surface coal mining. Because much of the strip mining in Appalachia is conducted adjacent to or near homes or rural settlements, the environmental, social, and property damage from this type of mining has affected many citizens. This has not been true to the same extent in Region West, where there are relatively few mines that tend to be located in remote areas away from family farms and settlements. Moreover, in Appalachia grass-roots movements openly express feelings of pent-up frustration concerning the perceived venality and powerlessness of state regulatory authorities. When OSM arrived on the scene, citizens were urged to exercise their rights under the SMCRA and told that only by doing so would past abuses be corrected and curbed [see Center for Law and Social Policy, 1978]. One Appalachian group, based in Region East, filed suit in 1979 to compel OSM to comply with the act by developing an aggressive, literal enforcement program (*Council of the Southern Mountains, Inc. et al. v. Andrus*, U.S. Dist. Court, D.C., Civil Action #79–1521).

There is a clear, substantial difference between Regions East and West in the number of citizen complaints received about harmful or dangerous mining practices. During 1979–1980, Region East received 445 citizen complaints while Region West received only five. It is to be expected, perhaps, that some difference would occur, given the large number of mines in Region East. Consequently, we converted the number of citizen complaints to a rate that makes comparison across regions more meaningful. These data are contained in table 6-4.

The data in table 6-4 show clearly that even when alternative measures are used for the base, the rate of citizen complaints in Region East far exceeds the rate for Region West.[7]

OSM's Region East program and personnel were attacked on a variety of fronts. Industry was hostile and suspicious that enforcement was conspiratorily lax in other regions where larger companies mine coal. The states were critical because the federal government had usurped their primary regulatory role, and they feared their "own" coal producers would be disadvantaged by stringent regulation. And citizens' groups, emboldened and made more determined by passage of SMCRA, were vigilant in their scrutiny of Region East operations. In sum, the political environment in Region East was conflict-ridden, whereas Region West's was much more placid. Of what consequence is this difference in the two Regions' political environments?

Based on a review of the literature on regulatory agencies, Thomas has suggested that "To the extent that an agency must concern itself with a hostile or unpredictable political evnironment, it will attempt to control the discretion available to officials who must apply rules to individual cases" [1980: 121].

But did the alternative use of discretionary powers originate at the regional level, or in regionally different policies emanating from OSM headquarters? Our analysis suggests the former as the major reason why Regions East and West developed different enforcement styles. We determined that extraregional directives and constraints were not appreciably different for the two regions — both operated under similar policies and incentives from OSM headquarters.

Headquarters executives generally favored a "hard line" and advocated aggressive enforcement practices. They believed that environmentally harmful mining practices were ubiquitous and were fair game for a relatively literal application of the regulations. Regional managers and personnel were aware of this preference for a more legalistic enforcement style, as well as efforts by headquarters executives to determine if they were pursuing violations vigorously. For the most part, these efforts met with a polite resistance in the regions. For the first two years of OSM's operations, a continuous, mild tension existed over this issue. Generally, the regions regarded headquarters' efforts as meddling. Just as importantly, headquarters never had the opportunity to develop and impose on the regions a uniform, consistent policy and guidelines for the inspection and enforcement program. Headquarters operated under severe time constraints imposed by the act's rigidly mandated deadlines and OSM's late start-up, which was caused by its delayed funding. As a result, the regions operated in a vacuum of sorts and were compelled to develop their own inspection and enforcement approaches [OSM, 1980]. In any case, the evidence suggests that these hierarchical preferences and pressures were not of major importance in the development of different enforcement approaches in Regions East and West.

Thomas's comment indicates that regulatory agencies might adopt a policelike, impartial enforcement program as a strategem to separate the agency and its operations from a partisan, conflict-ridden political environment. Along the same lines, an investigator of a legalistic police department claims:

> [T]he administrators of these departments want high arrest and ticketing rates [in traffic enforcement] not only because it is right but also to reduce the prospect (or the suspicion) of corruption, to protect themselves against criticism that they are not doing their job or are deciding themselves what laws are good or bad, and to achieve, by means of the law, certain larger social objectives [Wilson, 1968: 180].

A similar dynamic occurred in Region East. Little wonder that managers there felt it necessary to "prove" that OSM was not corrupt, playing favorites, or conspiring with large coal producers to destroy their smaller competitors. In the manner of Caesar's wife, they would be above suspicion. At the same time, they favored impartial, consistent enforcement throughout OSM's regions of operation. With respect to the more flexible enforcement style adopted in Region West, one Region East manager opined that personnel out there "never read the Act."

In the much calmer political environment of Region West, personnel could afford the luxury of more flexible enforcement. Relatively immune to the suspicions and criticisms of diverse groups, they were less concerned that weak enforcement in other regions would undermine their credibility with Region West operators. Consequently, there was little if any emphasis on the need for enforcement consistency across all five OSM regions. It is not surprising, therefore, that the Region West director would say that while the SMCRA "is a national Act, . . . in fact, there are distinct regions of coal mining with different histories and cultures and, therefore, there also will be distinct programs implementing this national Act. It isn't a regionalization of the objectives. It's a regionalization of the implementation" [*Energy Daily,* 1978].

There is an additional way in which local conditions in the two Regions affected their respective enforcement programs. The mining "community" in Region West is much smaller and more homogeneous than in Region East. Further, the mining company representatives with whom regulators interact usually are well-educated and outwardly sympathetic to the goals of regulation. Put another way, the Region West mining community enjoyed a much higher degree of consensus on mining and regulatory objectives than Region East. In communities where there is a substantial consensus, according to an observer of the police, they are likely to

> feel that they can use their judgment in a particular case without having to choose, or without being thought to have chosen, between competing standards of order held by different persons or subcultures. And if the community is small in addition, the police are more likely to have information about the character of a large number of citizens

and thus some grounds for making a valid judgment about their likely future conduct. Stated another way, the police in a small town may believe that they are treating equals equally even when they do not treat everybody the same [Wilson, 1968: 219–20].

In the small, normatively homogeneous community, enforcement takes on a personalized flavor. For example, while inspectors in Region East were assigned to areas of the states in which they worked and were responsible for inspecting all mines in their area, Region West managers made individual assignments to particular mines and inspection visits. This was done to achieve what they believed would be the optimal match of inspectors with mine personnel or mine problems. According to one manager:

> [W]hat I try to do is find out what strong points and what weaknesses each different inspector has, and make your assignments accordingly. (Unless it's to the point where you find a weakness that you have to correct.) . . . If you have an inspector who is a, who's able to get along with people well, then you'd make your decision, you know — if you have a company that the people that are running the company are technically oriented . . . then you send a technical guy up there. They know how to communicate. If you got somebody that's running a company who's a little bit difficult to deal with, then you send your diplomat.

A final difference in the local environments of Regions East and West must be noted. In the West, where there is a high level of consensus and, presumably, compliance, there is little need for vigorous enforcement. Those already voluntarily in compliance will be relatively unaffected by what happens to those who do not comply. However, in areas such as the East, where the rate of compliance is rather low, regulators must stand ready to employ aggressive enforcement against violators lest the rate erode even further. Harsh enforcement serves as a signal of reassurance to voluntary compliers that they will not be harmed economically by their compliance.[8] As Wilson notes about legalistic police department: "[T]he law must be enforced with a special vigor in those areas where community norms appear weakest; failure to do so would penalize law-abiding persons in those areas and inhibit the development of a regard for community norms among the law breakers" [1968: 285–286]. Our data suggest the same relationship is true of regulatory agencies.

The environmental differences we have discussed here were the principal determinants of the development of somewhat different styles of enforcement in Regions East and West. However, we do not believe they account for all the variation in the respective enforcement styles; conditions or characteristics of the task OSM personnel were required to perform also played a part.

Regulatory Task

Inspection and enforcement personnel in Regions East and West were mandated by the act to perform identical tasks: inspection of surface coal mines. However, this equality of legal task obscures very real differences in the social organization of mining and inspecting in Regions East and West. And these differences are of such a nature that they created a difference in the nature and difficulty of the task which inspectors in the two regions were called on to perform.

Because the mines in Region West are large and complicated, their organization and staffing patterns are more complex than in Region East.

> Most of the mines in the West have a resident environmental specialist, either at the mine or at least someone who is assigned those duties. A lot of the larger mines — most of them, in fact — have people who are trained in [the] regulatory compliance function. And those are the people you deal with. The people back in the East — at least when I was back there — the people that you deal with are the pit foreman or the mine superintendent, who's actually at the mine. And his main job is production . . . you're dealing more with production-oriented people in the East. And in the West, most of the people you deal with are not *production* oriented but environmentally oriented.

It is the responsibility of these specialized reclamation personnel to monitor developments in the regulatory matrix in which mining is conducted, to stay abreast of advances and alternatives in reclamation practices, and to plan for reclamation in a legal, cost-effective manner. Specialized personnel are fellow salaried technicians, generally are well educated, and tend to accept the principle, if not the content, of regulation. Also, they possess a long-range understanding of mining and reclamation plans on particular mine sites. They can demonstrate to the inspector how apparent deviations from the regulations are integral parts of comprehensive plans and to suggest alternative methods for accomplishing reclamation objectives. In a word, specialized personnel are much more likely to be civil and "reasonable" toward inspectors.

The picture is very different in Region East. There, when inspectors arrive at a mine site they are more likely than not to encounter and deal with production personnel. Such persons tend to be poorly educated, to lack a detailed understanding of the regulations, and to be unsympathetic toward any interference with production activities and schedules.

> Q.: What are the relative advantages and disadvantages, from the inspector's standpoint, of having to deal with production people, as opposed to specialists in reclamation?
>
> A.: The guy . . . the production people — you have to explain, re-explain. He doesn't even know what part of the regulations you're talking about. The reclamation guy, that's his job. I mean, you don't even have to, probably, cite

the regulations. He knows it. In other words, he *knows* he may be incorrect. Or he knows how to articulate: "Gee, I'm trying to do this instead of doing that. So I'm not in violation." He knows how to properly — for his side — articulate the argument against some sort of enforcement action, possible enforcement action. Or, he can demonstrate: "Here's what we're doing, here's how the mine will proceed," you know. "Here's how I'm going to do this, and later, when I come around to this cut, I hope to take this point off and put the pond over here, relocate or divert." He can sort of look into the future, and look at what you've done since the last time [the inspector] was there. He can demonstrate what they did. He's *knowledgeable* of those regs. Production guy — I mean, I've been on sites with inspectors where some of the *simplest* violations . . . have to be explained ten times. Often [the] production guy will take his reclamation plan and never look at it. Throw it in the truck, that's it.

Q.: It's much easier to deal with specialists?

A.: Right.

Q.: Makes the job more manageable and, I would imagine, just less of a headache?

A.: Oh yeah. Oh yeah. Oh yeah, that's for sure. Even if you get in an argument, I think it's less of a headache. At least you're arguing with someone who can articulate with you and speak to you on the level of the regulations, rather than "I hate these goddamned things. And I can't do anything with them and I wish they were. . . . They're a bag of shit and they're costing me a million dollars".

But while specialized personnel pose no physical threat to inspectors, they can be a threat nonetheless. As an inspector told us: "[Back in the East], with small operators, it [is] more of a 'down home attitude.'"

Q.: "Good-ole'-boy" type thing?

A.: "Good-ole'-boy" approach. Whereas out here, when you're dealing with, like a large technical staff, with a person in every specific field you're much more on your guard for technical issues and addressing things technically rather than just, you know, a broad, sweep-of-the-hand type approach.

Q.: Do the large companies ever intimidate you, just because they have so many experts in each different field?

A.: Sure.

Q.: How do you deal with that?

A.: Well, I personally am more careful. When I'm writing a violation, I'm real careful that I have "the goods," so to speak, before I act. But the problem out here is a lot of the people that you're dealing with have a better technical understanding of the problems than perhaps I do. Which makes it difficult. . . .

Q.: Well, what do you do in that case, just concede to a greater amount of knowledge?

A.: Well, I think in some cases I probably do, realistically. . . . It's pretty hard to try to — the correct word is *argue* — about a specific situation and you don't know as much about it as the person you're arguing with.

On both counts then — because specialized personnel are reasonable *and* knowledgeable — Region West inspectors may approach their duties with a degree of deference, circumspection and, therefore, conciliation that is less common in Region East.

The lessons here, while commonplace, are important nonetheless. First, a civil clientele begets a civil, conciliatory enforcement style. Conversely, an angry, disrespectful, or defiant clientele begets a more aggressive, determined enforcement style, on the assumption that only by such actions can future problems of a similar nature be deterred [see Reiss, 1971]. And second, regulatory encounters in which the enforcement agents feels less knowledgeable than the other party contain the potential for overly deferential and, therefore, lenient treatment.

Conclusion

We have indicated some of the ways that differences in the personnel, political environments, and nature of their regulatory task produced somewhat different enforcement emphases or styles in two regions of a newly-created regulatory agency, the federal Office of Surface Mining. While all three factors played some part in shaping the two enforcement programs, certainly the substantially different political environments of Regions East and West were of major importance. There is ample support in our analysis for Kagan's [1980: 7] suggestion that ''inspectorates . . . confronted with rising legal contestation and challenges to their authority, respond with enhanced mistrust and legalism.''

Further research is needed, however, if we are to increase and refine our understanding of the relationships between environmental conditions and emergent styles of regulatory law enforcement. Doubtless, environmental pressures do not always and everywhere result in a legalistic style of enforcement. Therefore, we should endeavor to specify, via empirical research, the *conditions* under which specified environmental pressures produce specific types of enforcement strategies. With respect to OSM, our own research, for example, calls attention to some potentially important characteristics of OSM and its political environment. For the most part, OSM developed its enforcement program(s) with at least some respect for, and sensitivity to, a variety of constituencies and groups. At the same time, it received strong political support (protection) from the Carter administration and from important members of Congress. Certainly it is conceivable that a different combination of internal conditions and external political forces would have produced a lessened sensitivity to the full range of environmental pressures. In the absence of a sensitivity toward a multiplicity of groups, not all claims would be treated equally and the resulting enforcement program would be less legalistic and more partisan.

Additional research also is needed to determine the kinds of forces that tend to *transform* various types of regulatory styles. Our study suggests that legalistic enforcement programs may be subjected to unusual or unique internal *and* political constraints that ultimately erode their stringency. This is another way of saying that legalistic enforcement programs may be particularly or peculiarly "unstable" and rather easily transformed, therefore, into programs with other emphases. The fact that OSM is a new agency, has been subjected to intense criticism, and has been a primary target of the Reagan administration's move toward deregulation suggests perhaps that stringent or legalistic enforcement programs are especially difficult to maintain even for relatively short periods of time.

Finally, much more research is needed if we are to develop an empirically-based understanding of the full range of regulatory law enforcement styles. Our study suggests that programs perhaps do not conform very neatly to the typologies which have been proffered thus far. The largely ad hoc distinction between conciliatory and legalistic enforcement styles, although it possesses considerable intuitive appeal, must be examined and elaborated further before we can be confident that it orders and predicts styles of regulatory law enforcement in the real world.

Notes

1. This chapter is based on a preliminary report from a study of OSM's development and impact on the coal industry, primarily during its first four years of operation.
2. The Reagan administration has reorganized OSM. In early 1982, regional offices were replaced by (1) offices in each of the coal-producing states, and (2) two technical service centers.
3. OSM provided us with copies of regional inspection reports, inspector activity summaries, and manpower records, beginning with their initial enforcement efforts (May 1978) and continuing to the present. We also acquired intraagency memoranda, media reports, court decisions and records, public testimony, and copies of *Federal Register* notices regarding OSM and its operations. Finally, we collected publications and reports from environmental and industry groups.

    Thus far over 100 open-ended interviews have been conducted with OSM employees, coal operators, mining consultants, representatives of environmental groups, and representatives of industry groups at various levels. Most of these interviews were conducted in Washington, D.C. and in Regions East and West. Each interview was tape recorded and lasted approximately one hour. Of the total number of interviews, 43 were conducted with OSM inspectors, supervisors, and managerial personnel in Regions East and West.

    A questionnaire was used to assess the attitudes of OSM field-level personnel on a variety of issues related to inspection and enforcement. The questionnaire was mailed to all inspectors employed by OSM during summer, 1981. Questionnaires were mailed to 159 persons. After one follow-up letter, we received completed questionnaires from 126 respondents, a return rate of 79 percent.

4.   These numbers are conservative estimates based on statistics furnished by OSM's Division of Inspection and Enforcement. The numbers include only personnel empowered to conduct inspections and issue notices of violation. They do not include field supervisors or district managers because they do not issue citations.

5.   In mining parlance, a short ton is the equivalent of 20 short hundred-weights, or 2,000 pounds.

6.   In 1979, 18 of the nation's largest coal producing surface mines were located in Region West. None were located in Region East National Coal Association, 1980.

7.   We do not mean to imply that Region West operated in complete freedom from oversight by citizen's groups. See, e.g., Johnson et al, 1980.

8.   A special irritant to Region East personnel was OSM's centralized office for assessing civil penalties. They believed assessments should have been decentralized, so that the regions could fix penalties. Presumably, such a procedure would have permitted them to tailor penalties flexibly and thus reward operators who were making a good faith effort to comply with the regulations.

Table 6-1. Summary Measures of OSM Inspection and Enforcement Activity, July 1, 1979 to June 30, 1980

Region	Number of NOVs Per:			Number of COs Per:		
	Inspector	Ten Inspections	Million Short Tons of Coal[a]	Inspector	Ten Inspections	Million Short Tons of Coal[a]
East	54.23	2.62	17.22	15.02	0.73	4.77
West	12.14	2.34	0.44	0.71	0.14	0.03
Total (U.S.)	32.31	2.01	8.45	6.54	0.40	1.66

[a]U.S. Department of Energy, 1981; 1981a.

Table 6-2. Regional Variation on Dimensions of Regulatory Enforcement Styles

Dimension	Region East			Region West			U.S. Total		
	X̄ Score	S.D.	N.	X̄ Score	S.D.	N	X̄ Score	S.D.	N
Legalism[a]	4.95	3.05	44	2.33	1.63	6	4.59	2.57	126
Conciliatory[b]	9.18	1.82	44	9.33	2.07	6	8.51	2.35	126

[a]A three-item scale (Cronbach's alpha = .67). Items are: "Generally the requirement that OSM inspectors write an NOV on every violation they observe is not an effective regulatory strategy." [0 Strongly Agree; 1 Agree; 2 Undecided; 3 Disagree; 4 Strongly Disagree]; "The best way for inspectors to do their job is to go strictly 'by the book.'" [4 Strongly Agree; 3 Agree; 2 Undecided; 1 Disagree; 0 Strongly Disagree]; and "I have tried to enforce the interim regulations strictly and uniformly, much as a police officer would do" [4 Strongly Agree; 3 Agree; 2 Undecided; 1 Disagree; 0 Strongly Disagree]. Responses to the three items were summed.

[b]A three-item scale (Cronbach's alpha = .77). Items are: "Compliance with the regulations is easiest to obtain if the inspector advises and works to educate the operator"; "In my work I have tried primarily to educate and consult with coal operators"; and "The best way for inspectors to do their job is to consult with and try to educate mine operators." Response alternatives to all three items were: [4 Strongly Agree; 3 Agree; 2 Undecided; 1 Disagree; and 0 Strongly Disagree]. Responses to the three items were summed.

Table 6-3. Regional Differences Among Inspectors in Perceptions of Coal Operators and State Regulatory Authorities

Perceptions of:	Region East			Region West			U.S. Total		
	$\overline{X}$ Score	S.D.	N.	$\overline{X}$ Score	S.D.	N	$\overline{X}$ Score	S.D.	N
Degree of Willful Noncompliance by Coal Operators[a]	1.70	0.63	44	0.83	0.41	6	1.59	0.70	126
Coal Operators' Trustworthiness[b]	1.05	0.91	44	1.33	0.82	6	1.20	0.98	126
Distrust of State Regulatory Authorities[c]	2.61	0.97	44	1.83	0.75	6	2.59	0.98	126

[a] "Based on your personal experience, how often do mine operators willfully and knowingly violate the federal regulations?" [3 Very Frequently; 2 Frequently; 1 Infrequently; 0 Almost Never]

[b] "Most coal operators can be trusted to do the right thing and to mine their coal in an environmentally sound way." [4 Strongly Agree; 3 Agree; 2 Undecided; 1 Disagree; 0 Strongly Disagree]

[c] "Most of the progress that OSM has made toward curbing mining abuses will be lost when state regulatory programs are implemented." [4 Strongly Agree; 3 Agree; 2 Undecided; 1 Disagree; 0 Strongly Disagree]

Table 6-4. Summary Measures of Citizen Complaint Activity, July 1, 1979 to June 30, 1980

| Region | Number of Complaints | Number of Citizen Complaints Per: | | |
		Inspector	Inspections	Million Short Tons of Coal
East	445	7.42	0.67	2.35
West	5	0.71	0.31	0.03
Total (U.S.)	1043	6.56	0.61	1.28

References

Bordua, David J. (ed.) (1967). *The Police: Six Sociological Essays*. New York: John Wiley & Sons.

Brauson, Bramley A. (1974). Stripping the Appalachians, 83 *Natural History* 52.

Caudill, Harry (1971). *My Land is Dying*. New York: E.P. Dutton.

Center for Law and Social Policy (and) Environmental Policy Institute (1978). *The Strip Mine Handbook*. Washington, D.C.: Brophy Associates, Inc.

Clelland, D. A., J. P. Lynxwiler, N. Shover and S. Groce (1981). Sources of Enforcement Strategies Among Surface Mining Inspectors: A Preliminary Analysis. Paper presented at the annual meeting of the American Sociological Association, Toronto (August 22).

Edelhertz, Herbert (ed.) (1980). *The Development of a Research Agenda on White Collar Crime*. Seattle: Battelle Human Affairs Research Centers.

Energy Daily (1978). Surface Mining Law Takes on a Regional Flavor. Tuesday, August 1.

Gardiner, John A. (1969). *Traffic and the Police*. Cambridge, Mass.: Harvard University Press.

Geis, Gilbert and Ezra Stotland (eds.) (1980). *White Collar Crime: Theory and Research*, Beverly Hills, Cal.: Sage Publications.

Hawkins, Keith (1980). The Use of Discretion by Regulatory Officials: A Case Study on Environmental Pollution in the United Kingdom. Draft paper presented to Baldy Center for Law and Social Policy, Conference on Law, Discretion and Bureaucratic Behavior (June). State University of New York at Buffalo.

Johnson, C. R., D. S. May and G. W. Pring (1980). *Stripping the Law on Coal*. Denver: Public Lands Institute.

Kagan, Robert A. (1978). *Regulatory Justice*. New York: Russell Sage Foundation.

——— (1980). The Positive Uses of Discretion: The Good Inspector. Paper presented to the Law and Society Association, Madison, Wisconsin, (June).

Lynxwiler, John P., and Stephen B. Groce (1981). Violative Behavior and the Negotiation of Public Identities in the Work Setting: An Analysis of Appalachian Mine Operators.

Paper presented at the annual meeting of the Southern Sociological Society, Louisville, Ky. (April 9).

Manning, Peter K. (1977). *Police Work*. Cambridge, Mass.: M.I.T. Press.

——— (1980). *The Narcs' Game*. Cambridge, Mass.: M.I.T. Press.

National Coal Association (1980). *Keystone Coal Industry Manual* New York: McGraw Hill.

National Research Council (1981). *Surface Mining: Soil, Coal, and Society*. Washington, D.C.: National Academy Press.

Nivola, Pietro S. (1978). Distributing a municipal service: A case study of housing inspection, 40 *Journal of Politics* 59.

Office of Surface Mining (1980). *Management Evaluation of the Division of Inspection and Enforcement and I&E Regional Operations*. Washington, D.C.: Division of Planning and Evaluation (January).

——— (1981). Inspectable Units. January 6.

President's Commission on Coal (1980). *Coal Data Book*. Washington, D.C.: U.S. Government Printing Office.

Reiss, Albert J., Jr. (1971). *The Police and the Public*. New Haven, Conn.: Yale University Press.

Reiss, Albert J., Jr., and David J. Bordua (1967). Environment and Organization: A Perspective on the Police, in Bordua [1967].

Shover, Neal (1980). The Criminalization of Corporate Behavior: Federal Surface Coal Mining, in Geis and Stotland [1980].

Thomas, John M. (1980). The Regulatory Role in the Containment of Corporate Illegality, in Edelhertz (1980).

U. S. Department of Energy (1981). *Energy Data Report*. Washington, D.C.: Energy Information Administration, January 9.

——— (1981a). *Energy Data Report*. Washington, D.C.: Energy Information Administration, July 17.

Wilson, James Q. (1968). *Varieties of Police Behavior*. Cambridge, Mass.: Harvard University Press.

——— (1978). *The Investigators*. New York: Basic Books.

——— (ed.) (1980). *The Politics of Regulation*. New York: Basic Books.

7 THE CONSEQUENCES OF RESPONSIVE REGULATION

Susan S. Silbey

Introduction

The public regulation of business for the common good has been declared a failure in America. A consensus has developed among scholars that things never quite work out as they ought when legislation is translated into administrative action. Much effort has been devoted to understanding how agencies mandated to serve the public become ineffective and indolent [Lowi, 1969; McConnell, 1966; Bernstein, 1955; Edelman, 1964; Shapiro, 1968; Herring, 1936; Leiserson, 1942; Kolko, 1965; Hamilton, 1957; Orren, 1974; Stone, 1975; Huntington, 1952; Morgan, 1952; Huntington et al, 1953; Argyris, 1978; Lilley and Miller, 1977]. Why do public regulatory agencies seem to serve the interests they were designed to regulate and control?

Various explanations have been suggested. These explanations range from analyses of the symbolic nature of a legislative process that produces inconsistent mandates [Edelman, 1964], to analyses of the segmented structure of a system that encourages a division of the commonweal among interested parties to the exclusion of the unorganized public [Lowi, 1969; 1978]. Examinations of organizational activity emphasize the rational dynamics of decision making and the self-maintenance functions of organizational behavior. Traditional diffidence about

The research for this paper was partially supported by the Behavioral Sciences Fund of Wellesley College.

rigorous enforcement is attributed to limited resources, and sometimes to mediocre personnel. Resource constraints cause litigation delays and encourage a standard of performance that rests upon closing files rather than winning cases [Ross, 1970]. The result is a pattern of enforcement characterized by weak commitment and high turnover in cases and personnel.

It has been suggested that excessive discretion, especially among low ranking "street-level" agents entrusted with day-to-day enforcement responsibilities impedes the efficacy of regulatory schemes [Davis, 1969; 1972; Lipsky, 1976; 1980; Wilson, 1973; 1978]. Uncontrolled discretion undermines the rule of law because, irrespective of resource and organizational capabilities, it leads to lax, inconsistent, and unfair enforcement. Discretion is responsible for the intrusion of nonlegal and political considerations into the regulatory process. The response to the discovery of discretion has been proposals for more formal control through rulemaking to confine, structure and review administrative and law enforcement discretion [Davis, 1969; 1972; Lowi, 1969; 1978].

Kagan suggests that the enforcement style of governmental regulators and inspectorates has changed as a result of demands for greater control of discretion. Where regulators had been flexible and cooperative, they have become inflexible and legalistic. "The shift has been away from a traditional enforcement style that relied heavily on persuasion, warnings and informal negotiations, and towards a legalistic style that stresses strict application of legal regulations and prompt imposition of heavier legal sanctions for all detected violations" [Kagan, 1980:1]. While it is not clear how pervasive this "new" enforcement style is, Kagan is no more sanguine about the prospects of legalistic enforcement for effective regulation than others have been about cooperative efforts.

The thesis of this chapter is that the "failure" of public regulation is the result of the responsiveness of regulatory agencies to their public constituencies. The problems of public regulation are not located solely within the internal structure of the agencies themselves, so that if one reorganized an office, one could predict the consequences for law enforcement. Regulation is produced from the interaction of an agency with other organizations and its environment. Poor organization and inadequate resources may contribute to ineffective regulation but do not fully account for it. It is not simply a matter of excess discretion or legalization; nor can public regulation be adequately described as subversion, dereliction, or incompetence. The apparent failure of public regulation persists because many things happen along the way from mandate to implementation that are reasonable and consistent with empirical as well as legal demands. These activities are seen as evidence of regulatory failure because they produce no unidirectional policy; competing demands engender responses that are not in a single direction.

The daily activities of officials are not specifically authorized by a governing mandate although they are undertaken to achieve it. They are not irrational within the agent's interpretation of the mandate because they are responsive to articulated demands for service, including the demand for regulation. In fact, they are the agent's interpretation of the mandate. Nevertheless, it does not make sense to think of these activities that fully occupy inspectorates and law enforcement offices as goals of regulation; and the consequences of responsive organizations cannot be measured as a direct relationship between means and ends. This provides an overrationalized conception of organizational behavior. Rather, policy implementation must be viewed as a series of adjustments and responses.

This chapter describes how a particular law enforcement agency responded to the competing demands of its environment by incorporating them within its implementation strategy. It focuses on one aspect of consumer protection practice — the adoption and consequences of a policy of case-by-case mediation of consumer complaints. The mediation of consumer complaints became the behavioral and legal mechanism through which private interests influenced their own regulation, thus constituting cooperation between regulators and the regulated. By meeting the demands of competing constituencies, the Massachusetts Consumer Protection Division (CPD) replicated the relations between consumer and business that public policies were designed to regulate. This thesis suggests that the normal operations of responsive organizations account for the patterns and "failure" of public regulation.

A Mandate for Consumer Protection

The Massachusetts Consumer Protection Act (Mass. Gen. Laws Ann. ch. 93A) was the culmination of a long history of trying to define the rights of consumers under law. The process is older than capitalism itself, and contemporary efforts to provide consumer protection through state regulation are a response to earlier attempts to correct market failures and abuses. These thrived in an environment that was hostile to ventures that would bolster the legal protection of consumer interests at the expense of the prevailing organization of the market.

Consumer protection is not a modern notion. It goes back to classical and medieval times when regulation of trade based upon religious and social precepts was common. Caveat emptor, the antithesis of consumer protection, is the by-product and symbol of the emergence of the market economy[1]. Neither existed before the last 400 years. They were historically new and radical concepts that, despite concerted attacks by the growth of the welfare state, continue to characterize the moral and social ordering of consumer business relations.

Caveat emptor incorporated the rising spirit of individualism into the law of market relations by expressing the principle that the consumer would heretofore bargain in the marketplace without any legal protection.[2] It is understood to be an ordinary rule of prudence, urging the reasonable person to use his or her faculties to assess the quality and quantity of the goods he or she purchases. The significance of the concept lies not so much in the meaning of its words, however, but in the social and economic policy of which it is a graphic symbol[3].

Caveat emptor and the market economy were consistent with the dominant philosophy of the Enlightenment and of emerging liberalism — a conscious abandonment of each individual to his or her own devices with a minimum of control, a minimum of standards of fair practice, and consequently, maximal individual autonomy. The belief prevailed that the aggregated consequences of each individual acting independently as agent and arbiter of his own interests achieved the common good of all, which was, after all, the achieving of the unfettered exercise of self-interest and the satisfaction of human wants. The market was the most efficient and effective mechanism for securing individual wants and interests because it was self-regulating. The self-interested buyer would not patronize for long purveyors of shoddy merchandise, thus driving out the unscrupulous and rewarding the honest and productive tradesman.

The context of contemporary consumer protection emerges from two empirical qualifications upon the classical model of the market. First, the self-regulation of the market was a myth. From the outset, the market economy was founded upon aggressive legislative activity, and its self-regulation has always depended upon protective legislation. Measures were needed to control the effects of periodic traumas due to unstable currencies, inflationary spirals, monopolies, and the like. A critical tension emerged between the free market and its consequences.

Second, *if ever there were localized conditions where the model of the free market approximated empirical reality, the modern world is a changed place.* It is questionable whether the consumer's even unencumbered wants are actually reflected in market choices. Technological advances have rapidly increased the development of new and complex products and the cost of information about these commodities has been significantly increased by the subtlety and intricacy of the information. Under present conditions there are too many products, the information is too sophisticated, and the market may not be sufficiently open and competitive in important areas to drive out inferior products and services. Critical expenditures involving large sums of money or life itself may be one-time, nonrepetitive transactions. In these cases errors of information are costly, and yet may not be avoidable. In principle and in fact, all consumer problems are generated by just this issue — the difficulty of obtaining reliable information in order to make rational market choices. Thus, consumer protection activities are about securing more and better consumer information.

Caveat emptor, although firmly established in English and American law, has never been so absolute as to deny the possibility for limited remedies against some market losses [Morrow, 1940; Traylor, 1969]. Private remedies at law for deceit

and misrepresentation, scores of malum prohibitum statutes, licensing and registration regulations, federal regulation of business, and assorted claims adjustment
services offered a range of remedies for consumers [*University of Pennsylvania
Law Review,* 1966; Rice, 1968; *Columbia Law Review,* 1956; Llewellyn, 1936;
Williston, 1948]. Yet these private legal remedies, mediating agencies and public
attempts at prospective regulation did not effectively meet the needs of consumer
protection. The costs were too high, the proof too difficult, the enforcement too
inadequate, and the machinery of administration and judicial review too
cumbersome.

The time had come for a new approach: the climate was ripe for consumer
protection. By this time, the Commonwealth of Massachusetts had three years
experience with a consumer's council of advisors to the governor, and a small
consumer protection agency in the attorney general's department that was established by administrative fiat, without statutory authority. In recent sessions of the
legislature, several bills had been submitted urging study and investigation of the
laws relative to unfair methods of competition and deception in the Commonwealth [Silbey, 1978: chap. 3). These were symptomatic of the general attention
consumer protection received during the 1960s. Ralph Nader had begun his
campaign against unsafe automobiles and developed this interest into a sustained
research and publicity effort directed at the efficacy of government regulation for
consumers. In 1963, David Caplovitz's *The Poor Pay More* was published and
commanded attention as the first systematic inquiry into the plight of low-income
consumers. In 1966 Congress passed five consumer laws, whereas it had passed
only two between 1962 and 1965. Consideration was given to creating a department of consumer affairs, and Senator Warren Magnuson was conducting investigations into what he called the "dark side of the marketplace" [Magnuson and
Carper, 1968]. In 1964 the president appointed a committee on consumer interests
to monitor and report on consumer problems [Nadel, 1971].

The consequences of these efforts were to mobilize public support on behalf
of consumers and to raise to the fore two principal concerns: (1) the inability of
consumers to obtain satisfaction either through the market in terms of reliable
products and services or to obtain satisfaction through existing remedies for the
failure of these products and services, and (2) the especially acute economic plight
of less advantaged consumers whose position was exacerbated through lack of
knowledge on how and where to shop, lack of capital to make cash purchases or
obtain favorable credit, lack of access to alternative markets, and lack of access to
the legal system.

Massachusetts had taken a large step toward providing broader statutory protection for consumer interests the year before with the passage of a truth-in-lending
retail installment sales act. The lines of battle had been drawn; consumers had won
when the bills had been passed over vociferous and organized opposition. Now in

1966, some members of the legislature wanted to provide a resource to handle consumer problems in a general and comprehensive manner. But, the passage of Chapter 93A of the Massachusetts General Laws cannot be said to represent any clear set of interests. True, it was designed by its author, and supported by the Federal Trade Commission (FTC), in order to provide a new kind of remedy for consumers through programmatic prosecutions against consumer frauds, and through intervention in unsatisfactory transactions where fraud was often a rarity.

But the leadership of the Massachusetts legislature could hardly have been considered consumer advocates, and yet, without their support there would have been no consumer protection act. The leadership rose from the ranks of the Democratic party regulars whose base of support lay in the inner core of the state's cities. By 1967, they were an entrenched, yet threatened leadership, who appeared to be conservative, lethargic, and corruption-ridden collaborators with powerful business and private interest groups in the state. The party leadership was challenged by a growing coalition of representatives who, supported by the burgeoning suburban middle class, were seeking to wrest control of Massachusetts politics from the State House politicos [Litt, 1965; Mayhew, 1968]. Consumer protection seemed to be an inevitability; it was just a matter of how and when. Therefore, it was an issue that the leadership had to support; they could worry about its implications at some future, less observed, moment. The legislation was finally enacted with support from both liberal and conservative factions.

When there is unanimous assent for a piece of legislation, the how and when — the technical mechanics and details — become extremely pertinent. In this instance, the supporters of the bill joined the bill's natural opponents in rewriting it to accommodate the claims and demands of represented, organized interests. Major corporations in the state resolved, through the Associated Industries of Massachusetts, to support the legislation while working to limit its effect. Language was inserted that gave businessmen opportunities to challenge and delay enforcement.

Nevertheless, the bill almost died, not from public exposure and public opposition, of which it received very little, but because it was buried in the deepest recesses of the legislature. Various explanations have been offered to account for the fact that a bill that apparently had public support from all quarters was languishing deep in the legislative process: organizational rivalries between the Better Business Bureau and an aggressive new consumer protection agency, fear of a power grab by the popular attorney general, and undercover opposition by business groups unwilling to publicly denounce the bill. Its eventual passage has been attributed to the power of appeals to the public interest and to the demands of political ambition. It was just not the time to oppose consumer protection. The threat of public notice on those who were bottling it up after bipartisan consensus had been reached was sufficient to bring it to the floor for the unanimous vote.

It is not accurate to say that the Consumer Protection Act fulfilled a single or unidirectional purpose. In any case, statutes are best understood as opportunities, not prescriptions. This much was clear to the participants active in the process of writing and promulgating Chapter 93A. The statute seemed to open the way for aggressive action on behalf of consumers and came to be regarded as a very progressive piece of legislation. Observers understood, however, that the law's effectiveness would depend upon the nature of its enforcement [National Association of Attorneys General, 1971: 441; Steele, 1975a]. As an opportunity, the statute itself created only a pressure on the political system, rather than channels or fixed routes for public administration. The interesting issue concerns how enforcement policy was organized, structured, and worked out in practice.

Implementing a Mandate for Consumer Protection: Case-by-Case Mediation of Consumer Complaints

The major contribution of the Consumer Protection Act was the establishment of an agency, under the attorney general, specifically mandated to protect the consuming public from deceptive and misrepresentative trade practices. The legislation delegates to the CPD the tasks of investigating consumer complaints concerning deceptive trade practices, initiating action in courts of equity and law in cases involving deceptive trade practices, promulgating rules and regulations in the area of deceptive trade practices, and enforcing the provisions of the Consumer Protection Act and supplementary rules and regulations.

To compel compliance with the law, the CPD is empowered (1) to file suits to obtain injunctive relief; (2) to file law suits for the restitution of damages sustained by consumers due to deceptive trade practices (including the demand of treble damages); (3) to file motions requesting the imposition of fines of up to $10,000 for the violation of injunctions; (4) to initiate a process leading to the subpoena of records and persons to uncover deceptive trade practices or to resolve consumer complaints; and to levy fines of up to $5,000 for failure to comply with the investigative process; (5) to demand and to receive binding assurances of discontinuance of allegedly deceptive trade practices; (6) to initiate a process leading to the imposition of penalties for violations of specific provisions of the Consumer Protection Act, such as the alteration of automobile odometer settings; and (7) to initiate a process leading to the abrogation of the right to engage in business in the Commonwealth for repeated violation of the statute or regulations promulgated under its authority [Mass. Gen. Law. ANN. ch. 93A].

To implement the Consumer Protection Act, the attorney general's staff adopted a policy of attempting some resolution of all consumer complaints received. Case-by-case investigation and negotiation of complaints is a widely used mode of enforcement [Palamountain, 1965; Cox, 1969; Bardach and Kagan, 1982]. Although other complaint handling agencies seem regularly to screen complaints [Nader, 1980; Serber, 1980], government agencies whose primary function is consumer protection generally do so less frequently [Steele, 1975a; 1975b; King and Mc Evoy, 1976; NAAG, 1971; Cranston, 1979]. The policy of the CPD was typical in this regard.

A policy of case-by-case investigation means that the activities of the CPD are set into motion by complaining consumers. Thus, for example, people who feel that they have been shortchanged in their dealings with trademen or merchants, or people who feel that they have been illegally and/or unfairly deprived of something they felt entitled to in some business dealings, came to the CPD seeking redress. The lawyers and investigators spent of their time processing cases: investigating, negotiating, and resolving consumer complaints. The agency's activities were reactive and followed the victimized consumer's perception of where protection was needed rather than the more direct enforcement policies that are explicitly authorized by the act. As a result, consumer protection was limited to ordering priorities in incoming business.

A case-by-case approach to consumer protection was responsive to several demands. First, it provided immediate help for consumers, thus overcoming the inadequacies of earlier consumer protection efforts which relied upon criminal enforcement or private legal actions [*Harvard Law Review,* 1967; *University of Pennsylvania Law Review,* 1966; Ball and Friedman, 1965; Kadish, 1963; Callman, 1948]. Criminal sanctions were rarely enforced and provided no redress for individual losses. Private legal actions were so costly as to be largely unavailable. The successful resolution of a consumer complaint by the attorney general's office meant that the consumer received a specific saving or refund. Consumers as a class have an interest in ending deceptive trade practices; but individual consumers who suffer a loss due to a misrepresentative transaction are primarily interested in what can be done for them. Effective consumer protection had to meet these individual consumer interests as well as deal with the generalized patterns of abuse. The CPD decided to become that place in government where the consumer could be assured of representation. As a first step, the agency chose to focus on the consumer's immediate demand for redress, on dispute resolution rather than law enforcement, on the needs and demands of the complaining consumers rather than the violation of standards of business conduct as such.

At the same time, case-by-case mediation of consumer complaints was responsive to a highly politicized environment. The attorney general was sensitive to the interests of active and supportive constituents such as the Associated Industries of Massachusetts. He did not wish to alienate the business community without whose support he could not be reelected and without whose cooperation he could not affect the nature of routine business transactions. Business interests had little reason to feel threatened. Faced with the demands of vocal consumer groups and the fears of powerful business interests, the policy of case-by-case mediation eliminated the politically hazardous problem of choosing sides. The personnel of the CPD refused to describe themselves as consumer advocates.

The CPD's policy reflected a benign view of business practices as unintentionally disadvantageous to consumers. Businessmen were not depicted as sly and predatory schemers who defrauded unwary and innocent victim-consumers. Rather, consumer grievances were the result of a dynamic market beyond any individual's control, the result of breaches of contract, misunderstandings, inevitable failure of communication, and unintentional human error. Admittedly, some losses resulted from illegal activities, but these were few in number. Most businessmen, however, are honest. Moreover, the line between fraudulent practices and acceptable activities is so unclear that punitive law enforcement was not the appropriate response. Where losses and disputes occurred, the CPD would intervene on a case-by-case basis to help promote profitable and equitable relations between consumers and business.

Moreover, case-by-case mediation also seemed to reflect the ultimate goal of consumer protection: controlling deceptive practices and driving incorrigible transgressors out of business. The Consumer Protection Act was specifically directed against patterns of deception and contains increasingly serious penalties for "repeating," "continual," and "habitual" offenders. A complete record of the results of investigation, the determinations of violations, and the resolution of complaints is crucial for implementing the provisions of the law. Therefore, the first problem for any administrator of this statute was how to bring the enforcers of the law and the instances of misrepresentation together. If the staff allowed the deceived consumers to bring their complaints to the attorney general, the CPD would not only help the individual consumer and correct troublesome (but not necessarily illegal) trade practices, but they would also identify and possibly prosecute violators of the law. Any other policy, such as programmatic prosecution, industry-by-industry attack on consumer fraud, or emphasis on proactive consumer education would also require accumulation of some history of consumer practices within the state. The case-by-case approach provided the necessary first step toward any policy of consumer protection.

The policy for consumer protection also took account of CPD's limited resources. The CPD began with essentially no administrative or legal precedent, an inexperienced staff, and few organizational resources. "The heavy investment of resources required to use formal institutions to resolve disputes created pressure to resolve them by more informal means," such as case by case negotiation [Steele, 1975a:1116; Serber, 1980; Macaulay, 1963; 1966; Cranston, 1979].

Indeed, the CPD was characterized by a lack of coordination and leadership. There was little differentiation of roles; channels of communication were haphazard and irregular. Investigation of consumer complaints was, from 1968 through 1975, the responsibility of both attorneys and "investigator" staff members who were usually not members of the bar. There was no formal division of labor, such that investigation of complaints was reserved for those members of the staff who were designated as "investigators". Attorneys had, in addition to their responsibility for the office's formal legal work (e.g. the preparation of subpoenas, bills of complaint, briefs on a variety of subjects), obligations to investigate and mediate consumer complaints. Because formal action by the division was limited, investigation of complaints was a primary responsibility of attorneys and "investigators."

Although the entire staff reported directly to the chief of the division, the assistant attorney general for consumer protection, their discretion was unchecked by any regular process of review. Very soon after its creation, the workload of the office grew beyond the ability of any chief to oversee the work of the entire staff. Resources for control such as sanctions, rewards, and incentives were lacking because the agents were either civil servants or political appointees. Moreover, members of the staff acknowledged that they were responsible only to the attorney general who had appointed them and not to the divisional chief who was responsible for their work. Yet because the attorney general was removed from the daily affairs of the division, he was also unable to review individual performance. Therefore, the investigators and attorneys operated as autonomous law enforcement units.

Initially, the case-by-case mediation policy seemed practical given the agency's resources. It provided the division with a sense of reasonable orderliness; officials knew what they had to do and knew why it had to be done.

The institution of a policy of case-by-case mediation forestalled a court test of the authorizing statute. The consumer protection act had dramatically altered the burden of proof between business and consumers, but the CPD attorneys were, nevertheless, reluctant to bring suits under the law before state court judges. They feared that the law's radical shift from earlier statutory precedents and common law traditions would not be understood or well received by a business-oriented judiciary.

Furthermore, they feared that the law would not be able to stand up against charges of vagueness. The statute summarily prohibited all deceptive and misrepresentative practices and all practices that had a tendency to deceive. The statute contained no additional language defining the proscribed activities. Since the law has remained virtually untested, it is difficult to resist the suspicion that this was a belief of convenience. It is true that most cases that come to the CPD do not involve easily identifiable and recognizable illegal practices. In many cases there are no clear or unquestionable rights or illegal practices involved on either side. Most issues fall into a grey zone of still unspecified deceptions, probable deceptions, or disagreements that have not yet been sufficiently generalized to be categorized as misrepresentation either through litigation or regulation. Common consumer complaints are often the product of the breakdown of consumer business relations for which the law provides no clear or possible remedy [see Ross and Littlefield, 1978; Caplowitz, 1963; Andreasen, 1975; Best and Andreasen, 1975; Nader, 1980]. The specific strengths of the Massachusetts statue reflected a belief that some unpatterned and undefinable consumer business disagreements were inevitable. The statute was purposely written to be as broad and encompassing as possible.

Nevertheless, there is little reason to believe that the law is vague under judicial interpretation. The terms correspond to the language of the Federal Trade Commission Act. The records of the legislation's author and of supporters of the original bill are clear about the intended meaning of this language [Greenberg, 1967, 1968; Meade, 1968; Shea, 1967; Dixon, 1966]. The process of explication has been continuing for 40 years at the FTC. But the staff of the CPD, especially a legal staff that was inexperienced for a long time, felt unsure of their own skills and often attributed their reluctance to proceed formally to the language of the law.

The policy of the CPD also seemed to respond to the fact that buying is far less methodically organized than selling. Because the character of many consumer transactions is haphazard and their terms, conditions, and circumstances unrecorded [see Macaulay, 1963], in any dispute settlement procedure, purveyors are better equipped than consumers to render plausible accounts of their side of the story and to support it with written records. Of course, there is no lack of resolute and resourceful consumers who keep records that match the records of business establishments, but they are not usually the ones who need the intercession of the CPD. Moreover, for most consumers, complaining is an unusual endeavor; for businesses, however, the handling of complaints is routine. Therefore, an informal mechanism that relied upon persuasion and negotiation rather than documentary proof and evidence was more likely to win tangible benefits for consumers.

In general, then, the staff of the CPD believed that the objectives of consumer protection were best served by responding to consumer complaints individually. For example, staff members argued that litigation could force tottering businesses, from whom the agency was able to wring compromise settlements, into bankruptcy. It could cost more to prepare a case for court than to convince offending businesses to settle. Litigation costs automatically reduce agency resources for mediating complaints, and the aggregate savings to the state's consumers would be reduced. Therefore, although the CPD was established to banish illicit practices from the marketplace, its routine work consisted of helping complaining consumers recoup losses. It was believed that with time, intercession by the attorney general on behalf of consumers would succeed in changing the marketplace. And in the meantime, the office was able to produce tangible results for the individual consumer where alternative enforcement strategies could produce less.

Indeed, in the period between May, 1968 and December, 1974, the CPD managed to function quite effectively without using any of its legal weapons. The office's effectiveness consisted of receiving, investigating, and disposing of between 250 and 400 complaints per week, more than half of which it resolved to the satisfaction of the complaining consumer[4]. These resolutions resulted in about 4 million dollars of restitutions and savings to consumers.

Though disposition of consumer protection cases may necessitate the use of subpoenas or other forms of legal coercion, routine cases are negotiated and concluded without employing formal legal process or punitive or restitutive authority[5]. The accomplishments of the CPD are products of laborious and frequently repetitious bargaining with businesses. This bargaining consists primarily of badgering businessmen, or convincing and often coercing them into making some sort of refund to complaining consumers [Silbey and Bittner, 1982]. Nearly 80 percent of consumers' complaints are silenced by securing a refund or restitution of some sort. The business practice that gave rise to the complaint is rarely addressed as a matter of interest in and of itself, or as a matter of possible interest to other consumers or the commonwealth. When a complaint is silenced, the case is completed [Silbey, 1981].

For example, consider the case of the Pontiac radiators. A consumer complained that the radiator in his six-month-old Pontiac cracked and that General Motors was unwilling to honor the warranty on the car. The manufacturer claimed that the device had been damaged by the consumer's negligence and misuse. The consumer had not used General Motors antifreeze or the equivalent as the owner's manual specified. But the manual did not describe an equivalent antifreeze and the consumer had used a nationally known brand. The investigator made numerous phone calls to Detroit to discuss the case with Pontiac's divisional counsel. He learned that General Motors had complaints from other consumers in Massachusetts, as well as from consumers in other states. He also learned that attorneys general in other states were initiating action against Pontiac on several grounds including deceptive practices. The investigator finally obtained an agreement from Pontiac to honor this consumer's warranty and to pay for any associated damages to the car. The investigator explained his success by saying that "Pontiac was on thin ice" and did not want to deal with yet another attorney general. The investigator was aware that General Motors had additional complaints from consumers in Massachusetts exactly like the one just settled. Yet he did not attempt to negotiate a settlement for them by having their radiators repaired, getting their money refunded, or securing a commitment to have the warranties honored now or in the future. The investigator commented: "It is not my affair. I do not have the complaints, and I am not going to dig them out and resurrect the dead."

This case is illustrative of the hundreds that are processed by the CPD each week. All cases begin with a complaint brought by an aggrieved consumer. When an agent receives a complaint, he or she immediately contacts the respondent business to report that a consumer has lodged a complaint and that an investigation has begun. The investigator does little more than ask the parties what happened. After speaking to both the consumer and the business, the agent makes a decision about what the complaint actually involves.

The staff's freedom of action is literally unchecked with respect to the investigation of complaints because the assessment of whether a complaint contains grounds for negotiation or resolution is entirely the investigator's — in practice it is never reviewed. All future questions about how to handle this complaint, possible routes of negotiation, the prospects of litigation, and the probable and likely dispositions depend upon this initial evaluation.

The agent assesses the veracity and integrity of the parties; ordinarily, he or she will not pursue a case if the parties do not substantially agree about the facts [Silbey, 1981:863]. The investigator also assesses the legal issues presented by the stipulated facts. Often the law provides no clear remedy; most cases that come to the CPD do not involve obvious illegal practices or assertions of unquestionable rights. Nevertheless, even if the complaint alleges a clear violation of law, the investigator must determine whether and how to attack it within the variety of legal means available, and may decide not to proceed with this investigation [Wilcox, 1972; Black 1974:38; Davis, 1972:88; Bittner, 1974; Lobenthal, 1970; Macaulay, 1979]. In the process of making these evaluations, the investigator forms an attitude about the "justice" of a complaint, and the likelihood of resolving it successfully. The investigator's best efforts are reserved for those "good" cases which have the best chance of a satisfactory disposition.

After a preliminary inquiry an investigator has two options: to drop the case because it seems without merit, or to continue with the case seeking a satisfactory disposition. If the agent decides to continue the case, he or she begins to negotiate with the parties; investigation gives way to mediation. The negotiations may be simple and the complaint resolved with one or two phone calls, or they may involve many calls such as in the Pontiac radiator case. More often than not, cases remain open in the investigator's file for months. Letters and telephone calls have not succeeded in securing any refund for the consumer. The case has reached what agents call a "state of limbo". It is open, nothing is happening, and the parties seem unable to reach any resolution. Most cases are neither open or closed — they are indeterminate.

Consumer protection is an endless process. It is endless because most cases have no clear boundaries or inherent conclusions. If a case cannot be resolved immediately to the satisfaction of the complaining consumer, it is the agent's tolerance and the agent's threshold of satisfaction that is critical for resolution. Despite the reactive stance of the agency, it is not the interested party's threshold of action that determines case disposition. Cases can be closed and resolved without grievances falling below the level of the consumer's or the businessman's interest because recourse to an alternative forum are costly and largely unavailable. Because consumer protection generally ends when the attorney general's agent closes a case, agents are reluctant to close cases unsatisfactorily. Thus, case mediation is frequently a series of impasses. The consumer wants his restitution, the business wants to be left alone, and the investigator wants a number to add to the office's record of success, i.e., satisfactorily closed cases. These interests govern case processing and militate against encouraging more consumers to complain, such as other Pontiac owners.

Consumer protection is also endless because complaints seemingly flow forever. There will always be more cases; there is no need to go looking for them. The endlessness of the case flow not only militated against looking for other like cases, it also worked against adopting other enforcement strategies. Once the attorney general began to accept consumer complaints, a reasonable decision in and of itself, the volume became overwhelming and the division became a victim of its own efforts: the more successful it was at resolving consumer complaints, the more complaints arrived and inundated the office. Coping with the flow of complaints required so much work that managing the cases fully occupied the office's resources. Consumer protection did not have to consist solely of case-by-case mediation; but once case-by-case mediation began, consumer protection ground to a halt. Coping with this first stage of consumer protection required so much work that, in effect, it co-opted any decision about what the job of consumer protection was to be.

Consequences of Responsive Implementation: Cooperation between Regulators and the Regulated

Both liberals and conservatives alike live comfortably with a public policy process in which power is delegated to those most immediately interested in it. It is a matter of incorporating parties having recognizably legitimate interests and effectively shutting out opposing positions and the public [See McConnell, 1963, 1966; Miller, 1959; Kolko, 1965, 1967; Weinstein, 1968; Weinstein and Eakins, 1970]. Participation replaces standards of implementation as contingency replaces law [Lowi, 1967:18]. This research suggests that the consequences of including private interests in the public policy process, in terms of problem definition and "self administration," is exacerbated by the effective incorporation of those same interests into the law enforcement process as well.

Mediation is generally regarded as a voluntary noncoercive process in which the third party has no power to impose a binding decision and relies upon the willingness of the parties to compromise. It allows an *equal* juxtaposition of the interests of each party, unconstrained by normative or legal priorities such as those contained in the consumer protection act. Mediation, in contrast to adjudication, arbitration, or some form of structured aggregation of interests, *incorporates* perspectives, values, and interests of *each* party *into* the outcome, thus legitimizing and enfranchising conflicting perspectives without choosing between them. It transforms the mechanism, the consumer protection law and its enforcement agency, that was created to provide some balance between these unequal interests from a mechanism for representing consumer claims to an agency for mediating them. When informal conciliatory mechanisms such as mediation and negotiation are adopted as law enforcement strategies, they become the behavioral means of cooperation between regulators and the regulated. Mediation of grievances and consumer disputes becomes a means through which the demands and perspectives of business can be incorporated into the definition of consumer protection itself. It is just this, for example, that Kagan suggests is the virtue of cooperative rather than legalistic enforcement strategies [Kagan, 1980].

Of course, mediation by an attorney general's office is not an example of classic mediation. Here, third-party intervention is inherently coercive. The CPD has the ability, if not to impose a binding solution, at least to ask a court to impose a compulsory solution. But the attorney general is not omnipotent and people succeed in not being coerced. In a six-year period from 1968 to 1974, the attorney general pursued only four consumer complaints through formal litigation. Case processing in the CPD can be characterized as mediation because in the negotiation of consumer complaints, there is a real gain for both sides. The CPD tended to accept whatever the defendant offered that, at the same time, satisfied the complainant. The consumer received something that mollified his interest in complaining further; the business continued operating as in the past and at the same time silenced the complaining consumer.

The satisfactory resolution of consumer complaints has been defined by consumer protection officials as meeting the demands of the complaining consumer without recourse to formal litigation. It is the most consistent and time-consuming work of consumer protection offices [Cranston, 1979; Steele, 1975a, 1975b; Nader, 1981; Daynard, 1979; Ramsey, 1981]. Satisfaction or success means negotiating a settlement between an aggrieved party and an offender. Success, according to this policy, requires the cooperation of business; it necessitates securing for the consumer what he or she did not receive from the original transaction — the product or service or money refunded.

What consequences follow from this policy? Responsive regulation fails to make law general. To Fuller [1969], this is a critical variable for determining legality. To Lowi [1969], this is characteristic of the replacement of the commonweal by private interest groups. Indeed, this policy is a failure to enforce and apply the law. It reduces law enforcement to a circumstantial and private relationship between the negotiating parties [Gulliver, 1973; Aubert, 1963] in which the public and third parties have no roles in this exclusive relationship. The elimination of public representation and the exclusivity of the negotiating situation are the most distinctive and telling aspects of cooperation. They are the key to understanding the practical meaning of public regulation.

Responsive regulation, by failing to make law general, incorporates business interests into law enforcement. Cooperative regulation protects trade because the market remains in the control of business. We have increasingly numerous accounts of the ways in which sellers accommodate customers through the complaint process [Ross and Littlefield, 1978]. This accommodation of business to the complaining consumer, encouraged, supported and facilitated by the CPD, also determines what relief will be granted. Thus, the level and extent of consumer protection depend in part on the goodwill of those against whom the protection is supposed to function. Through accommodation, the seller retains control over the outcome, thereby reducing additional costs of regulation [Ramsey, 1981].

By failing to make law general, consumer protection takes place in a sphere where one party is more powerful and where major advantages rest with business. First, the reliance upon case by case resolution of consumer complaints, that constitutes the major form of consumer protection in the United States, leaves the initiative with the complainant. Like the classical model of the market that consumer protection was intended to alter, case-by-case resolution of consumer problems relies upon the knowledge and aggressiveness of the consumer to obtain redress for unsatisfactory transactions. The consumer must bear the opportunity costs of satisfactory consumption, costs that are extraordinarily high in modern technological societies. Regulation is costly; it forces business to accept costs that have been heretofore "externalized".

The disaggregation of consumer complaints allows the business complained against to respond to consumer complaints individually. Although this may suggest that consumer complaints would therefore become more burdensome to business, because of their number, than if they were joined in their demands, it also allows a juxtaposition of the business's skills and resources to the consumer's already heavily taxed and diminished capabilities in the marketplace.

The accommodation inherent in cooperative and responsive regulation disguises political content by obscuring the inequality between consumers and business [see Abel, 1981]. For instance, an angry consumer confronting a mass seller or a recalcitrant merchant cannot help but see the confrontation as one of power. The mediation of the CPD transforms the dispute, making it appear to the consumer that the sides are now more evenly balanced. In other words, the seller, an adversary, is replaced by the mediator, apparently neutral (or even predisposed to the consumer) hiding the imbalance of the struggle. Of course, the individuation of grievances inherent in law disguises their political content. And yet, the neutrality and passivity of negotiation and mediation in the attorney general's office allowed inequalities and power differentials to affect the outcome. Therefore, the disaggregation of issues, typical of the legal process, is exacerbated when mediation is used as a regulatory process.

Moreover, from the businessman's point of view, this policy makes consumer protection a new kind of tax on business activities. Traditional wisdom assumes that law functions either as a deterrent, in the sense that behavior will be changed to accommodate or at least take account of legal proscriptions, or in more contemporary analyses, as a factor to be considered in a cost analysis of doing business. For example, Malcolm Feeley suggests that law should be looked at as a means of altering the costs of engaging in certain activities; law should be viewed as a pricing system that is more elaborate than a simple calculus of compliance. "Law creates categories through which people must filter their thinking and organize their lives." It creates "a complex pricing system which not only puts a value on the wants people may be inclined to pursue, but also affects them indirectly in that people also must adjust their wants to the behavior of others whose preferences in turn are shaped by law" [1976:515; see Holmes, 1897].

When an investigator notifies a businessman that a complaint has been lodged against him, he usually responds to the attorney general's representative by saying, "I'll see what I can do." A few weeks or months later, the businessman may get another call, or perhaps he will never be called again. The consumer has given up; the attorney general's agent has other cases to pursue [Silbey, 1981]. But, if the businessman does receive a subsequent call, and he is induced to make a refund or perform some service, there is no assurance that he will have adopted practices that conform to law. The merchant will have acceded to this consumer's demand in this particular case.

The consumer protection agency, in this sense, acts not as a regulatory agency establishing rules and regulations for business practice, but more like a police officer giving out parking tickets to those parties who get caught violating the law [see Packer, 1968]. In nine out of ten unsatisfactory transactions, businesses will not be approached about a complaint by the consumer or by the attorney general's office [Best and Andreasen, 1976; 1977]. But if on that tenth time, the business is required by the CPD to make a refund, the satisfaction of this consumer's complaints acts as a fine that symbolically covers the other unsatisfactory transactions that were not complained about. The CPD will have functioned as a tax collection agency, and like all taxes that permit a business to continue its normal operation, the costs will be passed on to the consumer. Law enforcement can never get at all violators; in this case, regulation does not even control calculating violators.

There is a sense in which cooperation means not only achieving less compliance than what was hoped for or possible, but in also achieving something different than compliance. It means that cooperative regulation will be accommodating. It will acclimate consumers to the ways of business; it will educate business to the demands of consumers. For example, a roofing contractor does more or less the same job at all times. If sometimes a roof leaks after it is installed, and if every once in a while he receives a complaint about poor workmanship from the attorney general's office, he will most likely regard these complaints as a nuisance. Will the roofer change the way he regularly does his job? A search of the literature suggests that the problems of the market are pervasive, small injuries, errors, miscalculations, and insufficiences that are often unpredictable and irreparable [see Rice, 1968; University of Pennsylvania Law Review, 1966; Silbey, 1978; Best and Andreasen, 1976; 1977; Nader, 1980]. Is the effort to resolve these individual consumer complaints merely acclimating consumers to the realities of the market at the expense of providing structural remedies to correct the source of the problem? If the most pervasive problems of the market are really roofs that sometimes leak, automobile repairs that are only sometimes effective, and toasters that last only six months, can one realistically legislate corrections for consumer complaints in general? Are the efforts of the CPD to satisfy the complaining consumer providing Band-Aids and thereby creating a mechanism for accommodating the consumer to the prevailing organization of production and business? Is this not what cooperation really means?

Summary and Conclusion

The CPD adopted a policy of case-by-case mediation of consumer complaints as a means of enforcing the Consumer Protection Act. It seemed a reasonable and practical thing to do given the limited resources, lack of administrative and legal history under the legislation, and cross pressures of consumer and business lobbying. The CPD could help individual consumers with immediate needs hoping that eventually these would accumulate to change the market and improve generally the situation of all consumers. At the same time, the agency could begin to educate the business community about their responsibilities under the law, allow them opportunity to adjust their practices, and develop the voluntary compliance that would be necessary to actually change market conditions.

Often all parties were satisfied. The consumer received some moderation of his loss; the businessman met a particular consumer's demand without necessarily having to change ordinary practices, or respond to consumers who had not complained. And the attorney general's agent could claim one more consumer case satisfactorily resolved by the good efforts of this public office, thus testifying to the effectiveness of legal regulation. An issue, complaint, dispute, however one wishes to label the event, was resolved within the limited domain of these parties. The activities of the CPD reflected what the agency understood its mandate to be.

Nevertheless, the apparently mundane routine of mediating consumer complaints has cumulative and systematic effects, the clearest of which is the incorporation of business interests and perspectives into law enforcement processes. Dynamic responsiveness seems to protect the ongoing organization of business, its relationship to the consuming public and the distribution of power, rights, obligations and resources between them. Cooperative regulation protects trade because it continually uses up all available resources, and, in the case of consumer protection, does not address itself to the elimination of deceptive practices. It helps compensate complaining victims and the silencing of complaints protects the organization of trade.

In this chapter I have not meant to be ironic, nor to begrudge sympathy to those who claim that they are doing as well as could be expected. I have not argued that subversion of the law is intended; but neither is it unusual. Indeed, I have not suggested that consumer protection ought to be or can be "fixed up" at the point where individual case resolution is adopted as a policy. A reactive, complaint-based system does not necessarily preclude the possibility that an agency could take on bad business practices. The agency itself is a repeat player, after all, and can adjust its policies to reflect the consequences of its past strategies; policy implementation is cyclical and responsive in this way. Although changing case-by-case mediation to something else will change what consumer protection is, that too will entail its own consequences. Any form of regulation of trade will have its own consequences, and weaknesses.

Finally, it is important to ask if there is any value in responsive and cooperative regulation? Obviously there is.[6] If there are situations where pro forma compliance does not achieve the intent of the law, for example, communication and protection of rights inherent in Miranda warnings or informed consent, then incremental and cooperative modes of regulation may be necessary. But where there are genuine abuses, questions of scale, repetitiveness and a desire for economy of effort, direct enforcement may be more effective [see Gifford, 1980]. The appropriateness of a particular enforcement strategy cannot be defined in advance; it will evolve in response to particular situations and mandates. However, the integration of mandates with environments requires a dynamic vision of social responsibility lest it degenerate into co-optation or unreasonableness. This tension is not easily resolved, because responsibility is not consonant with accountability and the requirements of law are not necessarily the requirements of justice.

Notes

1. *Caveat emptor* is latin and derived from *caveo,* to be on one's guard, to beware, or to avoid, and *emptor* is defined as a buyer or purchaser; thus, it can be translated as an injunction, to the buyer, to beware. The words are of Roman origin but were inconsistent with classical mores and law. If they were actual in Roman or later use, they must have had specific intent, limited usage and could never have been meant as a general rule, principle or philosophy (Hamilton, 1931: 1133, 1157).

2. Caveat emptor first appears in written works in 1534 in the course of a legal discussion by Fitzherbert on horse trading, "if he be tame and have been ryden upon, then caveat emptor". Fitzherbert further cautioned the "buyer to make make sure of the goodness of his bargain in horse flesh while yet there is time, if the horse be sold without a warranty it is 'at the other's peril', for his eyes and his taste ought to be his judge" (Hamilton, 1931: 1164). By the beginning of the seventeenth century the maxim is well known, and at least twice set down by Coke in his treatises. The commonly cited passage from Coke runs, "by the civil law every man is bound to warrant the things he selleth or conveyeth, albeit there is not express warranty, either in deed or in law; but the common law bindeth him not, for caveat emptor". The phrase is first discovered in the law reports in 1601 as an aside in a case concerning the ravishment of a wealthy ward (*Moore v. Hussey Hobart, 93 Eng. Rep.* 243) but it is in 1603 in *Chandeloa v. Lopus, 79 Eng. Rep.* 3, that the principle of the vendor's nonresponsibility for his wares is formulated in such authoritative manner that it has been cited as the foundation for succeeding decisions over the centuries.

3. Since the caveat emptor was not compatible with the principles of civil law, not a product of the law merchant, and inconsistent with the values and organization of traditional society, Walton Hamilton hypothesizes that it must have been a product of the folk thought of the masses. Perhaps it was a response to the growing presence of vagabond traders, wayfaring palmers, "peripetetic peddlers with gew-gaws and ornaments, strangers here today and there tomorrow, wayfaring men of no place and without law." These men plied their trade outside the market towns and regulated commerce. "In such wares, and among such men, one had to trade at his peril." Caveat emptor came to be the thing we know today from increasingly common situations of unremedial grievance. "The wisdom seems to be the afterthought of the good man who has bargained . . . once too often" [Hamilton, 1931: 1163].

4. Fewer than 1 percent of all consumer complaints resulted in litigation. During the period between March 1968 and December 1974, the CPD received, investigated, and disposed of anywhere between 200 and 700 complaints per week, depending upon how they were counted. It attained some sort of satisfactory resolution in approximately half of them. Satisfaction was determined by the consumer's acceptance of what a business offered in negotiation with the attorney general's agent. These resolutions created about four million dollars of restitutions and savings to consumers. But the records of formal legal proceedings entered into by the CPD is infinitesimally small in relation to the number of cases handled. There were altogether fewer than 30 petitions for orders of discontinuance and no more than four suits seeking injunctions. Steele [1975a] states

that approximately 4.5 percent of the cases received in the Illinois attorney general's office were litigated. While the difference in the two states is significant if contrasted to each other, in neither state did litigation represent a sizable portion of the office's work.

5. It has been suggested that mediation rarely approximates the ideal of noncoercive dispute resolution [Silbey and Merry, 1980].

6. Bardach and Kagan [1982] present an articulate and thorough argument against unreasonableness (the imposition of uniform regulatory requirements in situations where they do not make sense) and unresponsiveness (the failure to consider arguments by regulated enterprises that exceptions should be made).

References

Abel, Richard (1981). *The Politics of Informal Justice.* (2 vols.) New York: Academic Press.

Andreasen, Alan R. (1975) *The Disadvantaged Consumer.* New York: Free Press.

Argyris, Chris et al. (1978). *Regulating Business: The Search For an Optimum.* San Francisco: Institute for Contemporary Studies.

Aubert, Wilhelm (1963). Competition and Dissensus: Two Types of Conflict and Conflict Resolution, 7 *Journal of Conflict Resolution* 26.

Ball, Harry and Lawrence Friedman (1965). The Use of Criminal Sanctions in the Enforcement of Economic Legislation: A Sociological View, 17 *Stanford Law Review* 197.

Bardach, Eugene and Robert A. Kagan (1982). *Going by the Book: the Problem of Regulatory Unreasonableness:* Philadelphia: Temple University Press.

Bernstein, Marver (1955). *Regulating Business by Independent Commission.* Princeton, N.J.: Princeton University Press.

Best, Arthur and Alan Andreasen (1976). *Talking Back to Business: Voiced and Unvoiced Consumer Complaints.* Washington, D.C.: Center for the Study of Responsive Law.

——— (1977) Consumer Response to Unsatisfactory Purchases: A Survey of Perceiving Defects, Voicing Complaints and Obtaining Redress, 11 *Law and Society Review* 701.

Bittner, Egon (1974). Florence Nightingale in Pursuit of Willie Sutton, in H. Jacob (ed.), *The Potential for Reform of Criminal Justice,* Beverly Hills: Sage Publications.

Black, Charles (1974). *Capital Punishment.* New York: W. W. Norton.

Callman, Rudolf (1950). *Unfair Competition and Trade Marks.* Chicago: Callaghan.

Caplovitz, David (1963). *The Poor Pay More.* New York: Free Press.

Columbia Law Review (1956): Regulation of advertising, 56 *Columbia Law Review* 1018.

Cox, Edward F., Robert C. Fellmeth, John E. Schutz (1969). *The Nader Report on the Federal Trade Commission.* New York: Grove Press.

Cranston, Ross (1979). *Regulating Business: Law and Consumer Agencies.* London: The Macmillan Press, Ltd.

Davis, Kenneth C. (1969). *Discretionary Justice.* Baton Rouge: Louisiana State University Press.

———— (1972). *Administrative Law Text*. St. Paul: West Publishing Co.

Daynard, Richard Allen (1980). *Informal Resolution and Formal Adjudication of Consumer Complaints by a Licensing Authority: A Case Study*, M.I.T. Ph.D. Dissertation.

Dixon, Paul Rand, (1966). Federal State Cooperation to Combat Unfair Trade Practices, 39 *State Government* 37.

Edelman, Murray (1964). *The Symbolic Uses of Politics*. Urbana: University of Illinois Press.

Eovaldi, Thomas L. and Joan E. Gestrin (1971). Justice for Consumers: The Mechanisms of Redress, 6 *Northwestern University Law Review* 281.

Feeley, Malcolm (1976). The Concept of the Law in Social Science: A Critique and Notes on an Expanded View, 10 *Law and Society Review* 497.

Fuller, Lon (1969). *The Morality of Law*. New Haven: Yale University Press.

Gifford, Daniel J. (1980). Discretionary Decisionmaking in the Regulatory Agencies: A Conceptual Framework. Paper delivered at Law and Society Meeting, Madison, Wisconsin, June 1980.

Greenberg, Joel H. (1967). Speech to the Massachusetts House of Representatives. Unpublished, July 26, 1967.

————. Memorandum to Robert Quinn, Speaker of the Massachusetts House of Representatives, March 13, 1968.

Gulliver, P.H. (1973). Negotiation as a Model of Dispute Resolution: Toward a General Model, 7 *Law and Society Review* 667.

Hamilton, Walton (1931). The Ancient Maxim Caveat Emptor, 40 *Yale Law Journal* 1133.

———— (1957). *The Politics of Industry*. New York: Alfred Knopf.

Harvard Law Review (1967). Developments in the law of deceptive advertising, 80 *Harvard Law Review*, 1005.

Herring, E.P. (1936). *Public Administration and the Public Interest*. New York: McGraw Hill.

Holmes, O.W. (1897). The Path of the Law, 10 *Harvard Law Review* 457.

Huntington, Samuel (1952). The Marasmus of the ICC: The Commission, the Railroads and the Public Interest, 61 *Yale Law Journal* 467.

Huntington, Samuel, E. Morgan, and D. Williams (1953). The ICC Revisited: A Colloquy, 63 *Yale Law Journal* 44.

Jowell, Jeffrey (1975). *Law and Bureaucracy: Administrative Discretion and the Limits of Legal Action*. Port Washington, N.Y.: Dunellen Publications, Kennikat Press.

Kadish, S. (1963). Some Observations on the Use of Criminal Sanctions in Enforcing Economic Regulation, 30 *University of Chicago Law Review*, 423.

Kadish, Mortimer H. and Sanford H. Kadish (1973). *Discretion to Disobey*. Palo Alto: Stanford University Press.

Kagan, Robert (1980). The Good Inspector. Paper presented at Law and Society Meeting, Madison Wisconsin, June 1980.

King, Donald W. and Kathleen A. McEvoy (1976). *A National Survey of the Complaint Handling Procedures Used by Consumers*. Rockville, Md: King Research, Inc., Center for Quantitative Sciences (conducted for Technical Assistance Research Programs Inc., and Office of Consumer Affairs, U.S. Department of Health, Education and Welfare.)

Kolko, Gabriel (1965). *Railroads and Regulation*. Princeton: Princeton University Press.

———— (1967). *The Triumph of Conservatism*. Chicago: Quadrangle Books.

Leiserson, Avery (1942). *Administrative Regulation: A Study of Interests*. Chicago: University of Chicago Press.

Lilley, William and James G. Miller III (1977). The New Social Regulation, 47 *The Public Interest 49*.

Lipsky, Michael (1976). Toward a Theory of Street Level Bureaucracy'' in Willis D. Hawley (ed.), *Theoretical Perspectives on Urban Politics*. Englewood Cliffs, New Jersey: Prentice-Hall.

——— (1980). *Street Level Bureaucracy*. New York: Russell Sage Foundation.

Litt, Edgar (1965). *The Political Cultures of Massachusetts*. Cambridge: Massachusetts Institute of Technology Press.

Llewellyn, Karl (1936). The Warranty of Quality, 36 *Columbia Law Review* 699.

Lobenthal, Joseph, Jr. (1970). Buying Out, Selling Out, Copping Out: Law in the City, 30 *Antioch Review* 195.

Lowi, Theodore (1967). The Public Philosophy: Interest Group Liberalism, 61 *American Political Science Review* 5.

——— (1969; 1978). *The End of Liberalism*. New York: W.W. Norton.

Macaulay, Stewart (1963). Non-Contractual Relations in Business: A Preliminary Study, 28 *American Sociological Review* 55.

——— (1966). *Law and the Balance of Power*. New York: Russell Sage Foundation.

——— (1979). Lawyers and Consumer Protection Laws, 14 *Law and Society Review* 115.

Magnuson, Warren and T. Carper (1968). *The Dark Side of the Marketplace*. Englewood Cliffs: Prentice-Hall.

Mayhew, David (1968). Massachusetts Split Level Bipartyism, in G. Goodwin and Victoria Schuyck (eds.) *Party Politics in New England States*. Durham, New Hampshire: New England Center for Continuing Education.

McConnell, Grant (1963). The Spirit of Private Government, 52 *American Political Science Review* 754.

———. (1966). *Private Power and American Democracy*. New York: A. Knopf.

Meade, Robert (1968). Memorandum of Assistant Attorney General Robert Meade to Joel Greenberg, Massachusetts State Representative. Unpublished, March 1968.

Miller, Arthur S. (1959). *Private Government and the Constitution*. Santa Barbara, Calif.: Fund for the Republic.

Morgan, Charles S. (1952). A Critique of the Marasmus of the ICC, 62 *Yale Law Journal* 171.

Morrow, C. (1940). The Warranty of Quality, 14 *Tulane Law Review* 327.

Nadel, Mark (1971). *The Politics of Consumer Protection*. Indianapolis: Bobbs Merrill.

Nader, Laura (1980). *No Access to Justice*. New York: Academic Press.

National Association of Attorneys General, Committee on the Office of Attorney General (1971). *Report on the Office of Attorney General*.

Orren, Karen (1974). *Corporate Power and Social Change*. Baltimore: Johns Hopkins University Press.

Packer, Herbert (1968). *The Limits of the Criminal Sanction*. Palo Alto: Stanford University Press.

Palamountain, Joseph Jr. (1965). The Dolchin Case and the Federal Trade Commission, and The Federal Trade Commission and the Indiana Standard Case, in Edwin A. Bock (ed.) *Government Regulation of Business*. Englewood Cliffs, New Jersey: Prentice-Hall.

Ramsey, Iain D.C. (1981). Consumer Redress Mechanisms for Poor-Quality and Defective Products, 31 *University of Toronto Law Journal* 117.

Rice, David (1968). Remedies, Enforcement Procedures and the Duality of Consumer Transaction Problems, 48 *Boston University Law Review* 559.

Ross, H. Laurence (1970). *Settled Out of Court*. Chicago: Aldine.

Ross, H. Laurence and Neil O. Littlefield (1978). Complaint as a Problem-Solving Mechanism, 12 *Law and Society Review* 199.

Schrag, Philip (1972). *Counsel for the Deceived*. New York: Random House, Pantheon Books.

Serber, David (1980). Resolution and Rhetoric: Managing Complaints in the California Department of Insurance, in Laura Nader (ed.) *No Access to Law*. New York: Academic Press.

Shapiro, Martin (1968). *The Supreme Court and Administrative Agencies*. New York: Free Press.

Shea, Dermot (1967). Executive Secretary of Massachusetts Consumer's Council. Remarks before Mercantile Affairs Committee, Massachusetts, July 10, 1967.

Silbey, Susan S. (1978). Consumer Justice: The Massachusetts Attorney General's Office of Consumer Protection. University of Chicago, Ph.D. Dissertation.

——— (1981). Case Processing: Consumer Protection in an Attorney General's Office, 15 *Law and Society Review* 881.

Silbey, Susan S. and Egon Bittner (1982). The Availability of Law. 4 *Law and Policy Quarterly* 399.

Silbey, Susan S. and Sally E. Merry (1980). Coercion and Legitimacy in Informal Community Justice. Unpublished manuscript.

Steele, Eric (1975a). Fraud, Dispute and the Consumer: Responding to Consumer Complaints, 123 *University of Pennsylvania Law Review* 1107.

———. (1975b). The Dilemma of Consumer Fraud: Prosecute or Mediate, 61 *American Bar Association Journal* 1230.

Stone, C. (1975). *Where the Law Ends*. New York: Harper and Row.

Traylor, William (1969). Consumer Protection Against Sellers' Misrepresentations, 20 *Mercer Law Review* 414–431.

University of Pennsylvania Law Review (1966). Translating Sympathy for Deceived Consumers into Effective Programs for Protection, 111 *University of Pennsylvania Law Review* 667.

Weinstein, James (1968). *Corporate Ideal in the Liberal State: 1900–1918*. Boston: Beacon Press.

Weinstein, James and David Eakins (1970). *For A New America*. New York: Vintage Books.

Wilcox, Albert F. (1972). *The Decision to Prosecute*. London: Butterworths.

Williston, Samuel (1948). *The Law Governing Sales of Goods at Common Law and Under the Uniform Sales Act*. New York: Baker Voorhies Co.

Wilson, James Q. (1973). *Political Organizations*. New York: Basic Books.

——— (ed.) (1980). *The Politics of Regulation*. New York: Basic Books.

8 THE ECONOMICS OF REGULATORY ENFORCEMENT

Cento G. Veljanovski

Introduction

Regulation seeks to alter the behavior of those regulated. Whatever the form of legal rules, compliance must be induced by some means; the law must be enforced if it is to have any impact. Thus it is legal rules and their enforcement that together shape the incentives and deterrents that attempt to alter the behavior of those regulated and induce compliance with the law. It would follow from these self-evident statements that a full account of the regulatory process would seek, as a matter of crucial importance, a thorough understanding of enforcement and compliance processes. Unfortunately, the research to date has compartmentalized the study of regulation, focusing usually on only one stage of the regulatory process, such as standard-setting, enforcement, bureaucratic behavior or the impact and efficiency of specific regulations. With few exceptions surprisingly

An early version of this chapter was presented to the conference Perspectives on Regulation: Law, Discretion, and Bureaucratic Behavior, May 1980, jointly sponsored by the Baldy Center for Law and Social Policy and the Oxford (England) Center for Socio-Legal Studies at the State University of New York-Buffalo. The comments of conference participants and Keith Hawkins are gratefully acknowledged.

little attention has been devoted to explaining the interrelationships between different stages of the regulatory process. In this chapter enforcement and compliance behavior will be related to the nature of legal rules using an economic framework.

Penalty and Compliance Enforcement Models

Reiss and Biderman [1980:274–299] distinguish two stylized "forms" or "models" of regulatory law enforcement — penalty and compliance systems. The penalty system is what most people have in mind when thinking about law enforcement. The objective of this model of enforcement is to detect and prosecute violations of the law and to use the legal penalties to punish lawbreakers. A penalty system is a very legalistic approach to enforcement that employs prosecutions and legal sanctions as the routine enforcement instruments. It is a popular misconception that regulatory enforcement pursues such a penalty approach. Yet there is an increasing body of evidence indicating that many enforcement agencies in areas of social regulation pursue a different strategy.[1] They seek to induce compliance with the law through extralegal methods using legal sanctions as an enforcement device of last resort. The enforcement/compliance process is typically one involving direct negotiations, accommodations, threats, and tradeoffs between enforcement official and violator that result in compromises and modifications of the law that are sensitive to the economic and practical difficulties surrounding compliance. Compliance systems involve a high level of discretion in law enforcement and infrequent, highly selective prosecutions thus merging rule-making and enforcement decisions with the *effective* legal (i.e. judicial) decisions being made by the enforcement official. Moreover the motive for invoking legal sanctions is quite different in a compliance system; it is not so much to punish the violator but to signal the breakdown of negotiations and to prevent future law breaking.

Underlying the compliance system is a radically different model of regulation. Regulation is not viewed as a threat that is externally imposed on the firm but is, to use Holden's [1966] phrase, "regulation as bargaining." The bargaining features of law enforcement are, it is suggested, pervasive. In all areas of law, justice is negotiated: over 95 percent of tort claims and criminal cases in the United States are resolved not by formal legal procedure, but informal "bargains" between the parties in the form of out-of-court settlements and the negotiated guilty plea respectively [see Ross, 1970 and Lachman and McLaughlin, 1979][2] In civil, criminal, and regulatory areas there are sound economic reasons why law enforcement should emphasize cooperative solutions — it is often a cheaper method of enforcement.[3] Enforcement is thus best viewed initially as an implicit bargain between regulator and violator motivated by the cost-savings to both parties from avoiding legal proceedings and behaving cooperatively.

Rule Efficiency — the Inclusiveness Problem

Enforcement activities are facilitated and constrained by the form, stringency, and coverage of the law. In the regulatory area the primary motive for law breaking is economic: compliance is too costly and offenses are usually the by-product of a profitable activity. Often they are connected with some socially productive pursuit of benefit to society, e.g., the production of goods. This fact leads to a certain moral and legal ambivalence towards regulatory offenses (e.g., Why are fines in Britain usually so low?) that, to the economist at least, has a rational basis. Those offenses that cost more to avoid (in terms of direct expenditures and foregone production) than the harm they impose should ideally not be deterred because compliance would impose greater costs on society. This efficiency criterion implies that a rational enforcement strategy will not seek to induce full compliance nor even maximum feasible compliance with the law, but cost-justified compliance.[4] Moreover, the performance of a regulatory system should be measured by the extent to which it achieves social objectives and not by legalistic criteria or indices such as prosecution and conviction rates.

In practice the structure of legal rules may depart radically from that which would induce cost-effective compliance. The law will be both under- and overinclusive. Many socially undesirable activities and practices will be unregulated so that the law will be limited in coverage i.e. underinclusive. Also, the body of legal rules may embrace activities that are socially desirable and which should not be deterred or they may be too stringent, compelling practices that are excessively costly and/or ineffective. This is the problem of rule overinclusion. It is this problem of rule overinclusion that is an important factor in understanding enforcement and compliance behavior.[5]

Regulatory offenses give rise to losses; deterring these offenses is costly. The efficiency of a regulatory system involves comparing the avoided social losses with three principal costs: the costs of designing and implementing legal standards (rulemaking costs), the costs of enforcing the standards (enforcement costs) and the costs that they impose on the regulated industry (compliance costs). An "efficient" system of enforcement is one that minimizes the sum of these three costs plus social losses inflicted by regulatory offenses.[6] Since this chapter is concerned with enforcement, rule-making costs will be ignored except insofar as they explain the overinclusion problem. As far as the day-to-day enforcement of the law is concerned, rule-making costs are a sunk cost, i.e., one that has been incurred and does not influence the enforcement officials' decisions. A rational enforcement official will therefore suboptimize; that is, he will minimize the sum of the social losses and enforcement and compliance costs given the legal standards in existence, and other legal, budgetary, and political constraints. In this framework, a regulation is overinclusive if compliance is excessively costly or results in an insignificant amelioration of the harm to be avoided for a subset of regulated firms and/or industries. Or, defined somewhat more technically, over-inclusion results when the marginal avoided social or external losses from complying with a standard are less than the sum of compliance and enforcement costs.

The problem of overinclusion arises from the costs of designing and redrafting standards (rule-making costs). In order for legal standards to be cost-effective, the standard-setting body must possess considerable information on the technological and economic conditions surrounding abatement and the degree of harm caused by hazards. The cost of collecting and processing this information will tend to limit the extent to which standards match the least-cost method of abatement. These information and implementation costs will tend to be greater the more complex, heterogeneous, and/or extensive the activity that is being controlled. In addition, the standard-setting body will be involved in consultation with those regulated and interested parties, such as trade unions, giving rise to another set of costs (negotiation and consultation costs) associated with the standard-setting process itself and delay in the enactment of regulations.

The combination of these factors will lead to a regulatory framework that is poorly matched to the cost-effective means of achieving regulatory objectives. Many breaches of the law will be technical ones that have very little to do with encouraging socially desirable behavior or that achieve incremental improvements at disproportionate costs. The problem of overinclusion thus arises and will be accentuated over time, especially when changes in technology and economic conditions are rapid.

Overinclusiveness can be dealt with in a number of ways. The most obvious response is more discriminating regulations tailored to the specific technological and economic circumstances of the regulated industry. However, the rule-making costs of this approach will be prohibitive so that, at best, the individualization of standards will be crude. The individualized standards approach also increases both the number and detail of regulations and this complexity will affect the level of compliance because it requires those regulated to have extensive knowledge of the law. Moreover if enforcement costs are related to the number and complexity of regulations to be enforced, as it seems reasonable to assume, this approach will give rise to relatively high enforcement costs. Finally, individualized standards do not adequately deal with the problem of obsolete standards. Indeed, this problem is exacerbated because of the greater number of more detailed regulations.

A second rule response to overinclusion is the contingent standard that determines the offender's obligation to comply with the law on the basis of a ''cost-benefit'' test. Those regulated would have a legal duty to comply with a specific regulation only if the gravity of the risk (social loss) that would be avoided exceeded the compliance costs, that is, when compliance would be socially cost-minimizing.[7] This approach makes the firm's liability to comply with the law contingent on a standard not being overinclusive. A drawback of the contingent standard is that it creates uncertainty as to the firm's legal obligations and this in turn will impair the effectiveness of the law in deterring offenses. Regulations that employ a ''cost-benefit'' criterion to determine liability require those subject to the law to have fairly detailed information about enforcement practices and case law. However, the trade-off between the precision of legal obligations and the flexibility needed to deal with overinclusion is one that is pervasive and has to be dealt with in most legal contexts.

The third, and probably most effective, way to deal with rule overinclusion is to adopt a flexible and discretionary enforcement approach. This approach involves the selective use of legal and extralegal sanctions based on firm-specific circumstances such as the ability to comply and the gravity of the offense.[8] Discretionary enforcement shifts the cost-effectiveness decision out of the rule-making phase of the regulatory process onto the enforcement official who can be expected to have more detailed knowledge of the compliance potential of different classes of offenders. Those standards that are obsolete or overinclusive for some firms are not enforced, while others that are too stringent are modified in direct negotiations between the inspector and the firm. The crucial importance of enforcement procedures in understanding regulation is graphically illustrated by the discretionary law enforcement alternative: rule-making and enforcement processes merge, with effective legal rules being determined by enforcement officials.

In this chapter it is suggested that regulatory enforcement can be best explained in economic terms. It is hypothesized that enforcement officials behave *as if* they are conscious of the overinclusion problem and seek only to induce efficient compliance from industry. That is, they attempt to minimize the sum of social, compliance, and enforcement costs when allocating their resources.

A Positive Theory of Regulatory Enforcement

As Diver [1980] has stressed, a positive (i.e. an explanatory or predictive) model of enforcement must be able to ''explain'' both the *extent* and *pattern* of enforcement. An economic approach to regulatory enforcement is capable of satisfying this requirement by emphasizing the role played by overinclusion and the relative cost-minimizing properties of compliance and penalty enforcement strategies.

Underlying the economic model is a particular view of corporate criminality. It ''portrays the business firm as an amoral, profit-seeking organization motivated by rational calculation of costs and opportunities.'' (Kagan and Scholz, see above, chapter 4). Such a firm's decision to obey the law will depend solely on the costs and benefits of compliance; if a violation attracts an expected penalty in excess of the costs of compliance the firm will obey the law, otherwise it will not. A profit-maximizing firm will always choose the cheaper course of action. It follows from this model of law breaking that the more overinclusive the law the lower the compliance rate. Overinclusion leads to a high level of law breaking and the need for more severe and intensively enforced penalties. However, the adoption of such a penal and legalistic enforcement strategy will not necessarily be the best means of promoting economic efficiency (or other regulatory objectives) nor will it be the most effective use of the resources available to the enforcement agency.

Penalty Model

The penalty model of enforcement is based on a belief that industry should comply with all regulations and that those firms that break the law should be punished.[9] The penalty model thus suggests a strategy of intensive enforcement activity and high fines. This view of enforcement is usually modified to take account of the limited resources available to the agency (which limitation may be used to "justify" the fact that only a fraction of violations are prosecuted). However, the observation that regulatory law is often not vigorously enforced indicates to proponents of a penalty system government insincerity and agency capture, if not corruption.

The normative economic version of the penalty model differs from others by placing heavy emphasis on fines as the primary enforcement instrument.[10] The likelihood that a firm will comply with the law increases the higher the *expected* sanction. The expected penalty is the product of two elements: the likelihood of conviction and the nominal fine or other penalty that may be imposed. If the firm is risk-neutral, the same level of compliance can be achieved by varying one with a compensated variation in the other so as to maintain the value of the anticipated fine. That is, a $100 fine imposed with certainty would achieve an identical compliance rate as a $200 fine imposed on only 50 percent of violations.

The optimal penalty structure will therefore be determined solely by the costs to the enforcement agency of invoking these two policy variables.[11] Fines achieve compliance at zero enforcement costs because they deter by the fear that they will have to be paid. Inspecting, detecting and prosecuting offenders on the other hand is a very costly method of deterrence. Since a decrease in enforcement activity accompanied by an increase in the fine achieves the same level of compliance at lower enforcement costs, an optimal penalty structure will rely on heavy fines. The economist's "case-for-fines" suggests that full compliance can be achieved at relatively low enforcement costs by setting the fine at an extremely high level and the prosecution rate close to zero — a policy of infrequently bankrupting firms found in violation of the law.[12]

In practice, a penalty approach is undesirable because it ignores the overinclusiveness of many legal standards. A policy of prosecuting all violators, even if financially feasible, would fail to allocate enforcement resources rationally. Small and trivial offenses would rank equally with larger ones inflicting greater social harm. Clearly some scaling of penalties, based on the degree of harm caused by an offense, would be needed to ensure that potential violators are given appropriate incentives.[13] In Britain this policy is not pursued and fines are frequently not high nor exclusively relied on. The constraint imposed by low fines has led enforcement agencies to adopt a more flexible enforcement strategy.

An enforcement agency conscious of the undesirability of enforcing overinclusive standards would pursue a flexible and selective prosecution policy. The problem confronting such an agency can be described simply as one of suboptimizing, i.e., pursuing the goal of economic efficiency subject to a set of institutional, political, cost and budgetary constraints. Although the institutional constraints will differ from agency to agency, in Britain it is generally the case that the nature of offenses and maximum penalties are determined by statute, the actual fines by the courts, and the enforcement budget by the legislature.

The only variable that such an enforcement agency can vary is the prosecution/ conviction rate. The optimal strategy can be formalized in terms of a cost-effective deterrence model[14] using the following notation:

c^i = probability of conviction

e^i = net external damage per offense

f^i = fine imposed per offense

O^i = number of offenses

Assume that the costs of detecting, prosecuting (and convicting) offenders are proportional to the number of convictions, i.e. kcO, where $k > 1$ is the unit cost. Again for simplicity, *net* marginal external damage (the social loss per offense costs) is assumed to be a constant amount of $\$e$ per offense of each category and that there are $i, \ldots, n$ categories of offenses each associated with a specific regulation. A regulation is overinclusive if the net marginal (social) external costs of an offense are "insignificant" or negative, i.e. $e^i \leq o$. Alternatively, e^i can be redefined more loosely as an index of the gravity of an offense as determined by, say, the physical severity of the injury. The number of offenses is assumed to be negatively related to the expected fine.

$$0^i = O^i(c, f)$$

$$0^i_c = \frac{\partial 0^i}{\partial c^i} < 0$$

$$0^i_f = \frac{\partial 0^i}{\partial f^i} < 0 \tag{8.1}$$

Given these assumptions the enforcement agency seeks to minimize the net social (or external) costs of offenses E,

$$\text{Min. } E = \sum_{i}^{n} e^i0^i(c^if) \tag{8.2}$$

subject to the agency's enforcement budget

$$B = \sum_{i}^{n} k^ic^io^i + F \tag{8.3}$$

where B is the inspectorate's enforcement budget and F fixed administrative costs. For each category of offense the optimal detection/conviction rate will, for a given f, satisfy the condition (ignoring superscripts)

$$e - \lambda ck(1 - \frac{1}{\eta}) \tag{8.4}$$

where λ is the Lagrangian multiplier and $\eta = \frac{c}{0} \ 0_c > 0$ is the responsiveness or deterrability (elasticity) of offenses with respect to increases in the conviction rate. The optimal conviction rate for the ith category of offenses is given by the condition

$$c = \frac{e}{\lambda k \ (1 - \frac{1}{\eta})} \tag{8.5}$$

Equation 8.5 indicates that the optimal conviction rate for each regulation increases with e and the elasticity of offenses and decreases with the average costs of conviction k. If equation 8.5 is used as a predictive or explanatory theory, it indicates that an enforcement agency guided by considerations of economic efficiency would not prosecute offenses arising under overinclusive regulations or regulations for which marginal enforcement costs are relatively high. Also if it has at its disposal a number of enforcement instruments that differ as to their enforcement costs and offense elasticities there will be a tendency to use those instruments that are less costly (low k) or that encourage greater compliance (higher η).

Compliance Model

The enforcement costs of pursuing a penalty approach are often very high. As a result many agencies will use extralegal and informal methods to induce compliance that rely in part on the *threat* of prosecution but not its frequent use. The selective prosecution model developed above only considers one part of the activities of enforcement agencies. It does not deal with enforcement behavior once a violation has been detected: it is an "ex ante" model of enforcement focusing on the cost-effective deterrence of violations, and ignores the essentially sequential character of enforcement and compliance processes.

Before dealing with the economic aspects of a compliance system of enforcement, several important characteristics of regulatory offenses should be noted.[15] First, they differ from nonregulatory criminal offenses, such as murder, rape, and theft, in two important ways: they generally do not involve a positive act, but rather a failure to act, and the offense is often not a discrete event but a continuing state of affairs. Also, regulatory offenses normally occur within an organization where the responsibilities for compliance are often diffused, and noncompliance is the result either of ignorance or a conscious profit-maximizing decision that compliance is too costly. Whereas regulatory offenses are frequently the by-product of the pursuit of some otherwise socially beneficial activity such as industrial production, common crimes simply redistribute and destroy wealth. Thus enforcement officials, and society, are bound to take a more permissive attitude toward regulatory offenses, particularly when it can be shown that the law is overinclusive. Finally, regulatory enforcement is an activity in which personality and offense-specific factors play a more important part in the enforcement/ compliance process than in penalty system. The fact that they do is the essential element of discretion. Thus the penalty model of enforcement does not capture the essence of regulatory law enforcement. In regulatory situations involving inspection agencies, detection is linked automatically to the identity of the offender and creates an immediate bilateral relationship between inspector and offender that is conducive to bargaining over compliance. Finally, most public law enforcement bodies have a virtual monopoly over enforcement. This is a necessary condition for discretionary enforcement since, as Landes and Posner [1974] have shown, the private enforcement of law by ''informers'' encouraged by the payment of ''bounties'' will not be discretionary.

The enforcement setting of regulation is what may be called a ''relational'' one[16] in which, to quote Hawkins [1980: 5], ''regulatory enforcement . . . takes place in the context of continuing relationships'' and ''is carried out in personal, private transactions.'' The bilateral nature of this relationship suggests that the enforcement/compliance process is initially one of *bargaining for compliance,* what may be called a strategy of *negotiated compliance.* Prosecution is by no means the primary enforcement instrument but one of last resort that signals the failure of bargaining over compliance.

Inducing compliance by negotiation involves elements of exchange between the inspector and firm and is motivated by the cost-savings to each party from not going to court. It is best characterized as an ''enforcement game'' where strategic bargaining and bargaining power play crucial roles. What the enforcement official must do is persuade the offender that compliance is the cheapest course of action, whereas it will be in the offender's self-interest to persuade the official that compliance is infeasible or extremely costly.

The factors that will influence the terms of "implicit compliance bargains" can be identified easily although their precise effect on the outcome of negotiations is problematic.

An enforcement official concerned with gaining cost-effective compliance has three devices at his disposal; forbearance, advice, and threats. These devices will be used because they are cheaper than prosecution and if successful, will yield tangible results. Forbearance can induce compliance in two ways. First, the inspector can make it clear that he will not regard overinclusive rules as warranting compliance. He will exercise his discretion by not applying the law provided the firm acts reasonably when asked by the inspector to comply with regulations giving rise to more serious offenses. Such forbearance can be used to "buy" compliance with cost-effective regulations. Secondly, the official can forbear from prosecuting particular offenses. A prosecution can be threatened on the clear understanding that if acceptable compliance is assured it will not be undertaken. Here the inspector can behave strategically, that is, he may threaten more prosecutions than feasible or than he actually intends and/or exaggerate the magnitude of the penalties thereby making compliance more attractive. The use of prosecutions as a threat rather than as an automatic penalty offers the violator with a reward for complying. Kelman [1981: 205] stresses that this type of forbearance is a crucial aspect of a compliance system: "Punishment [in this case fines] tends to cause resentment because in exchange for the change in behavior, there is no improvement in one's original state but merely an avoidance of worsening. This tends to be perceived as an unfair exchange."

The absence of an exchange on the part of both enforcement official and violator may give rise to resentment that has policy implications. This is graphically illustrated by the early experience in enforcing the U.S. Occupational Safety and Health Act. Inspectors were required to cite all violations regardless of whether the firm had complied or not. This generated much hostility toward and contributed to the general unpopularity of Occupational Safety and Health Administration, which found expression in political activity to alter enforcement procedures.[17]

Another component of the compliance transaction is the provision by the inspector of free information to the firm that can be used to buy greater compliance. The information supplied by the inspector can be of two kinds; concerning the law and the least-cost method of compliance. Here the inspector adopts the role of adviser rather than policeman.

Given the number and detailed nature of standards, firms will often have a hazy perception of the law, their legal obligations, and the sanctions that will be imposed for noncompliance. This will obviously impair the effectiveness of the law. As Kelman [1981: 252] aptly puts it: "Ignorance of the law may be no excuse, but it certainly is a sufficient explanation for failure to obey it." The detection of breaches of the law and the inspector's visit can be used to provide the firm with information on its legal obligations at zero cost. Instead of the firm incurring the costs of fully acquainting itself with the law, the inspector informs the firm as part of his routine activities. Since prosecutions are not automatic and occur infrequently, there is no immediate cost, but rather considerable gain in avoided information costs to the firm from adopting a strategy of "wait-and-see." Thus the information supplied by the inspector can increase compliance without the need to prosecute.

The second, and possibly more important, type of information that can be supplied by enforcement officials concerns least-cost methods of compliance. An implicit assumption of most discussions of enforcement is that firms are not only aware of the law but have perfect information on efficient abatement techniques. Obviously this is frequently not the case, particularly in the small firm that does not possess the necessary expertise. Enforcement officials can give advice and information on the best methods of abating hazards. This provision of free information can not only be used to "buy" compliance by showing that it pays, but can generate improvements where hazards are not covered by specific regulations.

These inducements offered by the enforcement official operate in part against the background of the legal penalties available. However, the fact that formal penalties are low does not necessarily mean that the offender's incentive to comply with the law is also low. Prosecution imposes numerous other costs such as the prospective psychic costs to managers confronted with the threat of prosecution, third-party sanctions imposed by workers on trade unions and the loss of goodwill within the local community. These nonlegal sanctions will tend to be greater the more there are relational (i.e. personal) third-party links. Thus a firm in a small community polluting a local river will be more sensitive to the extralegal costs of being prosecuted, as will a large corporation that expects adverse publicity to follow.

For the enforcement official's part, there are several forces working towards a compliance strategy. Prosecution is costly and its impact on compliance is not immediate or even known. The enforcement official who refrains from prosecuting saves the agency money and time and if compliance is successfully obtained, this will yield tangible results. Also enforcement officials may wish to avoid conflict and be willing to adopt a less stringent approach not necessarily to gain compliance but to maintain a cozy relationship with those regulated.

Although enforcement officials may be willing to forbear and advise, a violator persuaded that the benefits of compliance are greater than he originally perceived may still not comply. If the compliance costs to the firm exceed the expected cost-savings from avoiding prosecution, a cooperative solution will not be agreed to and the firm will prefer to pay the fine and related legal and extralegal costs. The cost-minimization model indicates that the likelihood of negotiated compliance will be higher the larger are the expenses and sanctions associated with litigation, the perceived probability of conviction and the more information that can be supplied when noncompliance is due to ignorance.

An Illustration — Occupational Health and Safety Regulation in Britain and the United States

The importance of overinclusion to a full understanding of regulatory processes and impact is graphically illustrated by the contrasting experience with recent occupational health and safety (OHS) legislation in the United States and Britain.

In the early 1970s both Britain and the United States reformed the legislative and enforcement framework of OHS regulation. In the United States, the *Occupational Safety and Health Act* (OSHA) 1970 was enacted and four years later in Britain the *Health and Safety at Work Act* (HSWA) 1974 became law. Both of these acts grew out of a general concern that previous regulatory attempts to improve workplace health and safety were failing.[18] The general reaction to these reforms in each country has been very different. OSHA (1970) is almost universally unpopular and has become a symbol of meddlesome government interference. HSWA, on the other hand, has been well received. For example, a recent survey of employers' attitudes about various protective labor legislation found the response to HSWA "unusually favourable" [Daniel and Stigloe, 1978]. A recent British government report on the efficiency of administrative agencies suggested that the Health and Safety Executive was probably following cost-effective procedures in setting standards [Pliatzky, 1980]. This contrasts with OSHA's explicit mandate to ignore economic considerations.

It is clear from even a cursory examination of the activities of Occupational Safety and Health Administration (OSHA) and the British Factory Inspectorate, which enforces HSWA in manufacturing industry, that there are substantial differences in enforcement styles and philosophies. These differences correspond, at least superficially, with the penalty and compliance models respectively. OSHA has interpreted its role as strictly one of law enforcement. The dominant view within OSHA, states Kelman [1981, p. 191], "is that regulations must be enforced according to the book." The reason for this policy appears to be the fear that "unrestrained discretion" will get out of hand and the agency will be "captured" by those it regulates. Moreover, OSHA's "standard-setting process specifically rejects weighing of costs and benefits as a criterion for judging the desirability of standards"[19] and compared to British statutory safety regulations are more detailed specification standards.

The enforcement philosophy and style of British OHS is definitely a compliance system.[20] The Factory Inspectorate, which enforces OHS regulations in factories, has adopted an enforcement approach that emphasizes advice, persuasion, and negotiation as the officially preferred means of securing compliance. The Factory Inspectorate devotes most of its resources to the factory visit and is reluctant to prosecute. When it does prosecute, however, the choice of cases is highly selective, based on a fault criterion[21] and until recently has tended to follow an accident. This selective prosecution policy deals with the overinclusion problem by penalizing only those regulatory offenses that are clearly related to accident prevention. The work of the British factory inspector has been summarized as one of ''instruction (on matters within the law) and advice (on matters outside the law), rather than compulsion.''[22]

The characterization of the OSHA inspector as a policeman and his British equivalent as an adviser captures the essence of the difference in enforcement approaches. Part of the explanation for this difference in roles can be found in the different institutional and political constraints confronting each enforcement agency. In Britain, average (and maximum) fines tend to be low and violators must be prosecuted in *criminal* proceedings that are expensive and time consuming. OSHA, on the other hand, enables heavier *civil* penalties to be imposed administratively by the enforcement official without the need to go to court. The observation that OSHA has adopted a penalty approach is consistent with the economic model since these civil penalties are cheaper to impose for the enforcement agency. In this regard it is interesting to note that the availability of administrative notices under HSWA, which enable an inspector to order compliance or stop work, has led the Factory Inspectorate to reduce the number of prosecutions it undertakes annually and to rely more heavily on these notices. This again is consistent with the predictions of the economic model because the latter are cheaper and will induce greater compliance because they permit the inspector to order the firm to stop production.

OSHA's rulemaking and enforcement approaches also explain the mounting evidence that it has failed to improve the level of workplace.[23] The legislative ban on the use of economic criteria in the setting of standards suggests that overinclusion will be a serious problem. This coupled with a penalty enforcement strategy may lead to greater compliance than a negotiated compliance strategy but not necessarily to fewer accidents. To illustrate this point, consider the extreme example of a regulatory system where all regulations are overinclusive and where only a small percentage of safety inputs are regulated. In such a situation increased enforcement and higher penalties will induce greater compliance. But it will also change the relative *net* price (price minus expected fine) of regulated and unregulated safety inputs in favour of the former. The net price of regulated safety inputs will fall and this will induce the firm to decrease the level of unregulated safety inputs which, by assumption, are more effective in reducing the accident rate. Such a regulatory system will lead to the perverse result of higher safety-related costs *and* a higher accident rate.[24] Although anecdotal evidence is not proof of the proposition, Kagan and Scholz in their chapter in this volume (chapter 4) give a very graphic example of this type of adaptation to rule-oriented penalty systems: a steel company embroiled in conflicts with OSHA "replaced the trained safety engineer who headed its accident-prevention program with a lawyer."

The analysis so far has given a very favorable interpretation to the administrative exercise of discretion. However, it is important to appreciate the different views of discretion held in two countries and the influence that this will have on the relationship between rules and enforcement. In the United States the exercise of bureaucratic discretion is disliked and discouraged, whereas in Britain it is considered an essential part of the regulatory system. In the United States the abuse of discretion by enforcement officials is seen as a major problem to be controlled rather than rule overinclusion and inefficiency. The role of rules in the United States system, as Kelman has found, is not only to regulate safety but to control the discretion of enforcement officials in order to avoid abuses and agency capture. The British (and Swedish) approach deemphasizes these problems: rules and enforcement techniques are not designed to control officials but to achieve desired regulatory goals. This difference is explained by the different political traditions in the two countries, although it is interesting that President Reagan by Executive Order 12,291 now requires all executive agencies to focus on overinclusion by mandating the cost-benefit analysis of all new regulations.[25]

Conclusion

In this chapter I have attempted to cast the features of penalty and compliance systems of regulatory enforcement in economic terms. Many of these features have been shown to have an economic justification thus reinforcing the view that an economic approach based on the efficiency criterion can provide a theoretical framework for the study of enforcement. This is not, of course, to assert that enforcement can only be explained in economic terms. Obviously political and administrative considerations may dominate, as the example of OSHA clearly shows. One puzzle that has yet to be convincingly explained is why regulatory offenses typically attract insignificant, if not derisory, penalties. A wider efficiency analysis of regulation would show this to be inefficient, since, as discussed above, higher fines achieve compliance at lower enforcement costs. This systemic inefficiency has not been considered because I have been concerned to provide a positive theory of enforcement given that a first-best policy (i.e., higher fines) has not been adopted by Parliament and the courts. Economists have not generally tackled the question of what the efficient bureaucratic response should be to imperfectly designed rules and penalties and have therefore unnecessarily restricted the contribution that they can make to current research on regulation.[26]

Notes

1. For Britain, see the work and evidence in Beaumont, 1979; Carson, 1970a, b; Cranston, 1979; Gunningham, 1974; Hawkins, 1980, forthcoming; Law Commission, 1969; Rhodes, 1981; Veljanovski, 1983. Kelman, 1981 and Stearns, 1979 provide similar evidence on the enforcement of Swedish labor legislation. For United States studies see references cited in Hawkins, forthcoming. A feature of most of this work is the absence of a *theory* of regulatory enforcement; see Diver, 1980.

2. For a similar view of regulation as an ''implicit administered contract'' between those regulated and the agency see Goldberg, 1976.

3. For economic models of out-of-court settlement and plea-bargains see Landes, 1970 and Gould, 1973.

4. See Posner, 1980.

5. For two economic discussions of rulemaking that touch on the overinclusion problem but do not develop its implications for enforcement see Hirsch, 1974 and Ehrlich and Posner, 1974. Also see Mendeloff, 1981.

6. Cost-minimization approaches such as this have become popular among economists appraising legal rules, e.g., Becker, 1966; McKean, 1980; and Posner, 1977.

7. Negligence or fault liability is a contingent standard which Posner, 1972 has argued is determined in practice by comparing the costs of prevention with the expected losses.

8. Landes and Posner, 1974: 38–9, note this function of discretion as does an earlier paper by Stigler, 1970.

9. For economic theories of enforcement with a more penal emphasis than the model developed in the text see Becker, 1968; Harford, 1978; and Ashenfelter, 1979. Diver, 1980 is the only attempt to provide a more descriptive theoretical account of regulatory enforcement. Also see Feeley, 1970.

10. See Becker, 1968 and Posner, 1980.

11. This example implicitly assumes that offenders are risk neutral.

12. Accompanying the case-for-fines is the notion of an 'optimal' fine. Those offenders who are prosecuted should pay a fine that reflects *both* the social loss plus the enforcement costs expended to detect and prosecute each violation. Thus if e is the monetary value of the social (external) costs, k, enforcement costs, and c, the detection/conviction rate, then the optimal fine f^* is given by the expression $f^* = (e + k)/c$. Thus if $e = \$30$ and only 1 in 10,000 offenses are prosecuted then the optimal fine equals \$300,000. It hardly needs to be stated that such an approach is not likely to be used. Obviously, if c is near zero, f^* tends toward infinity. This example and discussion in the text assume that the offenders are risk neutral. If they are not then, as Polinsky and Shavell, 1979 show the ''case-for-fines'' is somewhat weakened and a finite fine will be optimal.

13. Block and Sidak, 1980 provide a number of reasons why this policy may be inefficient. The principal inefficiency they identify are error costs which in a regulatory context are the result of overinclusion. Stigler, 1970 has pointed out that the case-for-fines is marred by its failure to take account of marginal deterrence. If fines do not discriminate among offenses causing different levels of harm (social losses) firms will not have an (higher) incentive to avoid the more serious harms.

14. The model is a modified and simplified version in Becker, 1968. A more rigorous model is developed by Veljanovski, 1982.
15. Reiss and Biderman, 1980: 274–276 provide a similar list of attributes.
16. The term *relational* comes from MacNeil's, 1974 work on contract.
17. Kelman, 1980: 260 notes that the main congressional activity regarding OSHA has been directed to altering enforcement procedures.
18. *See* discussion in Robens Report, 1970.
19. Cornell et al., 1976: 487.
20. A more detailed account of the enforcement procedures of the Factory Inspectorate can be found in Veljanovski, 1983 and Rhodes, 1981: ch. 4.
21. *See* Law Commission, 1969, Carson, 1970a, b, Hadden, 1970, Smith and Pearson, 1969.
22. *Annual Report of H. M. Chief Inspector of Factories 1932* (Cmd. 1933) p. 9. Interestingly some of the same contrasts that can be drawn between OSHA and the Factory Inspectorate have been identified by Kelman, 1980 (see also Stearns, 1979 in her comparative study of Swedish and United States OHS regulation.
23. E.g. Viscusi, 1980. A full account and review of these studies can be found in Veljanovski, 1981: ch. 7. *Cf.* Mendeloff, 1969 and Smith, 1979. The only comparable econometric study of the impact of British OHS legislation provides tentative evidence that the compliance approach has lowered the accident rate in manufacturing industry: Veljanovski, 1980.
24. This type of response points to the importance of having a full account of the firm's compliance and safety decisions. For rigorous discussions of such perverse adaptive responses to regulations see Peltzman, 1975; Viscusi, 1980; and Veljanovski, 1981: ch. 7.
25. See Baldwin and Veljanovski, 1984.
26. However, see Viscusi and Zeckhauser, 1979; Harford, 1978; and Diver, 1980.

References

Ashenfelter, O. and R. S. Smith (1979). Compliance with the Minimum Wage Law, 87 *Journal of Political Economy* 333.

Baldwin, R. and C. G. Veljanovski (1984). Regulation and Cost-Benefit Analysis, 62 *Public Administration,* forthcoming.

Beaumont, P. B. (1979). The Limits of Inspection: A Study of the Workings of the Government Wages Inspectorate, 57 *Public Administration* 203.

Becker, G. S. (1968). Crime and Punishment: An Economic Approach, 76 *Journal of Political Economy* 169.

Block, M. K. and J. G. Sidak (1980). The Cost of Antitrust Deterrence: Why not Hang a Price Fixer Now and Then?, 65 *Georgetown Law Journal* 1131.

Carson, W. G. (1970a). Some Sociological Aspects of Strict Liability and the Enforcement of Factory Legislation, 33 *Modern Law Review* 396.

———— (1970b). White Collar Crime and the Enforcement of Factory Legislation, 10 *British Journal of Criminology* 383.

Cornell, N. W., R. G. Noll, and B. Weingast (1976). Safety Regulation, in H. O. Owen and C. L. Schultze, (eds.), *Setting National Priorities*. Washington: Brookings Institution.

Cranston, R. (1979). *Regulating Business — Law and Consumer Agencies*. London: Macmillan.

Daniel, W. W. and B. Stigloe (1978). *The Impact of Employment Protection Laws*. London: Policy Studies Institute.

Diver, C. S. (1980). A Theory of Regulatory Enforcement, 28 *Public Policy* 259.

Ehrlich, I. and R. A. Posner (1974). An Economic Analysis of Legal Rule Making, 3 *Journal of Legal Studies* 257.

Feeley, M. (1970). Coercion and Compliance — A New Look at an Old Problem, 4 *Law and Society Review* 505.

Goldberg, V. P. (1976). Regulation and Administered Contracts, 7 *Bell Journal of Economics* 426.

Gould, J. P. (1973). The Economics of Legal Conflict, 2 *Journal of Legal Studies* 393.

Gunningham, N. (1974). *Pollution, Social Interest and the Law*. London: Martin Robertson.

Harford, J. D. (1978). Firm Behaviour Under Imperfectly Enforceable Pollution Standards and Taxes, 5 *Journal of Environmental Economics and Management* 26.

Hawkins, K. (1980). The Use of Discretion by Regulatory Officials: A Case Study on Environmental Pollution in the United Kingdom. Paper presented at the Conference on Perspectives on Regulation: Law, Discretion and Bureaucratic Behavior, sponsored by Baldy Center for Law and Social Policy and Oxford University Centre for Socio-legal Studies, State Unversity of New York at Buffalo, May.

——— (forthcoming). *Environment and Enforcement: Regulation and the Social Definition of Pollution*. Oxford: Oxford University Press.

Hirsch, W. Z. (1974). Reducing the Law's Uncertainty and Complexity, 21 *UCLA Law Review* 1233.

Holden, M. (1966). *Pollution Control as a Bargaining Process: An Essay on Regulatory Decision Making*. Ithaca: Cornell University Water Resources Center, Publication no. 9.

Kadish, S. H. (1963). Some Observations on the Use of Criminal Sanctions in Enforcing Economic Regulations, 30 *University of Chicago Law Review* 432.

Kagan, R. A. (1980). The Positive Uses of Discretion: The Good Inspector. Paper given at Law and Society Association Annual Meeting, Madison, Wisconsin.

Kelman, S. (1980). Occupational Health and Safety Administration, in J. Q. Wilson (ed.), *Politics of Regulation*. New York: Basic Books.

——— (1981). *Regulating America, Regulating Sweden: A Comparative Study of Occupational Safety and Health Policy*. Cambridge: MIT Press.

Lachman, J. and W. McLauchlin (1977). Models of Plea Bargaining in S. Nagel (ed.), *Modeling the Criminal Justice System*. Beverly Hills: Russell Sage.

Landes, W. M. (1971). An Economic Analysis of the Courts, 14 *Journal of Law and Economics* 61.

Landes, W. M. and R. A. Posner (1975). The Private Enforcement of Law, 4 *Journal of Legal Studies* 1.

Law Commission (1969). *Strict Liability and the Enforcement of the Factory Act 1961*. London: Working Paper No. 30.

McKean, R. (1980). Enforcement Costs in Environment and Safety Regulation, 6 *Policy Analysis* 269.

MacNeil, I. R. (1974). The Many Futures of Contract, 47 *Southern California Law Review* 691.

Mendeloff, J. (1981). Does Overregulation Cause Underregulation?, *Regulation* (Sept.– Oct.) 47.

Peltzman, S. (1975). The Effects of Automobile Safety Regulation, 83 *Journal of Political Economy* 677.

Pliatzky, L. (1980). *Report on Non-Departmental Public Bodies.* London: HMSO (Cmnd. 7797).

Polinsky, A. M. and S. Shavell (1979). The Optimal Tradeoff Between Fines and Probability of Conviction *American Economic Review* 880.

Posner, R. A. (1972). A Theory of Negligence, 1 *Journal of Legal Studies* 29.

——— (1977). *Economic Analysis of Law* (2nd ed.). Boston: Little, Brown.

——— (1980). Optimal Sentences for White-Collar Crime, 17 *American Criminal Law Review* 409.

Reiss, A. J. Jr. and A. D. Biderman (1980). *Data Sources on White-Collar Law-Breaking.* Washington, DC: National Institute of Justice.

Rhodes, G. (1981). *Inspectorates in British Government,* London: George Allen & Unwin.

Robens Report (1972). *Committee on Safety and Health at Work,* London: H.M.S.O. (Cmnd 5034).

Ross, H. L. (1970). *Settled Out of Court,* Chicago: Aldine.

Smith, R. S. (1979). The Impact of the OSHA Inspections of Manufacturing Injury Rates, 14 *Journal of Human Resources,* 145.

Stearns, L. R. (1979). Fact and Fiction of a Model of Enforcement Bureaucracy 6 *British Journal of Law and Society,* 1.

Stigler, G. J. (1970). The Optimum Enforcement of Laws, 78 *Journal of Political Economy,* 526.

Veljanovski, C. G. (1980). An Empirical Analysis of British Industrial Safety Regulation in *Perspectives on Regulation: Law, Discretion and Bureaucratic Behavior,* SUNY/ Buffalo: Baldy Center for Law and Social Policy.

——— (1981). *Regulating Industrial Accidents — An Economic Analysis of Market and Legal Responses,* University of York D. Phil.

——— (1982). A Positive Economic Theory of Regulatory Enforcement, manuscript. Oxford: Centre for Socio-Legal Studies.

——— (1983). Regulatory Enforcement — An Economic Study of the British Factory Inspectorate, 5 *Law and Policy Quarterly* 75.

Viscusi, W. K. (1979). The Impact of Occupational Safety and Health Regulation, 10 *Bell Journal of Economics,* Spring, 117.

Viscusi, W. K. and R. J. Zeckhauser (1979). Optimal Standards with Incomplete Enforcement, 27 *Public Policy,* 437.

Contributing Authors

Donald Clelland is Associate Professor of Sociology at the University of Tennessee (Knoxville). He has conducted research and published in the areas of social conflict and stratification. His central interest is the study of power.

Stephen Groce is a Ph.D. candidate in sociology at the University of Tennessee (Knoxville). His areas of interest include deviant behavior and phenomenological sociology.

Keith Hawkins is Senior Research Fellow at the Centre for Socio-legal Studies and a Fellow of Wolfson College, Oxford University. He took a Ph.D. at Cambridge University with a dissertation on decision-making in American parole systems. His research interests are in sociology of law and sociology of deviance, on which he has published a number of papers. *Environment and Enforcement,* his study of the enforcement of water pollution regulations in England, is to be published by Oxford University Press early in 1984.

Robert A. Kagan is Professor of Political Science at the University of California, Berkeley. He is the author of *Regulatory Justice: Implementing a Wage Price Freeze* (N.Y. Russell Sage Foundation, 1978); with Eugene Bardach, *Going by the*

Book: The Problem of Regulatory Unreasonableness, A Twentieth Century Fund Report (Philadelphia: Temple University Press, 1982); and several articles, with Lawrence Friedman, Stanton Wheeler and Bliss Cartwright, on the history of American State Supreme Courts.

Steven Kelman is Associate Professor of Public Policy at Harvard University, Kennedy School of Government. He is a summa cum laude graduate of Harvard College and received his Ph.D. from Harvard University. He is most recently the author of *Regulating America, Regulating Sweden: a Comparative Study of Occupational Safety and Health Policies* (M.I.T. Press, 1981), and *What Price Incentives: Economists and the Environment* (Auburn House, 1981). He has also written widely on regulatory issues and the application of ethical theory to public policy questions.

John Lynxwiler is a Ph.D. candidate in sociology at the University of Tennessee (Knoxville). His doctoral dissertation examines the social organization of field-level inspectors during the Office of Surface Mining's initial period of enforcement. His current interests include the social organization of accounts and deviant behavior in complex organizations.

Albert J. Reiss, Jr. is the William Graham Sumner Professor of Sociology and in the Institution for Social and Policy Studies, Yale University and a Lecturer in Law, Yale Law School. He is the author and co-author of major works on the police, organizational deviance, white-collar crime, and of law as a form of social control. He has contributed to methodological and technical developments in understanding changes in law violations and deviant behavior, especially in his work on understanding changes in rates and in measuring victimization by crime.

John T. Scholz is Assistant Professor of Political Science at the State University of New York at Stony Brook. He is currently doing research on corporate compliance strategies and stochastic models of organizational learning. He has written several articles on regulation, including "State Regulatory Reform and Federal Regulation" (Policy Studies Review 1:347–359, November, 1981). He has also written extensively on Nepal, including the book *Nepal: Portrait of a Himalayan Kingdom* co-authored with Leo E. Rose.

Neal Shover is Professor of sociology at the University of Tennessee (Knoxville). He received his Ph.D. in 1971 from the University of Illinois (Urbana) and has conducted research and published on a variety of issues related to crime and social control processes. He is interested particularly in the etiology and control of corporate and organizational crime. Currently, he and Professor Donald Clelland are examining the development of the Office of Surface Mining.

Susan S. Silbey is Assistant Professor of Sociology at Wellesley College and received a Ph.D. in Political Science from the University of Chicago. She is currently completing a book on the enforcement of consumer protection legislation and has grant support to study the public ordering of private disputes.

John M. Thomas is Director of the Center for Policy Studies, Associate Professor of Managerial Economics and Policy and Adjunct Associate Professor of Law at the State University of New York at Buffalo. He is Editor of the *Law and Policy Quarterly.* His current research examines the nature of policy formation and implementation in regulation.

Cento G. Veljanovski is Research Officer in Law and Economics at the SSRC Centre for Socio-legal Studies, Wolfson College, Oxford University, and Lecturer in English Law at University College London. He specializes in the application of economics to law and regulation particularly in the areas of the common law, social and telecommunications regulation and competition law. His latest publications include a monograph *The New Law-and-Economics* (Oxford: Centre for Socio-Legal Studies, 1982) and an anthology entitled *Readings in the Economics of Law and Regulation* (Oxford University Press, 1984) with A. I. Ogus.

Author Index

192

Subject Index